Management and Labor in Imperial Germany

The main steel-casting plant of the Krupp works.

Elaine Glovka Spencer

Management and Labor in Imperial Germany

Ruhr Industrialists as Employers, 1896–1914

Rutgers University Press
New Brunswick, New Jersey

Frontispiece: The main steel-casting plant of the Krupp works. Photograph reproduced by permission of Sidgwick & Johnson Ltd., from *The Last of Old Europe* by A. J. P. Taylor.

Library of Congress Cataloging in Publication Data
Spencer, Elaine Glovka, 1939–
    Management and labor in imperial Germany.

    Bibliography: p.
    Includes index.
    1. Industrial relations—Germany (West)—Ruhr River Region—History. 2. Steel industry and trade—Germany (West)—Ruhr River Region—Personnel management—History. 3. Iron industry and trade—Germany (West)—Ruhr River Region—Personnel management—History. 4. Coal mines and mining—Germany (West)—Ruhr River Region—Personnel management—History. 5. Employers' associations—Germany (West)—Ruhr River Region—History. I. Title.
HD8459.R8S68 1984   331'.0943'55   83–11089
ISBN 0-8135-1017-1

Copyright © 1984 by Rutgers, The State University
All rights reserved
Manufactured in the United States of America

To George

Contents

	Acknowledgments	ix
	Introduction	1
1.	Coal, Iron, and Steel	9
2.	The Entrepreneurial Elite	24
3.	Ruhr Workers	40
4.	Industry and Government	52
5.	Initial Challenges	63
6.	Company Welfare Programs	71
7.	The Terms of Labor	80
8.	Conflict and Readjustment	98
9.	Containment	114
10.	Unsolved Problems	130
	Conclusions and Comparisons	139
	Appendix A: Ruhr Coal, Iron, and Steel Corporations	149
	Appendix B: Members of the Ruhr Entrepreneurial Elite	151
	Notes	157
	Bibliography	189
	Index	205

Map faces page 9

Acknowledgments

Over the years it has taken to research and write this book, many individuals have generously provided me with guidance and assistance. I am happy to have this opportunity to acknowledge publicly their efforts on my behalf.

First on the list of those to whom I am indebted is Professor Hans Rosenberg, who, with patience and insight, directed the dissertation that was the precursor of this work. My dissertation also benefited from the suggestions of Professor Gerald Feldman, who shared with me some of his extensive knowledge of the history of German industry. Whatever the failings of this investigation, they did not result from any lack of good advice given me at its beginning.

Indispensable for my study of Ruhr employers was the aid offered by numerous archivists and librarians. Particularly generous with his assistance was Herr Bodo Herzog, who made available to me the vast archival collection of the Gutehoffnungshütte. With his help, I spent several very rewarding weeks working through a wealth of documents that illuminated not only the management of the metallurgical and mining interests of the Gutehoffnungshütte but also the relationship of that concern and its leaders to other companies, government officials, political associations, and interest groups.

Dr. Hedwig Behrens, though retired, took time to discuss archival sources with me. Dr. Gertrud Milkereit of the Thyssen archive and Dr. Lutz Hatzfeld of the Mannesmann archive made available small but useful collections of documents relating to entrepreneurial associations. The Bundesarchiv Koblenz and the Bergbau Archiv provided extensive documentation on two key organizations: the Verein deutscher Eisen- und Stahlindustrieller and the Zechenverband. The Bergbau Archiv also yielded much useful information on the administration of Ruhr mines, especially those subsequently acquired by Krupp.

The *Staatsarchive* in Koblenz, Düsseldorf, and Münster provided abundant government documents on a variety of relevant topics ranging from general economic conditions to safety, hours of labor, company welfare institutions, work orders, and worker committees. Since any manifes-

Acknowledgments

tation of labor unrest was certain to attract government attention, the reports of provincial and district officials and of the *Oberbergamt* Dortmund give particularly full coverage of strikes.

The Rheinisch-Westfälisches Wirtschaftsarchiv and the Industrieinstitut in Cologne proved useful sources for specialized literature about Ruhr industry. And the Bergbau Bücherei in Essen was invaluable for its collection of published protocols and reports of entrepreneurial associations.

The University of Chicago Press granted me permission to use parts of my article "Employer Response to Unionism: Ruhr Coal Industrialists before 1914," which originally appeared in *Journal of Modern History* 48 (Spring 1976). This material appears in chapters 8, 9, and 10.

Finally, my husband, George W. Spencer, has made a vital contribution to this book. At every stage of its preparation, I have relied upon his encouragement and his editorial skills.

Management and Labor in Imperial Germany

Introduction

No other social problem of Wilhelmian Germany has aroused as much interest and concern, both then and subsequently, as the question of the relationship of the industrial labor force to the rest of society. Speaking in Essen in 1912 on the occasion of the hundredth anniversary of the Krupp steelworks, Alfred Hugenberg, chairman of that firm's executive committee (*Direktorium*) from 1909 to 1919 and a key figure in this study, stated the problem as follows: "In whatever area of life we look, we face the task of integrating the workers of large-scale industry, a class of men which has grown to immense proportions in an unprecedented manner, into the slowly developing framework of our national life."[1] No one then in a position of authority in the German Empire would have denied the central importance of this task, though there were differences of opinion as to how it might best be accomplished. The efforts of the ruling elites of the Second Reich to resolve this problem to their own satisfaction—namely, to pacify the workers while excluding them from meaningful participation in decision making in industrial, communal, and national affairs—is a theme of major significance in German history. Indeed, subsequent fateful developments in the twentieth century can be ascribed in no small measure to the bitter social and political legacy of this determined rear guard action.

Crucial to any assessment of the consequences for Imperial German society of the rapid emergence of a massive industrial labor force is an understanding of the actions of German employers. Given the importance of these actions, the response of industrial leaders to changes in the size, composition, aspirations, and expectations of the working class has not failed to attract scholarly attention. However, if for no other reason than the sheer magnitude and complexity of the question, investigations with the usual national focus have been able to illuminate only selected facets of the problem, particularly those relating to interest politics, social legislation, centralized antistrike tactics, and the fight against union recognition and collective bargaining.² Studies that focus on the workplace and the local community, still too few in number, reveal further dimensions of the problem but are often divorced from broader social and political considerations.³

The purpose of this study is to investigate the efforts of one important group of German employers to come to terms with labor at all levels and in all spheres of interaction: on the job and off, in local as well as in national affairs, and with unorganized as well as organized workers. My intent is to cover the full range of employer-employee relationships from personnel administration to union-management relations to the class struggle in the political arena. I will attempt to identify areas of increasing and decreasing friction and tension, keeping in mind that some facets of the employer-employee relationship might have been improving while others were deteriorating. I will also note the extent to which changes in all aspects of labor relations proceeded along lines dictated by the requirements of large-scale organizations and economic rationality and, furthermore, the ways in which they reflected the peculiar circumstances of German industrialization as well as social and political developments under the empire.

This book concentrates on the years from the industrial boom of the late 1890s to the outbreak of war in 1914. This was a period of general, but not unbroken, prosperity for German big business. It stands in contrast to the deflation that had characterized most of the 1870s and 1880s and to the renewed economic reverses of the early 1890s. My choice of 1896 as the beginning date for this investigation is based upon a pronounced increase, discussed in chapter 1, in industrial prices and profits and a more positive tenor of business reports. Although this periodization was initially suggested by theories proposed by Joseph Schumpeter and others about long waves in the development of industrial economies, the justification for it does not depend on the validity of such extended cycles for other countries and periods.⁴

Renewed prosperity had psychological effects. Members of Imperial Germany's entrepreneurial elite were greatly relieved to see a decade and a half of low prices and profits give way, initially in the late 1880s and more substantially a decade later, to improved prospects for basic industry. The economic determinants of relations between management and labor in primary production as well as expectations and priorities on both sides were different from what they had been in the age of Bismarck. To what extent German industrialists adapted their employment practices to these changed circumstances or failed to do so because of other considerations is central to this study.

In order to encompass the widest possible range of employer activi-

Introduction

ties and concerns, this book focuses on a single industrial region rather than on the nation as a whole, though the national context will be kept very much in mind. The choice of a particular group of industrialists to be investigated has been predicated upon the assumption that the group should consist of men who were deeply involved in attempting to come to terms with the most pressing and controversial labor issues of the day, such as those relating to the increasing size of production and administrative units, the growing complexity of industrial organization, the professionalization of management, the advent of unionization, the growth of cities, and the mounting public concern about and government intervention in industrial affairs. In other words, the group should consist of industrial leaders who were under considerable pressure to reevaluate and restructure their existing modes of relating to workers.

The leadership elite of the Ruhr coal, iron, and steel industries constituted such a group. The Ruhr was Imperial Germany's premier area of heavy industry; the most important, indeed, in Europe. It was crucial to the empire's economic well-being and status as a great power. Its business elite presided over large and complex enterprises and had to grapple with complicated labor problems. On labor questions, as on most other issues, these men frequently took it upon themselves to speak for German industry as a whole, though representatives of other industries and regions often protested. Given the vast economic and strategic importance of Ruhr heavy industry for the very survival of the German Empire, the attention of government, press, and political parties naturally focused on this group of employers more than any other.

This elite was small and tightly knit. The production of coal, iron, and steel in the prewar Ruhr was dominated by a mere handful of large firms, defined for purposes of this study as those employing five thousand or more workers. Between 1896 and 1914, twenty-nine companies, not all existent at any given moment, reached or surpassed this size, some several times over. These firms are listed in Appendix A.

The choice of five thousand workers as the lower limit for a firm's inclusion in this study presents no problem with regard to the Ruhr iron and steel industry. In ferrous metallurgy, companies either easily surpassed that size or came nowhere near it. In coal mining, there was much more of a continuum in company size. Nevertheless, in this industry, too, concerns with more than five thousand employees predominated. By 1912 such firms were producing 74 percent of Ruhr coal.[5]

In both mining and metallurgy, small and medium-sized companies usually had little choice but to follow the dictates of the giant concerns or to attempt through merger to join their ranks. The leaders of the large firms exercised an influence on the formation of industrial policy that extended regularly and significantly beyond the individual company and the single community. They virtually monopolized positions as high officials of the most important associations of Ruhr industry. Only in rare instances would an individual who was not associated with one of the giant concerns be admitted into the inner circle. Most conspicuous of such exceptions was Eduard Kleine, who served from 1905 to 1909 as chairman of the Verein für die bergbaulichen Interessen im Oberbergamtsbezirk Dortmund (usually known as the Bergbau Verein), the oldest and most comprehensive association of Ruhr coal industrialists. He was also chairman of the Zechenverband, the employer organization formed in 1908 under the auspices of the Bergbau Verein. Kleine's role in the councils of Ruhr industry was so prominent that he will be treated in this study as a member of the entrepreneurial elite even though none of the mining companies that he directed employed as many as five thousand workers.

In the large corporations of the prewar Ruhr, the separation of ownership, control, and management was the norm rather than the exception. Despite the stipulations of laws governing corporate structure under the empire, the official position of an individual within such an organization was not always a reliable indicator of his role in the decision-making process. In this study, men were selected to represent the Ruhr elite not because they held any particular position but because they appear to have been in actual practice more influential than anyone else in allocating resources and setting goals for the region's largest corporations.[6] The identity of the person who, regardless of his legal position, most frequently exercised such authority for each of the giant firms was determined case-by-case on the basis of biographical information and company histories, a procedure possible because of the small number of concerns involved.[7] An effort was made to limit the choice for each company to a single individual at any given time, that is, the person whom other members of the Ruhr elite would have consulted if they wanted a major commitment from that firm. I have made an exception in the case of the Krupp steelworks. Because control of that giant family-owned firm fluctuated between ownership and management, the successive heads of both the family and the executive committee have been included. I have made another exception in the case of the Gelsenkirchener Bergwerks-Aktiengesellschaft (Bergwerks-AG) by including not only its chief executive, Emil Kirdorf, but also its mining director, Paul Randebrock. Randebrock is included not because he was Kirdorf's deputy but because he was Kleine's successor as chairman of the Bergbau Verein and of the Zechenverband.

Introduction

After examining a variety of sources, such as company festschriften, biographies, trade journals, and collections of biographical sketches, I identified thirty-six men who met the above criteria and for whom biographical information was available. The addition of Kleine and Randebrock brought the number to thirty-eight. All of these individuals were resident in the Ruhr and active as industrial leaders during all or part of the era from the mid-1890s to the First World War.

Those thirty-eight men represented twenty-six of the twenty-nine biggest companies. Three of these industrialists, Carl Funke, Franz Haniel, and August Thyssen, each presided over more than one of these major concerns at the same time. For three of the twenty-nine corporations, only the names of their leaders or a mere smattering of information about them was available, so these men were excluded. The three firms in question, the Concordia, the Consolidation, and the Ewald mining companies, each employed fewer than ten thousand workers. Also omitted because of inadequate information were the managing director (*Generaldirektor*) of the Dortmunder Union from 1902 to 1910 and the managing director of the Graf Bismarck mining company before 1908. In total, at least five men, and perhaps two or three others not known to me, had to be excluded from this study because of insufficient data. The names of the thirty-eight men chosen to represent the leaders of Ruhr heavy industry in this investigation are listed in Appendix B, along with a summary of biographical information about each.[8]

This group, presiding over the greatest concentration of industrial power in the nation, ascribed to itself a major role in the preservation of the German Empire. These men viewed existing authority—their own and that of the state—as interrelated and fragile, subject to ever-increasing challenge in a progressively less deferential age. As a consequence, they tried in every way they could to prevent the weakening of established power, fighting against political and industrial democracy and against any encroachments upon the prerogatives of industrial leaders. In this struggle, their most pressing priority was to maintain effective control over the hundreds of thousands of workers who toiled in the mines and mills of the Ruhr.

In their relations with workers during the last prewar decades, Ruhr employers faced a number of problems. Especially pressing was the need to attract, discipline, and motivate masses of young men, many of them new both to the region and to industrial employment. Because Ruhr industry was a major importer of labor, the terms of employment had to be nationally competitive. Ruhr employers, however, viewed the resulting influx of workers into the region's mushrooming cities as both an economic asset and a potential threat. Increasingly large proletarian concentrations complicated efforts to monitor workers' off-the-job activities and fostered fears that protests could escalate to uncontrollable dimensions.

From the employers' perspective, their efforts to respond to problems inherent in the expansion of Ruhr industry were hampered by the advent of organized labor, a development that increasingly publicized and politicized industrial relations in the Ruhr as elsewhere in Germany. At the same time, increased government intervention, though sporadic and largely ineffective, was much resented by the region's industrial leaders and caused them to become more conscious of their public image. Beyond the Ruhr, political developments during the Wilhelmian era, especially the electoral successes of the Social Democrats, heightened employers' unease and their sense that it was their special mission to save Germany from subversion.

The response of Ruhr industrial leaders to these developments extended substantially beyond the antiparliamentary and antistrike activities that have attracted the most attention. Workers were cajoled as well as threatened. Punitive measures, both on the job and off, were coupled with those intended to reconcile workers to the existing order. Corporate paternalism and expanding employment opportunities, along with the harassment of dissidents, were the most commonly prescribed antidotes for manifestations of worker discontent. Given the vast economic resources at the disposal of Ruhr employers, their cohesiveness and determination as a group, the unwillingness of the government to attempt in more than a halfhearted fashion to curb their power, and a work force that included large numbers of unskilled newcomers, the entrepreneurial elite was largely successful in maintaining the upper hand, though some modest accommodation to changing circumstances was necessary. The employers' major success before the First World War was the containment, though not the elimination, of organized labor in their region. They were less successful in achieving the goal of a significantly more stable and compliant work force. Beyond the Ruhr, they continued to find the political situation frustrating but still preferable to the most likely alternatives.

The first four chapters of this book describe the growth of heavy industry in the Ruhr, the region's employers and workers, and the relationship between industry and government in Wilhelmian Germany. These topics are treated selectively, not exhaustively, with an emphasis on their relevance to labor relations. Chapters 5 through 10 provide an account of the employer strategies and tactics chosen and of the consequences of the

Introduction

choices made. The final section of this study includes not only a summary statement about Ruhr employers on the eve of war and beyond but also a brief comparison of their labor policies with those of their counterparts in England and the United States.

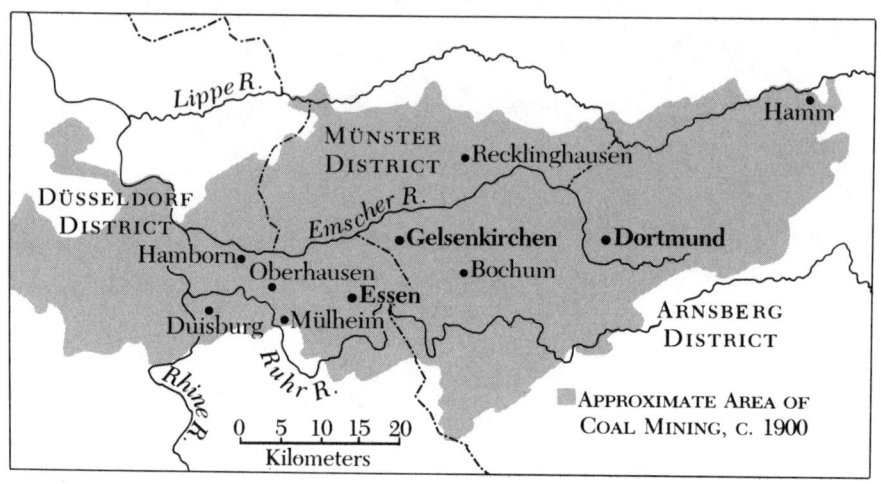

The Ruhr Coalfield around 1900.

1
Coal, Iron, and Steel

The Ruhr Coalfield

The foundation of the Ruhr's impressive industrial development was coal. Its abundance in the region permitted the growth not only of large-scale mining operations but also of a massive metallurgical industry. In the second half of the nineteenth century, the coal, iron, and steel industries of the Ruhr, economically interdependent and often linked by common ownership and leadership, eclipsed all other forms of economic activity in this previously insignificant corner of central Europe.

Small and compact, its geographic limits determined by the extent of profitably workable coal deposits, the Ruhr industrial region at the beginning of the twentieth century extended from the valley of the Ruhr River in the south to that of the Lippe in the north. In between, the Emscher River, like the Ruhr and Lippe a tributary of the Rhine, marked the center of large-scale mining activity. To the west, the frontiers of Ruhr mining extended across the Rhine into the county (*Kreis*) of Moers. The last outpost in the east was a few kilometers beyond the city of Hamm.[1]

Ruhr heavy industry was situated wholly within the state of Prussia, the laws of which were more immediately relevant to its day-to-day functioning than were those of the German Empire. Within Prussia, the Ruhr did not coincide even remotely with any major administrative units, such divisions being preindustrial in origin. The Ruhr encompassed parts of the provinces of Rhineland and Westphalia and of the government districts (*Regierungsbezirke*) of Düsseldorf (Rhineland), Arnsberg (Westphalia), and Münster (Westphalia).

For the historian, one unfortunate consequence of this lack of congruence between administrative frontiers and economic realities is that much otherwise relevant statistical information collected by the state does not apply directly or exclusively to the Ruhr. An important exception is the extensive body of quantitative material collected by the relevant regional mining authority of the Prussian state (*Oberbergamt* Dortmund). Although there were a few minor discrepancies between the boundaries of the *Oberbergamtsbezirk* Dortmund and the Ruhr coalfield, these were so slight that for all practical purposes the figures published for the former reflect developments in the latter.[2] One fact that those figures clearly demonstrate is the Ruhr's overwhelming domination of the coal industry of Imperial Germany. By 1913 the *Oberbergamtsbezirk* Dortmund was producing 110,812,000 metric tons of coal or 58 percent of Germany's total output of 191,511,000 tons. Upper Silesia was a distant second with 43,900,000 tons or 23 percent.[3]

The prewar Ruhr was also first in the production of ferrous metals. Although the area was without major iron ore deposits of its own, the good coking quality of the bulk of its coal made it Imperial Germany's foremost metallurgical region. By 1913 the Ruhr was producing 8,209,157 metric tons of pig iron or 42.5 percent of a total of 19,309,172 for the German customs area, which consisted of the German Empire plus Luxembourg.[4] The bulk of the remainder, 6,417,727 metric tons or 33 percent, was produced in Lorraine and Luxembourg but was smelted largely with coke produced in the Ruhr.[5] Close corporate ties linked the Ruhr coal industry with the iron production of the border areas to the west.[6] The prewar Ruhr enjoyed an even more substantial lead in the production of steel than in the production of iron, accounting in 1913 for 10,112,000 metric tons or 59 percent of the German total of 17,148,000 tons.[7]

Ruhr Industry before 1896

The rise of Ruhr heavy industry to its commanding position within the German economy had been precipitous. Before the middle of the nineteenth century, the Ruhr was still overwhelmingly agrarian. Among the twenty-nine largest corporations of the prewar Ruhr, only seven could trace their origins to the first half of the century and only two, the Gutehoffnungshütte and the Krupp steelworks, had evolved directly from companies that existed prior to 1840.[8]

Although still essentially preindustrial, the Ruhr in the 1830s and 1840s witnessed important innovations—facilitated with capital and entrepreneurship imported from the neighboring Rhineland and from Great Britain, Belgium, and France—changes that, in conjunction with the advent of railroads, made possible the subsequent rapid growth of its primary industries. The most important of these innovations was the sinking by Franz Haniel of Ruhrort and then Mathias Stinnes of Mülheim of the first shafts successfully penetrating the marl covering most of the coal deposits of the region. Such shafts were not only more productive than the traditional, small surface mines and tunnels along the Ruhr River, but they also made accessible the region's vast reserves of coking coal. The coal yielded by the older mines of the southern fringe of the Ruhr coalfield had proven unsuitable for coking. By piercing through the marl, the pioneers of modern mining in the Ruhr opened the way for the establishment of the region's first successful coke-fired blast furnaces at midcentury.[9] Then during the boom years of the early and mid-1850s, Ruhr heavy industry began to assume its modern aspect. In the course of this investment spree and that of the early 1870s, almost half of the giant corporations of the prewar Ruhr had their beginning.[10]

From the vantage point of the spectacular *Gründerjahre* (promoters' years) of the early 1870s, Ruhr business leaders had reason to be pleased with their accomplishments. In the district administered by the *Oberbergamt* Dortmund, the production of coal had risen from 1,999,000 tons in 1850 to 16,417,000 tons in 1873, an average annual increase of 9 percent.[11] Ruhr blast furnaces, producing a mere 11,500 tons of pig iron in 1850, were turning out 479,233 tons in 1873.[12] Inflated prices, their like not to be seen again until the twentieth century, insured handsome profits from this greatly expanded output. The unprecedented economic boom that followed German unification seemed a confirmation of entrepreneurial expectations about the salutary effects of a dual triumph of industrialization and national unity.

But the feverish expectations of the *Gründerjahre* were not fulfilled. Following the crash of 1873, the remaining years of the seventies were the most painful experienced by Ruhr industrialists under the empire. Prices declined drastically from their 1873 highs. Pig iron that sold in the Ruhr for 125.20 marks per ton in 1873 sold in 1874 for 79.80 and in 1879 for only 51.65.[13] Ruhr coal in 1873 brought an average of 10.99 marks per ton; by 1879 the average price had dropped to 4.14 marks.[14] A brief recovery at the beginning of the next decade was followed by a renewed slump lasting from 1882 to 1886. Pig iron prices fell to a low of 43.55 marks per ton in 1886.[15] Improved economic conditions in the late 1880s were cut short by the recession of the early 1890s.

Profit margins narrowed and often disappeared entirely in the mid- and late 1870s, remaining unsatisfactory through most of the next decade as well. Ruhr companies that had paid hefty dividends during the *Gründerjahre* now paid none at all, or at most very modest sums. Among the largest companies, the Hoerder Verein established a particularly dismal record. Beginning in 1875, it paid dividends in only five of the next twenty years. With prospects so bleak, the price of stock in Ruhr companies plunged. Shares in the Bochumer Verein, which traded at 240 percent of face value in 1873, fell to 120 by 1874 and to 20 by 1877.[16]

The difficulties of the years following the crisis of 1873 were clearly reflected in prices, profits, and entrepreneurial attitudes, but only to a much lesser extent in production levels.[17] Given the large amounts of capital tied up in the primary industries, it was very costly to allow productive capacity to remain idle. Reductions in output were initiated most reluctantly, especially as long as numerous competitors could be expected to take up any slack thus created. As a consequence, coal production reported by the *Oberbergamt* Dortmund suffered minor setbacks in only four of the years (1874, 1877, 1886, and 1892) between 1873 and 1896, registering an overall increase from 16,417,000 tons to 44,893,000 tons for an average annual rate half that of the years between 1850 and 1873.[18] In metallurgy, production of pig iron dropped in 1874, not surpassing the 1873 figure until 1877. But thereafter, for the rest of the century, production dipped slightly only in 1890. Overall output increased from 479,233 tons in 1873 to 2,086,662 tons in 1896.[19]

In general, unit costs, rather than output, were cut during the deflationary years following 1873. Initially, savings were realized by slashing wages. Whereas in 1873 Ruhr miners earned an average 3.75 marks per shift, by 1879 the average had fallen to 2.33 marks.[20] Shift earnings of hewers and haulers in Dortmund mines (1913 = index base 100) fell from 77 in 1873 to a low of 39 in 1879. At Krupp, daily earnings of metal workers (1913 = index base 100) fell from 63 in 1873 to 51 in 1879.[21]

Anxious to convince the state to intervene on their behalf, Ruhr industrialists argued that without protection they were unable to offer a decent living to their workers. Louis Baare, the influential managing director of the Bochumer Verein from 1854 to 1895, dolefully testified to the Iron Inquiry Commission (Eisen-Enquete-Kommission) in 1878: "The people are deprived. They cannot feed themselves properly, and wife and children, the whole family, suffer as a consequence. . . . Under the circumstances, it is very bad for the working classes. The people have lost their strength."[22]

With wage rates pared to a minimum by the end of the 1870s, production costs could be further reduced only by increasing the size and efficiency of industrial units and, especially in the fast-changing iron and steel industry, through the introduction of new production processes and technical improvements. The most important instance of such innovation was the adoption in 1879 by the Rheinische Stahlwerke and the Hoerder Verein of the new Thomas-Gilchrist basic process of making steel. Despite low or nonexistent profits for much of the period, capital continued to be invested. Indeed, investment in expanded and modernized production facilities was one reason dividends remained low through the 1880s.

To secure needed capital, Ruhr developers drew upon the resources of Germany's large joint-stock banks, most notably, the Schaaffhausen'scher

Bankverein in Cologne and the Deutsche Bank, the Disconto-Gesellschaft, and the Dresdner Bank in Berlin. The price Ruhr industrialists paid for such assistance was the acceptance of careful bank supervision of their affairs. When financial difficulties were particularly serious, bankers insisted upon the selection of someone who enjoyed their confidence to undertake the task of reorganization. The Hoerder Verein underwent two such reorganizations, in 1878 and 1893, resulting in capital losses of 17.1 million marks for its investors.[23]

Unable to keep pace, many smaller, less efficient, less favorably located, and poorly financed companies failed to survive the economic tribulations of the 1870s and 1880s. Those years left a lasting mark on entrepreneurial calculations. On the eve of World War I, the region's business elite still included men who had been among those called upon to cope with the aftermath of the crash of 1873, who had had to pick up the pieces, to reorganize and readjust.

Particularly traumatic was the experience of Robert Müser. In 1856, his father, Friedrich Wilhelm Müser, M. D., had been one of the founders of the Harpener Bergbau-AG and had served for eighteen years as chairman of the company's administrative board (*Verwaltungsrat*). The Harpener Bergbau-AG prospered spectacularly during the boom years of the early 1870s. In 1871–1872 the company paid dividends of 25 percent of firm capital, and in 1873–1874, dividends of 60 percent. At this point, the elder Müser died, and his son, age twenty-five, was recalled from employment with a New York bank and elected to the administrative board, only to be confronted immediately with a dramatic reversal of the company's fortunes. For 1875–1876 and 1876–1877, the company could pay no dividends at all and very little through the whole of the next decade.[24]

Such experiences impelled men like Müser to become determined advocates of collective action, willing to sacrifice a measure of freedom for greater security. This was also the view of Emil Kirdorf. In 1873 Kirdorf was just beginning his long association with the Gelsenkirchener Bergwerks-AG, itself a product of the boom of the early 1870s. Kirdorf fought long and persistently for the cherished goal of stability through industrial cooperation.[25] Significantly, Müser and Kirdorf represented the two largest coal-producing companies in the prewar Ruhr. Their advocacy of a cartel as a means of eliminating ruinous competition among mining companies was of key importance in the formation of a selling union or syndicate, the Rheinisch-Westfälisches Kohlensyndikat, in 1893 and in its subsequent perpetuation.[26] The syndicate, the most rigid form of cartel, represented at its establishment 86.6 percent of all coal produced in the *Oberbergamtsbezirk* Dortmund and dictate both production and price levels for member firms.[27]

Ruhr iron and steel industrialists also pursued the goal of regulating competition, though with less success than that achieved by coal producers. A pig iron syndicate for Rhineland and Westphalia (Roheisensyndikat), formed in 1896, had a troubled history and collapsed in 1908, unable to withstand competition from outsiders. It was, however, reorganized and strengthened in 1910.

In the steel industry, product diversity complicated efforts to establish a comprehensive cartel. Specialized organizations for different kinds of products were formed but were not merged into a single unit until 1904, when the Stahlwerksverband was created, representing 83.5 percent of German steel production. The Stahlwerksverband suffered from serious internal divisions and was gravely weakened in 1912 by loss of control over its members' more finished products.[28]

Cartelization took time. A more immediately successful collective response to the economic difficulties following the crash of 1873 was greater entrepreneurial attention to interest-group politics. An increasingly important function assumed by a major portion of the Ruhr elite was leadership of a broad array of industrial associations. Governmental receptiveness encouraged such efforts.

In the Bergbau Verein, formed in 1858, Ruhr mining already possessed a strong organization to represent its interests. The stimulus to joint action had been provided by the economic crisis of 1857. In the first years of its existence, the mine owners' association had devoted itself largely to securing cheaper and more efficient transportation for industrial products. Regionally organized, the Bergbau Verein of the *Oberbergamtsbezirk* Dortmund collaborated as needed with *Bergbau Vereine* in Germany's other mining districts. Adapting itself to the industry's problems as they emerged, the Bergbau Verein remained until after the First World War the primary representative of Ruhr mining, especially in its relations with the state.[29]

Less homogeneous than mining, the iron and steel industry was more difficult to organize for collective action. However, in the 1870s its commitment to a campaign for protective tariffs in response to market difficulties provided the stimulus for major organizational initiatives. Ruhr entrepreneurs were instrumental in the formation in 1874 of the influential Association of German Iron and Steel Industrialists (Verein deutscher Eisen- und Stahlindustrieller, or VdESI). The organization's membership consisted of a wide variety of sizes and types of production units located throughout the German Empire. But within the VdESI, by far the largest and most powerful regional organization was its Northwest Group, representing the iron and steel industry of Rhineland and Westphalia, especially that of the Ruhr.[30]

Leading Ruhr industrialists were also active in the formation of the Centralverband deutscher Industrieller, which claimed to speak for German industry as a whole. Founded in 1876 as part of the successful campaign for protective tariffs, it never realized its goal of embracing all of German industry. A primary reason for this failure, aside from the inherent difficulty of uniting such diverse interests, was that the Centralverband was always perceived as being closely associated with the narrow interests of heavy industry. Indeed, so close were the ties between the Centralverband and the VdESI that from 1893 to 1912 they shared a common administration, under the direction of their mutual business manager (*Geschäftsführer*) Henry Axel Bueck. In 1895 a rival organization, the Bund der Industriellen, was formed, representing manufacturers of finished goods who challenged the cartel policies of the primary producers within the Centralverband.[31]

During the protectionist campaign of the late 1870s, spearheaded by the Centralverband and the VdESI, the potential for creating a powerful alliance by joining the leading Prussian propertied interests, old and new, acquired concrete form.[32] This rapprochement was initially based upon the common interest of the iron and steel entrepreneurs in the west and the estate owners in the east in protective tariffs. Economic interest triumphed over earlier social and political prejudices. Managing Director Louis Baare of the Bochumer Verein blamed doctrinaire free traders in the liberal camp for forcing Ruhr iron and steel producers to ally themselves with otherwise uncongenial partners.[33] The resulting "Junker-industrialist alliance" was never a love match but always a carefully calculated and often contentious marriage of convenience. Increasing conflict of economic interests between industrial and agricultural producers in the 1890s subjected relations between those two groups to growing strain, but a common commitment to an authoritarian social order insured continued efforts to revive cooperation in national affairs. Especially on labor-related issues, Ruhr employers could usually count on the support of a landed elite fearful that any concessions made to industrial workers would ultimately inspire demands from agricultural laborers for similar benefits.

Prewar Prosperity

For much of the period from 1873 to the mid-1890s, the primary concern of Ruhr producers had been low prices and inadequate markets. In contrast, from 1896 to the war, the coal, iron, and steel industries were at times unable to meet demand, even with extensive overtime and expanded facilities. In the hectic boom years just before the turn of the century, the strong demand for iron and steel caused a temporary revival of the outmoded, labor-intensive process of puddling, a method of producing wrought iron requiring workers to stir the molten metal by hand.[34]

There were, to be sure, recession years during the last two prewar decades, and these served as reminders to Ruhr employers not to take good fortune for granted and as opportunities to cut wages and purge work forces of unwanted elements. But the prosperous years far outnumbered the lean years. The generally high level of prosperity of this period is of particular significance for this study as it partially eased the bitterness generated by the organizational conflict and the drive to create a more efficient and disciplined work force that also characterized the Wilhelmian era.

The period from 1896 to 1914 includes two and one-half short-term business cycles. If these are dated from one peak year to the next, then the delimiting dates would be 1890, 1900, 1907, and 1913. The economic contractions beginning in each of the first three of those years lasted until troughs were reached in 1894, 1902, and late 1908, respectively. The 1913 slump was terminated by the outbreak of war. In accordance with the above periodization, the years from 1896 to 1900 comprise the hectic boom portion of the cycle that began in 1890. The recession of 1901–1902, followed by two years of hesitant recovery, and then a boom lasting to mid-1907 constitute the next cycle. Two years of recession, 1908 and 1909, followed by recovery and prosperity to 1913, made up the last complete prewar cycle.[35] The fluctuations of these short-term cycles of business activity are significant because they can be correlated with fluctuations in the intensity of labor strife and the shifting of the offensive from labor to management and vice versa. On the whole, prosperous years favored labor organization and agitation whereas recession years favored employer countermeasures.[36]

In the last two prewar decades, when economically good years outnumbered the bad and demand was generally high, prices for coal, iron, and steel recovered in both nominal and real terms from the low levels of the late 1870s and the 1880s.[37] And due at least in part to the operation of the cartels formed at the end of the nineteenth and the beginning of the twentieth centuries, these prices were now more stable and predictable than those of earlier years. Large Ruhr companies were once more capable of paying substantial dividends with regularity, in addition to sums reserved for paying off obligations incurred in less favorable times past and for expanding production facilities.[38] For joint-stock companies of the Ruhr coal industry, dividends averaged 11.94 percent of firm capital between 1896 and 1911, with a low of 9.27 percent in 1909 and a high of 15.55 percent in 1900.[39] The stocks of Ruhr corporations once again became highly desirable and sold at levels comparable to those of the early 1870s. Thus, shares of the Bochumer Verein that hit a low of 20 percent of face value in 1877 and had recovered to 150 by 1895–1896, rose to 280 in 1899 and 1900.[40]

For the leaders of Ruhr heavy industry, the prosperity and profitability of the last two prewar decades meant greater security and greater freedom from outside intervention. Booming profits eased problems of industrial financing and strengthened the position of Ruhr industrialists vis-à-vis their bankers, reversing the trend of the 1870s and 1880s. At the same time, the process of concentration, discussed below, created in the new century concerns so vast that their financial needs could be met only by a consortium of banks, thereby reducing the immediate control exercised by any one of them.[41] Indeed, so great were the investments of the major banks in Ruhr industry and so vital was the well-being of that industry to the fate of Germany's most important investment houses that the region's industrial leaders had as much or more influence over the bankers as bankers had with industry.

Members of the Ruhr business elite, always cautious about admitting good fortune for fear of encouraging demands by government, labor, and consumers, nevertheless commented upon the marked improvement in the economic climate as the nineteenth century drew to a close. Thus, in 1897, Hanns Jencke, chairman from 1879 to 1902 of the Krupp *Direktorium*, speaking to the Bergbau Verein, contrasted the currently favorable prospects with the trials of years past: "Gentlemen! At the beginning of our deliberations I should like to emphasize that it is under favorable auspices that this year's meeting takes place, favorable in general and for mining in particular, and it would not be right to deny it. . . . In the course of the past decades, it has not always been so. The good years have been the exception, have been rare. Most years have brought little cause for joy."[42] Continuing, Jencke attributed the current improvements to the political stability guaranteed by the Second Empire, to the government's tariff policies, and to the stabilizing influence of the cartels. In 1913, in a retrospective evaluation, Wilhelm Beukenberg, managing director of the Phoenix steelworks from 1908 to 1922, referred to the long series of favorable years during the reign of William II, contrasting them to the tribulations of the 1870s and 1880s, and attributing these favorable developments to the cartels and to the hard work and dedication of the entrepreneurial elite. He warned, however, against being lulled by good times into an "all-too-rosy" vision of the future.[43]

To counteract accusations that the period's high profits were achieved at the expense of the rest of society, Ruhr industrialists always hastened to add to any commentary on business successes a recital of the blessings, especially higher wages and more abundant employment opportunities, accruing to the working class as a result. But they did not ask whether labor's gains were proportionate to those of capital. In employer rhetoric, the image of the undernourished and insecure worker, used in the 1870s to justify government protection for industry, gave way in the Wilhelmian era to the image of prosperous masses who ought to be grateful to those who presided over a flourishing economy.

Yet gratitude was not always forthcoming. The last two decades before World War I witnessed significant attempts at the economic and political organization of labor in the Ruhr and challenges to employer absolutism. In addition to the emotionally charged clashes thus engendered, Ruhr employers found themselves confronted with problems arising from the growing inadequacy of traditional forms of personnel management, unsuited to the vast multiunit concerns that by then had become the norm rather than the exception in heavy industry. Grudgingly, the Ruhr industrial elite found itself forced to turn substantial attention to labor problems of all descriptions, an unwelcome diversion from grander pursuits of the time such as organizational and technological rationalization. That the diversion was most unwelcome, viewed as the workers' willful and gratuitous obstruction of smoothly functioning production, helps explain why the responses given were all too often harsh and uncompromising.

Corporate Growth

The burgeoning size of industrial enterprises was one of the most commented upon developments relating to labor relations in the prewar Ruhr, overshadowed in the public consciousness only by the more dramatic issue of unionization. There was much discussion by government officials, social theorists, labor leaders, and industrialists of the impossibility of maintaining meaningful personal contact between management and workers in concerns employing thousands and tens of thousands, of the consequent undermining of the legitimacy of traditional patterns of labor relations, and of the need to devise new forms of internal industrial organization to cope with problems of supervision and delegation of authority.[44] Conservative critics of urbanization, industrialization, capitalism, and everything else deemed modern (and Imperial Germany had many such critics) lamented the passing of personalized relations between employer and employee, and saw this passing not only as morally regrettable but also as socially dangerous.[45] And even the Ruhr industrial elite, though committed to bigness for the sake of cheaper, more efficient production, for greater ease in the control of markets and resources, and for personal aggrandizement, shared the anxiety of the empire's other elites over the possible social costs.

The increasing size of Ruhr firms in the last prewar generation may be accounted for only in part by the overall growth of coal, iron, and steel production. Actually, the average annual rate of increase for coal production reported by the *Oberbergamt* Dortmund between 1896 and 1913 was not substantially higher than it had been between 1873 and 1896. During the last two decades before the war, growth in coal production was slowed by the restraints imposed by the syndicate, the difficulties of opening new mines at ever greater depths, and shortages of labor in peak years. But in absolute terms, the growth of the last prewar decades was impressive. Coal production more than doubled from 44,893,000 tons in 1896 to 110,765,000 tons in 1913.[46] And expansion of the iron and steel industry was even more impressive. Production of pig iron in the Ruhr (the figures are actually for Rhineland-Westphalia without the Saar, the Siegerland, and the Lahn and Dill districts) increased from 3,270,400 tons in 1900 (earlier available figures are for a slightly different area) to 8,209,200 in 1913.[47]

The growth of total output of coal, iron, and steel between 1896 and 1914 was not matched by increased numbers of production units. The number of mines in the Ruhr had peaked at 299 in 1857. The total had fallen to 159 by 1895, reflecting the failure of many of the less profitable mines to survive the deflationary years following the crash of 1873. There was little change before the war; the number of mines in 1913 was 168.[48] To be sure, additional mines—larger, deeper, more modern and efficient—continued to be opened in the Ruhr coalfield, especially in the industrial frontier north of the Emscher River. Nevertheless, during the last prewar generation, the number of Ruhr mines remained essentially constant because the sinking of new shafts was offset by the closing of older, smaller, less efficient mines, most of which were located on the southern fringes of the Ruhr.

The demise of these less profitable mines was hastened by the coal syndicate's quota system, which dictated how much each member could produce in a year. The larger, more prosperous companies could increase the amount of coal they were permitted to dig by purchasing marginal mines, closing them down, and transferring the production quotas of the closed mines to more profitable operations in the north. This practice, especially marked in 1904 and again in 1913, produced a bitter reaction in the Reichstag and the Prussian bureaucracy, sparked by the complaints of local officials, retailers, and landlords in the southern Ruhr who contended that the coal owners were irresponsibly depriving towns of their industrial bases. Government officials and local public opinion stood firm in the contention that the operation of basic industry is a public trust and cannot be suspended merely to bring greater profits to large firms. Industrial spokesmen did not attempt to refute this line of argument but contended that the closings, though socially regrettable, were economically inevitable. Public outcry and bureaucratic intervention could only slow, but not halt, the abandonment of older, less profitable mines.[49]

Ever-larger mines characterized the prewar Ruhr. Whereas in 1885 only seven Ruhr mines produced more than half a million tons a year, by 1900 thirty-six did so. By 1913 the number had increased to sixty-seven. In 1885 no Ruhr mine produced as much as a million tons. By 1900 five did, and by 1913 nineteen produced that amount.[50] Between 1895 and 1913 the average number of workers employed per mine rose from 973 to 2,279.[51]

In the primary iron and steel industry, there was no room for the small producer. In the summer of 1914 there were only eighty-three blast furnaces in operation in the Ruhr, linked in groups of from two to ten in only nineteen locations. In 1857, the largest blast furnace in the Ruhr had a daily capacity of only 25 tons. In 1914 the average daily capacity of a blast furnace was 284 tons. Those of the Deutscher Kaiser company produced an average of 540 tons per day.[52]

The growing size of production units in the coal, iron, and steel industries was only one aspect of the formation of massive industrial empires in the Ruhr. Even more striking was the process of concentration of control. Following the crash of 1873, the emphasis, particularly in the hitherto fragmented coal industry, was on horizontal integration. Intensified competition convinced many influential members of the Bergbau Verein that there should be a significant reduction in the number of independent coal producers in the Ruhr.

One of the foremost advocates of concentration was Eduard Kleine, a leading personality in the Bergbau Verein from 1874 to 1909. In 1885 he urged the members of the mine owners' association to consolidate their holdings into the largest possible units. Indeed, he suggested that the "most effective course of action would be the consolidation of all the mines in the region into a single company." He feared, however, that such a monopoly could not be realized because "the state and public opinion would oppose such a concentration of power."[53]

Indeed, even among Kleine's closest associates in the Bergbau Verein, there were those who, cherishing independence and respectful of the organizational and leadership problems posed by companies of unprecedented size, expressed reservations about unlimited consolidation. One was Emil Krabler, managing director of the Kölner Bergwerksverein from 1886 to 1907. Like Kleine, Krabler was also a leading personality in the Bergbau Verein from the 1870s into the new century. But unlike Kleine, who participated in the direction of a number of companies in which his wife's family had an interest, Krabler dedicated his entire career to only one, which he led cautiously. Observed Krabler: "There is a limit to everything as soon as a single person is no longer able to maintain complete overview. From that point on success depends upon the lucky choice of collaborators. The development of our company demonstrates, however, that good results are possible without expansion."[54] Yet Krabler's extreme caution, like Kleine's grand plan, was not tenable. Krabler's son-in-law and successor, Fritz Winkhaus, adopted a more expansive policy, more in line with the demands of the time, leading in 1912 to fusion with the Bergbaugesellschaft Neu-Essen.[55]

Significantly, both Kleine and Krabler were strong supporters of the 1893 formation of the coal syndicate, though Kleine viewed it as a less desirable option than massive consolidation. Its advocates viewed the syndicate not only as a means of limiting competition and curbing independence in a fragmented industry but also as a means of preserving a modicum of independence for modest-sized as well as large companies by supporting prices that made survival possible for all members. This was the promise. That the promise, as far as the small companies were concerned, was not fulfilled was attributed by syndicate leader Emil Kirdorf to higher wages and increased costs of complying with government safety and welfare legislation that bore most heavily upon marginal firms.[56] Yet, the syndicate itself, dominated by the largest companies, hastened the demise of many smaller mines through its provision for the purchase and transfer of production quotas from one member to another.

If horizontal integration characterized the years following 1873, vertical integration came to the fore during the last two prewar decades. Especially important was the forging of closer ties between coal mining and iron and steel production. The formation of the Kohlensyndikat in 1893 was to prove an important stimulant to the formation of mixed concerns. Iron and steel companies purchased coal mines in order to secure themselves against the impact of the syndicate's price and delivery policies.[57] By 1900, a fifth of all coal production in the Ruhr was controlled by the iron and steel industry. All of the major metallurgical companies had some investment in coal.[58] By 1912, the Phoenix steelworks was the fifth largest coal producer in the Ruhr, the Gutehoffnungshütte was eighth, and Krupp eleventh.[59]

By the turn of the century, the expanding production of the steel companies' mines, the *Hüttenzechen*, constituted an increasing threat to the coal syndicate. Coal produced by these mines beyond the needs of metallurgy was dumped on the market. In 1903 the *Hüttenzechen* were integrated into the coal syndicate on the basis of a major concession that excluded their coal produced for internal comsumption from the production quotas of the cartel. But this concession to the *Hüttenzechen* weakened the competitive position of companies exclusively committed to coal and motivated the largest of them, Emil Kirdorf's Gelsenkirchener Bergwerks-AG, to expand into iron and steel production. In 1904 the Gelsenkirchen concern merged with the Aachener Hüttenverein Rote Erde, headed by Kirdorf's older brother Adolph, and subsequently with the Schalker Verein, controlled by August Thyssen.[60]

The largest corporations of the prewar Ruhr not only fused the production of coal, iron, and steel but also added an ever-wider range of byproducts and finished goods, partly to take advantage of technological developments favoring integrated production, partly to circumvent cartel limitations, and partly to avoid dependence on a single market.[61] The effect on some companies was striking. Thus, in 1896 the profits of the Gelsenkirchener Bergwerks-AG from the manufacture of coal tar, ammonia, and benzene had amounted to only 114,751 marks, but by 1906 such profits amounted to 2,289,454 marks.[62] Ruhr heavy-industry firms also became increasingly involved in marketing, in transportation (controlling the most important navigation companies in the region), and in the production of energy, by supplying gas and electricity to cities in the Ruhr and even beyond.[63] Large Ruhr concerns also expanded their holdings (ore fields, manufacturing subsidiaries, sales, and shipping offices) in other parts of Germany and in other countries.[64]

During the last two decades before 1914, expansion from iron and steel into coal, from coal into iron and steel, or from either enterprise into finished goods was often achieved by acquiring existing units rather than establishing new ones. Fusion occurred not only when large companies absorbed small ones but also when giant concerns merged. Especially spectacular mergers of the early years of the twentieth century included not only the previously mentioned expansion of the Gelsenkirchener Bergwerks-AG but also the union of the Hoerder Verein and the Nordstern mining company with Phoenix in 1906–1907 and the 1910 merger of the Dortmunder Union with the Deutsch-Luxemburgische Bergwerks- und Hütten-AG. As a consequence of these mergers, the Gelsenkirchener Bergwerks-AG employed 45,640 workers in 1913–1914, Phoenix employed 40,260, and Deutsch-Luxemberg employed 53,347.

One Ruhr corporation was even larger: Krupp had 70,127 employees in the last year of peace. Other giants included the Harpener Bergbau-AG, the Gutehoffnungshütte, and Deutscher Kaiser with more than twenty thousand each; and Hibernia, the Bochumer Verein, the Rheinische Stahlwerke, and Hoesch with more than ten thousand each.[65] The growth in scale of such operations seems particularly impressive when we recall that the two giant employers of the Ruhr at midcentury had been

Jacobi, Haniel & Huyssen, the forerunner of the Gutehoffnungshütte, with about two thousand workers, and Mathias Stinnes with about one thousand.[66]

The huge, integrated concerns of the prewar Ruhr coexisted to the First World War and beyond, their rivalries limited by the cartels. The formation of trusts in American big business after the turn of the century did stimulate some discussion of a similar strategy in the Ruhr. Foremost advocate of this alternative was August Thyssen, owner of the Deutscher Kaiser company, who argued that the cartels were outmoded and the time had come to form a trust joining the most productive German concerns. Thyssen, a close observer of business developments in the United States, argued that only a German trust could meet American competition in the twentieth century.[67] In 1904, Thyssen and Hugo Stinnes, grandson of Mathias Stinnes and leading personality at the Deutsch-Luxemburg concern, entered the supervisory board (*Aufsichtsrat*) of the expanding Gelsenkirchener Bergwerks-AG, perhaps hoping to use that corporation as the nucleus of a trust.[68] A bitter struggle for control ensued, in which Gelsenkirchen's Managing Director Emil Kirdorf emerged victorious. In 1909, Thyssen gave up his seat on the Gelsenkirchen supervisory board and sold all but an insignificant portion of his holdings in that company.[69] The creation of a trust in Ruhr heavy industry had to wait until after the First World War. Until then, oligopoly was the order of the day in the Ruhr, a state of affairs strongly supported by the Prussian government, which preferred it to disruptive competition on the one hand or an all-powerful trust on the other.[70]

The small number of nearly coequal giants that were in the forefront of determining the policies to be pursued by heavy industry faced pressing managerial problems, problems both of sheer size and of increased internal heterogeneity. Given the tremendous investments represented by these huge concerns, there was great pressure to eliminate inefficient practices preventing optimum utilization of resources.[71] When enterprises grew through mergers and the acquisition of preexisting units, differing or even conflicting managerial policies and practices might characterize the individual components of the same company. In multiplant concerns where the central office was often far removed from actual production, there was the problem of remote control, only partly eased by the introduction of the telephone. And with regard to labor problems, the leaders of giant industrial combines found themselves confronted with an ever-broader spectrum of workers and working conditions.

2
The Entrepreneurial Elite

Owners and Managers

The men who presided over the largest concerns in the prewar Ruhr were fiercely determined to master the organizational problems posed by the increased size and complexity of production and administrative units without making any significant sacrifice in their personal authority. This was as true of salaried executives as it was of owner-entrepreneurs.

From the beginning of modern heavy industry in the Ruhr, the self-reliant owner-entrepreneur was rare. Among leaders in the prewar era, the clearest example of this type was August Thyssen. Born in 1843, Thyssen, with financial aid from his father and other relatives, became a partner in 1867 in a Duisburg rolling mill. He withdrew in 1871 to be on his own, and established the firm of Thyssen & Co. in Mülheim. In 1883 Thyssen began to purchase shares of the Deutscher Kaiser mining company in Hamborn. By 1891 he was sole owner. In building his empire, Thyssen took particular care to maintain his independence, relying upon loans rather than stock issues to finance expansion and utilizing family members as much as possible to staff key positions.[1] Besides the Thyssen enterprises, the only other family-owned firms in the Ruhr that employed over five thousand were three Haniel-owned mining companies (Zollverein, Neumühl, and Rheinpreussen), the Gutehoffnungshütte, the Hoesch steelworks, and the Krupp steelworks.

The governing boards (*Grubenvorstände*) of the Haniel mines were presided over after 1893 by Franz Haniel, grandson and namesake of the man who introduced deep mining into the Ruhr. The younger Franz Haniel was also chairman of the supervisory board (*Vorsitzender des Aufsichtsrates*) of the Gutehoffnungshütte, of which his energetic grandfather had been one of the cofounders.[2] The Gutehoffnungshütte had in Carl Lueg and later Paul Reusch managing directors who were prominent members of the Ruhr elite.

The Hoesch steelworks, though family owned, passed increasingly under managerial control at the end of the nineteenth century. Albert Hoesch, as chief executive of the firm, had maintained rigorous personal supervision. He himself, for example, took charge of the company's ledgers, considering the balance to be his personal secret.[3] But after his death in 1898, he was replaced not by a family member (his sons were still minors) but by Friedrich Springorum, who served as the company's managing director until 1920. Members of the Hoesch family did, however, remain the dominant force on the firm's supervisory board.

Family ownership of the Krupp concern was jealously guarded. When the firm was transformed into a joint-stock company in 1903, all but 4 of the 160,000 shares were kept in the possession of the family. The four other shares went to individuals close to the Krupps.[4] But during the years following Alfred Krupp's death in 1887, the family's leadership of the company had faltered. Friedrich Alfred Krupp, especially in his last years, was often absent from Essen for long periods, preferring Capri's more hospitable climate. Much of the burden of direction devolved upon the chairman of the executive committee, Hanns Jencke, who had held that post since 1879. During these years, it was not unknown for the executive committee to disregard the expressed wishes of the absent owner.[5] When F. A. Krupp died in 1902, he left no male heir. Since Jencke also retired in the same year and his successor, Max Roetger, was a less forceful individual, collegial but not always harmonious leadership at Krupp became the order of the day. The trend toward committee rule was, however, partially reversed by the marriage in 1906 of Bertha Krupp to diplomat Gustav von Bohlen und Halbach, who added the Krupp name to his own and became chairman of the supervisory board. In 1909, he chose Alfred Hugenberg to replace Roetger as chairman of the executive committee.[6]

The rarity of family firms in the Ruhr was a consequence of the initial scarcity of capital in that region in combination with the large sums needed to build a steel mill or to sink a mine shaft. Even in the middle of the nineteenth century, the amounts required were typically beyond the resources of a single family: 200,000–300,000 taler for a blast furnace; 500,000–1,000,000 taler for a coal mine; and 1,000,000–2,000,000 taler for a steel mill.[7]

Years might pass before production began, even more until dividends were forthcoming. Building a steel mill usually took two or more years. Mining was less predictable. Sinking a mine shaft typically took two to five years, but often much longer if geological conditions proved unfavorable. In an extreme case, twenty-seven years (1857–1884) were required to sink the Haniel mine Rheinpreussen in the difficult terrain on the Rhine's left bank. *Gewerkschaften*, the traditional form of corporate organization in Ruhr mining, made provision for unpredictability in the capital needs of new mines with the requirement that investors (*Gewerken*) had to supply whatever extra funds were needed beyond the original amount invested.

Until the middle of the nineteenth century, state officials had been responsible for the operation of all mines in Prussia, whether state-owned or private. As a consequence, the function of the *Gewerken* had initially been limited to the provision of capital. After mid-century, when state direction of private mines was dismantled, many *Gewerken*, given their lack of technical expertise in mining and the tradition of separation of ownership and control, were content to see direction pass from state mining officials to salaried executives in their own employ. Others, however, claimed a more active role for themselves.

Descendants of prominent *Gewerken* represented in the prewar industrial elite were the Waldthausen and Funke families in Essen and the Stinnes family in Mülheim. The Waldthausens and Funkes were, after the Krupps, the richest families in Essen. The most important interest of the Waldthausens was the Arenberg'sche AG, presided over to 1906 by Oskar von Waldthausen, and then by his nephew Otto Krawehl.[8] Much larger was the industrial empire controlled by Carl Funke, himself married to a Waldthausen. He built upon the fortune left him by his father, building contractor and mine promoter Fritz Funke. At the time of his death in 1912, Carl Funke controlled mining companies employing 25,240 workers. Among these companies were two employing over five thousand: König Ludwig in Recklinghausen and the Essener Steinkohlenbergwerke AG, the latter formed in 1906 in an attempt to consolidate and revive some of the older, smaller, less profitable mines around Essen.[9]

Similar in purpose to the Essener Steinkohlenbergwerke AG was the Mülheimer Bergwerksverein, formed in 1898 by Hugo Stinnes. In 1912 the Stinnes mines employed a total of 11,409. The most important enterprise with which Hugo Stinnes was associated was not, however, one of the Stinnes mines but rather the Deutsch-Luxemburgische Bergwerks- und Hütten-AG, founded in 1901. Its purpose was to combine metallurgy in Luxemburg with mining in the Ruhr. Stinnes, representing coal interests within the combine, was given a seat on the supervisory board in 1904 and became its chairman in 1906, replacing banker and promoter Bernhard Dernberg, who left to become colonial secretary.[10]

Great as was the personal fortune that Hugo Stinnes amassed, his industrial power was immeasurably greater. He sat on the supervisory boards of seventeen joint-stock companies (*Aktiengesellschaften*) and of five mining *Gewerkschaften*. He controlled, rather than owned, the huge Deutsch-Luxemburg concern. Indeed, since Stinnes relied heavily upon outside financing, he was subject to some of the same pressures as were corporate managers.

The career of Hugo Stinnes, born in 1870, was paralleled in many ways by that of Peter Kloeckner, born in 1863, even though Stinnes belonged to one of the oldest of Ruhr industrial families and Kloeckner, a native of Koblenz and the son of a dockyard owner, was a newcomer to the region. The careers of the two men intersected at an early stage as both, in pursuit of commercial experience, entered the employ of the prominent Koblenz iron merchant Carl Spaeter. Kloeckner was one of the firm's head clerks when Stinnes was a commercial apprentice there.[11] Family contacts had been instrumental in securing for both young men the opportunity of working with Spaeter. Kloeckner, like Stinnes, developed close ties with major banks and constructed an industrial empire on that basis. Like Stinnes, he amassed numerous industrial offices, sitting on the supervisory boards of twenty-five companies and serving as chairman of seven. His most important post was as head of the Lothringer Hüttenverein. Founded in 1897 in Brussels to combine Lorraine iron ore and Ruhr coal, the company was foundering when Kloeckner, at the behest of concerned banking interests, joined the supervisory board in 1903 and began the task of reorganization.[12]

Although the wealth and power of the leading industrial capitalists of the prewar Ruhr was awesome, the fact remains that the industrial elite of that region was predominantly a managerial elite. Devolution of control upon salaried entrepreneurs came early in the development of Ruhr heavy industry as a consequence of the generally dispersed nature of ownership and the multiple commitments of many leading investors.[13] Of the thirty-eight individuals selected to represent the Ruhr elite in this study, twenty-eight were managers without significant holdings in the companies they directed, though typically their investment of ego in these concerns was immense.

In the Ruhr as elsewhere, the first generation of corporate managers had to struggle for recognition and freedom of action. But in the long run, it proved difficult for shareholders to monitor closely the functioning of rapidly expanding enterprises. A vigorous and determined manager, possessing superior familiarity with the enterprise, held the advantage. This was the case with Louis Baare, first of the important managing directors in the Ruhr, who rose to effective control of the Bochumer Verein in the 1860s. That firm's supervisory board, composed of men who resided outside the region and who met together but once a month, could not long remain a formidable barrier to his ambitions. Baare's success provided the model for other ambitious Ruhr managers.[14]

By the end of the nineteenth century, members of the managerial elite had been largely successful in their struggle for recognition as industrial leaders. The growth of ever-larger concerns during the last two prewar decades enhanced the positions of salaried executives. The amount of capital invested was now typically so great that usually no single investor or group of investors could dictate policy or felt compelled to try as long as dividends were adequate, as they usually were during these years. Supervisory boards, legally empowered to monitor the activities of management, often become so bloated and cumbersome and were deliberately kept so poorly informed as to be useless as instruments of control.[15] An extreme example was the Gelsenkirchener Bergwerks-AG's supervisory board, which in 1905 consisted of twenty-five men from all parts of Germany. Even such powerful and determined board members as August Thyssen and Hugo Stinnes failed to carry the day against Gelsenkirchen's managing director, Emil Kirdorf.[16]

By the beginning of the twentieth century, as the careers of Thyssen, Stinnes, and Kirdorf illustrate, the formal distinction between owner-entrepreneur and salaried executive often meant little in actual practice. The managing directors of the largest corporations had won recognition as industrial leaders in their own right and could be just as imperious and jealous of their personal authority as were those men whose authority rested upon personal ownership. It is difficult to trace any direct correlation between changes in the owner-management relationship and changes in labor policies. The combination of family enterprise with large-scale production did produce some notable examples of extensive company welfare programs and relatively stable employer-employee relations. The most frequently cited example was Krupp. But the significance of such cases was certainly grossly exaggerated and romanticized by conservative observers who deplored the supposedly greater impersonality of joint-stock companies. Actually, the increased impersonality of labor-management relations of the last prewar decades was more a function of mammoth size and of the removal of the managerial elite from the site of production than of the emergence of professional managers as employers.[17]

Recruitment and Training

Those among the industrial elite of the prewar Ruhr who exercised their power and influence from the board room all came from families of industrial or commercial entrepreneurs of the Ruhr or the Rhine province, with the single exception of diplomat Gustav von Bohlen und Halbach, the husband of Bertha Krupp.[18] Most commonly, the preparation of these men for their future careers stressed apprenticeship in the family firm or in that of a relative or one of the father's business associates. Thereafter, family wealth and connections made possible early assumption of responsible positions. Hugo Stinnes founded his first firm at age twenty-three. August Thyssen became a partner in a rolling mill at age twenty-four. Carl Funke and Albert Hoesch began directing family enterprises at ages twenty-one and twenty-four respectively.[19]

The emphasis on early on-the-job experience normally precluded extensive formal technical education. Stinnes's technical training consisted of half a year at the Berlin Mining Academy. Friedrich Alfred Krupp, despite his personal interest in science and technology, was permitted only a short stay at the technical university in Braunschweig, receiving most of his instruction at the Krupp works under his father's watchful eye. The elder Krupp maintained that because one man could not oversee all aspects of a firm as large as Krupp's, administrative ability and experience were more important than technical expertise, which could be left to the second echelons of the firm's hierarchy.[20] Only three of the capitalists received extensive training at postsecondary institutions. Otto Krawehl was trained, at his father's insistence, as a state mining official (*Bergassessor*). Albert Hoesch and August Thyssen were educated to become acquainted with the most modern techniques in the manufacture of iron and steel.[21]

If family connections were vital to those who became board chairmen, they were scarcely less so to many managers. Five of the twenty-eight salaried executives in the prewar Ruhr business elite virtually inherited their positions. Thus, Carl Lueg of the Gutehoffnungshütte succeeded his father in 1864. Robert Müser, managing director of the Harpener Bergbau-AG, was the eleventh child of that company's original chief executive. Managing Director Fritz Baare of the Bochumer Verein was the third son and successor of Louis Baare. In 1904, Hermann Pieper, Jr., became managing director of the Constantin der Grosse mining company following the death of his father, Hermann Pieper, Sr. And Fritz Winkhaus assumed control of the Kölner Bergwerksverein in 1907 when his father-in-law, Emil Krabler, retired as managing director.[22]

At least four others were directly helped by family connections in their entry into Ruhr management positions. Emil Kirdorf began his career in Ruhr mining by accepting a position that had previously been offered to his brother Adolph. And Emil Goecke was appointed managing director of the Rheinische Stahlwerke in 1878 by his brother Feodor, who was chairman of the supervisory board, a post to which Feodor had been named the year before with the mission of reorganizing the tottering firm.[23] Eduard Kleine's career in Ruhr mining was helped along by his marriage to Mathilde Hueck, daughter of a prominent family of Dortmund *Gewerken*. And the career of his son, Eugen Kleine, benefited not only from his parents' contacts but also from those of his father-in-law, Theodor Schmieding. Schmieding was not only a brother of the mayor of Dortmund and a leading spokesman of Ruhr industry in the Prussian Landtag but also a member of the supervisory board of the Harpener Bergbau-AG. When Robert Müser gave up his position as managing director of that company to become chairman of the supervisory board, Eugen Kleine was appointed in his place.[24]

Altogether at least half of the salaried executives in the Ruhr entrepreneurial elite came from entrepreneurial or managerial families. Nine had fathers who were themselves managers of coal or of iron and steel operations, seven in private industry, two in the service of the state. Three more had fathers who were small-scale iron manufacturers, and two had fathers who had been active in other industries (one as owner, one as manager). As for the rest, there was one clergyman's son, two sons of estate owners, four sons of civil servants, and six whose father's occupations I could not definitely determine.

When it is recalled that nine out of ten of the capitalists in the elite came from entrepreneurial families, the homogeneity of the group in terms of social origins is apparent.[25] The families of origin of the capitalists were, of course, much wealthier than those of the future directors. But even the latter came from families that were generally quite well-to-do. Beginning a career leading to upper management normally required a significant investment at some point, for education and other purposes. A few would-be managers were hard-pressed to find the needed resources. For example, when Emil Kirdorf assumed his first post as commercial director of the Holland mining company in 1871, he had to put up a bond of 10,000 taler. Because the Kirdorf family textile firm had gone bankrupt not long before, his family was unable to cover this cost. The money was provided for the ambitious twenty-four-year-old by a friend of his fiancée's family.[26] A fortunate choice of financée also helped Wilhelm Beukenberg. His family was financially among the most modest of any that we are considering. His father was a *Steiger*, the lowest category among mining supervisors, and could not afford a technical education for his son. The necessary funds were provided by Beukenberg's betrothed, daughter of a well-to-do peasant family.[27]

Since family contacts counted for so much in the careers of those who became industrial leaders in the prewar Ruhr, it is not surprising that most of these men were born not far from where they were to spend the most important of their working years. Of the thirty-eight, seventeen (five owners and twelve managers) were born in the Ruhr itself. Ten more (four capitalists and six salaried executives) were born in other parts of the Rhine province or Westphalia. Ten managers were born elsewhere in Germany.

The only foreign-born member of the elite was Gustav Krupp von Bohlen und Halbach, who was born in The Hague where his father served as Baden's envoy to the Netherlands.[28]

But even for those born in the Ruhr, preparation for their careers usually required residence elsewhere for a time. Only five of the thirty-eight never lived any place else.[29] In contrast, eight members of the elite spent extended periods working or studying in other European countries or in the United States. The leaders of Ruhr industry as a group paid close attention to developments in other industrialized countries, a tradition established in the mid-nineteenth century when Ruhr industry was an importer of foreign capital and expertise and sustained subsequently by heavy industry's intense involvement in the world market. This interest extended not only to technological and commercial changes but to developments in labor relations as well.

Academic training necessarily took future industrial leaders out of the Ruhr. Prior to the First World War, none of the appropriate institutions was located in the Ruhr. Academic training was particularly important in the careers of prospective directors. Whereas the training of the capitalists was likely to stress on-the-job experience over academic preparation, future managers were more likely to have extensive postsecondary instruction. Of the twenty-eight managers, only six were without extensive academic training. Of the six, three had commercial apprenticeships, one a factory apprenticeship, and two had attended trade schools. Of the other twenty-two, ten were the product of mining academies, five were trained in the law, and seven were engineers.

The engineers, trained at technical institutes or technical universities, were to be found in the iron and steel industry. Their academic training was normally combined with early on-the-job experience. In general, technical expertise was accorded greater prominence as a qualification for leadership in metallurgy than in mining, where the pace of technological change was less hectic and where, because of the tradition of state direction, early private initiative had been primarily commercial.

Those future Ruhr managers who attended the mining academies did so as part of the prescribed preparation to become state mining officials. Men bearing the title *Bergassessor a. D.* (retired state mining official) were especially prominent in the highest managerial ranks of the coal industry, an important legacy of the period of state direction. To achieve that title required long preparation, usually nine or ten years beyond the Gymnasium, combining practical experience in mining, academic training, and state examinations. These were high-level positions. Even to be admitted to the program was not easy for men without the proper contacts. Thus, Fritz Winkhaus was turned down when he first applied. A second application was successful, however, his case being sponsored this time by a civil engineer, prominent in Ruhr mining, who was related to Winkhaus's grandmother.[30]

The men we are considering entered state service with the intent of later transferring to more lucrative positions in private industry. But spending approximately a decade as aspiring state officials was not without significant implications for their later lives. Especially important were the close bonds between state and private mining bureaucracies, since the two groups contained men of similar background and training. Also important was the extended exposure of these future Ruhr managers to bureaucratic models of organization.

For leadership personnel Ruhr industry drew not only upon the state mining bureaucracy but also, though to a lesser extent, upon other branches of state service. In addition to the ten managers in the elite who had been state mining officials, four others had begun careers in government: two in the administrative bureaucracy, one in the judiciary, and one as director of the Saxon state railroads.[31] These men were trained in the law, the normal preparation for high civil servants in Germany. Three of the four were selected in succession to become chairman of the executive committee of the Krupp steelworks, a company noted for its exceptionally close governmental ties.

Relations with Other Elites

The fact revealed most clearly by a survey of the families of origin and the training of the Ruhr industrial elite is the closeness of the ties between that group and the state bureaucracy. Of the thirty-eight members of the elite, sixteen had been trained for state service. If to that sixteen are added those whose fathers were bureaucrats or whose mothers or wives came from bureaucratic families, the number rises to at least twenty-two. The closeness of these ties both reflected and encouraged the accommodation of Ruhr coal, iron, and steel producers to the established social and political order of Prussia and Germany.

Initially, the most significant reference group for the first Ruhr entrepreneurs had not been any of the traditional elites of Prussian society—namely, the court, the officer corps, the high civil service, and the landed estate owners—but rather the financial, commercial, manufacturing, and professional leaders of Rhineland and Westphalia. These provincial notables provided much of the capital and initiative for early industrialization in the Ruhr. They also provided much of the liberal orientation of the emerging elite of coal, iron, and steel. This attitude was characterized by opposition to overwhelming aristocratic and bureaucratic domination of the Prussian state. But by the second half of the nineteenth century, especially after 1870, the ties between leading Ruhr industrialists and other business and professional men in the two western provinces had weakened, as a result of the growing exclusiveness of Ruhr industrial leaders, their rapidly expanding wealth and power, their growing involvement in national and international as opposed to local affairs, and their increasingly strained relations with German liberalism.

In terms of wealth, leading Ruhr capitalists were among the very richest individuals in Wilhelmian Germany. In 1911, the fortune of Bertha Krupp was estimated at 283 million marks, that of Franz Haniel at 65 million, that of August Thyssen at 54 million, and that of Hugo Stinnes at 34 million. Of the twenty richest individuals in the prosperous Rhine province, six were Haniels, two were Krupps, two were Thyssens, two were Hoesches, two were Waldthausens, one was Hugo Stinnes and one Carl Funke. The other four came from families of Rhenish iron manufacturers.[32]

Leading corporate managers in Ruhr heavy industry, of course, never amassed fortunes of equivalent size. Yet in the new century they too counted as rich men, having substantially improved their personal financial positions relative to their predecessors.[33] They benefited from prewar prosperity and industrial expansion. Profit-sharing plans for the managerial elite, income from personal investments, and the common practice of holding several lucrative seats on the supervisory boards of other companies yielded more than enough money to support an upper-class life style. Richest of Ruhr managers was Emil Kirdorf, who with an estimated eleven to twelve million marks in 1911 ranked twenty-second among Rhenish millionaires. Of the twenty-eight managers in the prewar elite, at least ten others besides Kirdorf were multimillionaires, and the actual total was undoubtedly higher.[34]

Increased wealth permitted an increasingly opulent life style by the end of the nineteenth century. One of the most conspicuous manifestations of the more luxurious style of life adopted by many Ruhr industrialists was the villa. Large and richly furnished, such houses provided the appropriate setting for entertaining important guests: military officers, high government officials, foreign dignitaries, and in the case of the Krupp family, the emperor himself.[35]

In contrast to their predecessors, who often lived on or near the factory grounds, later generations of industrialists built their houses as far from the smoking chimneys as time and money allowed. Most chose to reside in exclusive suburbs or on the outskirts of town.[36] The result of this withdrawal from the immediate factory area was an increasing spatial separation of the entrepreneurial elite from the workers, from the community, and from the less wealthy business and professional men of the region.

However, the proliferation of grandiose residences and the adoption of an opulent life style, including luxury motor cars, hunting preserves, and art collections, should not obscure the extent to which older attitudes and modes of behavior continued to characterize industrial leaders. More often than not, their elaborate villas were maintained for representative purposes, because they were expected and because they were useful in cultivating and impressing socially, politically, and financially important contacts, rather than because the owners derived inordinate personal gratification from a luxurious existence. The villa was a proud symbol of industrial accomplishment.

Often the owners of villas and landed estates lived with personal simplicity. For example, August Thyssen, who entertained large numbers of guests, still pinched his pennies when it came to personal expenditures. His much younger Mülheim neighbor, Hugo Stinnes, was also noted for living austerely relative to his wealth and power.[37] Long hours and hard work were essential elements in the lives of leading industrialists, making them particularly unsympathetic to demands from subordinates for shorter workdays or a less hectic pace. The prewar entrepreneur felt compelled to dedicate most of his time and effort to business in order to master the increasing complexity of industrial organization. As the industrialists became increasingly preoccupied with their professional roles, they showed less interest in filling honorary and communal offices that did not directly involve the interests of industry.[38]

Far more important than personal wealth and its trappings, especially for the managerial elite, were the vast resources these men controlled and the number of lives directly affected by their decisions. Emil Kirdorf, at the head of the giant Gelsenkirchen combine, operating with capital that was not his personal property, was nonetheless one of the towering figures of Ruhr industry. Even when income remained relatively modest—as in the case of Fritz Baare, whose exclusive commitment to the Bochumer Verein precluded serving on the supervisory boards of other concerns and collecting the generous fees—standing within Ruhr society could be high, reflecting economic and social power rather than personal wealth.[39]

Given the great wealth and power of Ruhr industrial leaders and their overwhelming preoccupation with business, there were few groups in Wilhelmian society with whom they associated on a basis of equality and mutual respect. Except for their ties with one another, Ruhr entrepreneurs maintained their closest business and personal ties with leading investment bankers. Although, as noted in chapter 1, Ruhr industrialists of the last prewar decades enjoyed a greater measure of independence vis-à-vis the banks than had their predecessors, they still had to cultivate carefully the representatives of the major financial institutions. Arranging financing for expansion was one of the most important functions of corporate leaders of the period. Bankers were prominent members of the supervisory boards of nearly all large Ruhr concerns. Most notable was Carl Klönne, director of the Deutsche Bank, intimate friend of August Thyssen and Carl Funke, and member of the supervisory boards of the Gelsenkirchener Bergwerks-AG, the Harpener Bergbau-AG, the Schalker Verein, the Nordstern mining company, and the Bochumer Verein. Leading Ruhr industrialists, in turn, were often members of the supervisory boards of major banks. The board of the Disconto-Gesellschaft, for example, included Ruhr leaders Emil Kirdorf, Hermann Brauns, Wilhelm Beukenberg, Jacob Hasslacher, and Friedrich Springorum. The Dresdner Bank had close ties with Thyssen and Krupp, with former Krupp director Hanns Jencke serving as chairman of that bank's supervisory board from 1904 to 1910.[40]

During the prosperous years prior to World War I, bank representatives rarely intervened directly in the internal affairs of healthy Ruhr concerns.[41] One area in which their intervention was particularly unwelcome was that of labor relations. Resistance to such interventions had emerged prominently as early as the Ruhr coal strike of 1889. In that instance, mine operators dismissed counsels of moderation from their bankers as reflecting misguided concern with the maintenance of short-term profits. Their own priority was the maintenance of employer authority, whatever the immediate costs.[42]

Relations of Ruhr industrialists with leaders of finance and commerce other than investment bankers were less satisfactory, especially since these groups favored freer trade than did the industrialists and, in some respects, a more liberal political and social development in Prussia and Germany. The same was often true of relations with manufacturers of finished goods. The prospect of a broad alliance of all of Germany's industrial, commercial, and financial interests that would constitute a counterweight, not only to democratic and socialist demands but also to excessive agrarian and bureaucratic pretensions, was welcome to the Ruhr elite so long as such an alliance would in large measure accept their leadership. But these claims to leadership by a group often considered by other German entrepreneurs to be too rigid, too self-centered, and too uncompromising were a persistent obstacle to formation of an alliance uniting all those representing German capitalism.[43]

Among German industrialists, the Ruhr elite had most in common with the men who presided over large industrial establishments in Upper

Silesia and the Saar. The Silesian magnates shared with the richest Ruhr capitalists the absolute pinnacle of wealth in Wilhelmian society, but differed from them in being primarily of aristocratic origin. However, the prominence of titled owners in Silesia, who were similarly reliant on salaried executives, does not appear to have been linked to any major differences in approach to labor problems.[44]

In most instances, regular contacts among Germany's heavy industrial regions were maintained by managers rather than by owners. Members of the Ruhr managerial elite found their closest counterparts in such men as Ewald Hilger, managing director of the Vereinigte Königs- und Laurahütte in Silesia (formerly director of state mining in the Saar), Adolf Williger, managing director of the Kattowitzer AG für Bergbau und Hüttenbetrieb in Silesia, and Edmond Weisdorff, managing director of the Burbacher Hütte in the Saar. Hilger, born in the Ruhr, was the son of the founder of the Ewald mining company in Herten in Westphalia.[45] A noteworthy link between Ruhr and Saar industry was the friendship between Friedrich Alfred Krupp and Carl Ferdinand Freiherr von Stumm-Halberg, most prominent of Saar industrialists.[46] More accessible to most Ruhr industrialists, however, than the haughty Stumm were the Röchlings of Völkingen-Saar.

Whereas Ruhr employers frequently criticized other German industrialists for being insufficiently firm in resisting organized labor, they never had occasion to direct such complaints against the leaders of heavy industry in the Saar and in Upper Silesia. Indeed, employers in those two border areas were even more unyielding in their antistrike and antiunion policies than were the leaders of Ruhr industry. Employers in Silesia and the Saar could afford to be relentless because of the nature of the work forces they confronted. The strong influence of the Catholic church in the Saar and in Silesia militated against the spread of both social democracy and unions.[47] In Silesia, the work force was particularly disadvantaged, being composed in part of women, minors, and seasonal workers, and consisting predominantly of members of Prussia's Polish-speaking minority.[48]

Whereas Silesia and the Saar were Catholic, the Ruhr was religiously divided, with a majority of Catholics in the west and a majority of Protestants in the east. As of December 1893, 47.91 percent of the miners in the *Oberbergamtsbezirk* Dortmund were Protestant, 51.82 percent were Catholic, and a handful did not identify with either of the major confessions.[49] The leaders of Ruhr heavy industry, however, were predominantly Protestant. Of the thirty-eight employers examined here, religious background could be determined for thirty-three. Of these, twenty-six were Protestants. Only seven came from Catholic families.[50]

There is little evidence that religion meant very much in the personal lives of most Ruhr industrialists. Only Carl Funke is recorded as having been particularly active in church affairs.[51] Among the leaders of Ruhr heavy industry, religion appears to have been more important in a political and social than in a spiritual sense. Protestantism constituted one link, though far from the most important one, connecting Ruhr industrial leaders and the traditional Prussian elites.

Since the second half of the nineteenth century, as the economic balance in Prussia shifted from east to west, from agriculture to industry, it had become increasingly difficult for the traditional Prussian elites to ignore the needs of Ruhr industry. They found their earlier exclusiveness vis-à-vis industrial entrepreneurs difficult to sustain. Ruhr industrialists, for their part, proved willing to leave largely unchallenged the existing social and political hierarchy in Prussia as long as the government showed itself responsive to their interests.

But if Ruhr industrialists supported substantial accommodation to the privileges of the traditional elites, they were far from being either subservient to or overawed by those groups. The Ruhr industrialists' isolation from the agrarian east, their work-centered life style, and their pride in their economic power, plus the remnants of aristocratic disdain for the bourgeois capitalist or manager, as well as clashes over specific issues such as transport policies, labor recruitment, and taxes, served to sustain in the entrepreneurial elite a strong sense of separate identity and worth. As practical men, Ruhr industrialists were aware that they had time on their side and that in any alliance with the older ruling groups they held the stronger position. Of the various elements of the German bourgeoisie, the Ruhr elite was the one most effectively protected from being mesmerized by the glitter of court and nobility by an awareness of their own power and importance.

The coal, iron, and steel magnates of the west were unlikely to be overly impressed by anyone whose claims to preeminent social position rested solely upon hereditary privilege or a noble title. Freiherr Eberhard von Bodenhausen, who became a member of the Krupp *Direktorium* in 1906, believed that his aristocratic name was the greatest obstacle he had to overcome in his efforts to make a career for himself in Ruhr industry.[52] That there was some basis for the prejudice he encountered is apparent in the distaste with which he admitted to being a businessman and his admission that his choice of career had been made solely in terms of the money it would bring him.[53] His attitude toward business was alien to members of the Ruhr entrepreneurial elite.

August Thyssen was horrified that three of his four children deserted the Ruhr to spend time in aristocratic company. His estranged son Heinrich went so far as to have himself adopted by his father-in-law and bore as a consequence the title of a Hungarian baron. The elder Thyssen stressed that the family's greatness and hopes for the future could only be built upon coal, iron, and steel, not upon aristocratic pretensions.[54]

The wealthiest and most powerful entrepreneurs, such as Thyssen, Stinnes, Kirdorf, and even William II's favorite, F. A. Krupp, turned down patents of nobility offered them.[55] Krupp's resonse was that he did not desire a name different from that of his father.[56] These were men of such wealth, power, and pride of accomplishment that they did not need to seek the patronage of anyone, even the kaiser.[57] Patents of nobility were accepted, it is true, by members of the long-established Haniel and Waldthausen families, but those involved were typically rentiers rather than active industrial leaders.

Industrial leaders active in the prewar Ruhr did accept titles, but these characteristically reflected their occupational accomplishments. Every reasonably successful industrialist with a fortune of at least two or three million marks and the properly conservative political orientation could expect to receive the title of *Kommerzienrat*. The wealthiest and most powerful entrepreneurs could expect the title of *Geheimer Kommerzienrat*. During the Wilhelmian period, these titles were granted to managers as well as to owner-entrepreneurs, constituting official recognition of the rise of the managing director into the ranks of industrial leadership.[58]

The granting and receiving of titles did not reflect complete social parity between Ruhr industrialists and the traditional social elites. The leaders of coal, iron, and steel production, despite their wealth and unquestioned service to the growth of German power, were still not favored with orders and titles to the same degree as members of the older ruling strata. Decorations such as the third or fourth class *Kronenorden* or *Roter Adlerorden* that were offered to leading industrialists in addition to their *Kommerzienrat* titles were also offered to junior army officers and middle-rank bureaucrats after a few years of service.[59]

In Imperial Germany, those few representatives of big business who moved in the highest social circles nationally, as opposed to regionally, did so as personal favorites of the emperor. Especially prominent among businessmen with personal access to the monarch were Albert Ballin, the managing director of Germany's largest shipping company, Saar industrialist Freiherr von Stumm-Halberg, and F. A. Krupp.[60] The favor shown by the kaiser for Krupp was very great indeed. When Krupp died in 1902 under a cloud of rumor and scandal, William II publicly made the following extraordinary pronouncement: "The unusual circumstances surrounding this unfortunate occurrence have caused me as ruler of the German Empire to be present [at the funeral] in order to place the shield of the German Emperor over the house and memory of the deceased."[61] The close ties between the house of Krupp and the house of Hohenzollern reflected the great wealth of the Krupp family, the firm's carefully cultivated reputation as a benevolent though strict employer, and the firm's special standing as the premier armorer of the empire. Indeed, among industrialists, weapons manufacturers generally enjoyed greater prestige than any others as far as the traditional elites were concerned.

The special relationship of the Krupps and the dynasty was not duplicated elsewhere in the Ruhr. Other Ruhr firms were less successful in developing a similar mystique. Because they were generally less dependent upon the state as a direct customer, there was less reason for them to curry favor quite so assiduously at the top. During the reign of William II, individual members of the Ruhr entrepreneurial elite often leveled harsh criticism at the emperor and his entourage. Initially, this reflected a pro-Bismarckian bias and irritation at the ruler's early attempts to pose as a friend of the working classes. Later, the most ardently imperialist and politically extreme elements of the elite, especially those associated with or sympathetic to the Pan-Germans, attacked the emperor as lacking the will to push consistently Germany's rightful claims to expand as a world power. Most outspoken of William II's critics in the Ruhr was abrasive Emil Kirdorf, who brusquely turned aside all attempts to reconcile him to Germany's current ruler.[62] However, within the entrepreneurial elite, criticism of the monarch did not entail criticism of the institution of monarchy, which was supported as part of the traditional authoritarian structure of Prussian-German society. Even Kirdorf, though he stated that he himself had long since lost any monarchical sentiment, saw democracy as the only alternative, and from his point of view that would have been much worse.[63]

Whatever their personal reservations about the monarch, Ruhr industrialists did make use of the integrative power of monarchical symbolism. Royal visits to the Ruhr with their attendant pageantry, publicity, and distribution of honors at all levels were most welcome as opportunities to foster among workers, company officials, and other residents of the region a sense of national solidarity and pride in local and national accomplishments. When, however, the monarchy collapsed in 1918, leading Ruhr industrialists wasted little regret on it. It was the authoritarian military-bureaucratic state they missed.

3
Ruhr Workers

The social and economic gulf separating the small, tightly knit entrepreneurial elite of Ruhr industry from the masses who toiled in the mines and mills was vast. Professional obligations of Ruhr employers often took them to Berlin to confer with business and government leaders but seldom to work sites in their own region and never to places where laborers spent their nonworking hours. Ruhr employers claimed that they were accessible to their employees and understood them better than did government officials, bourgeois social reformers, or labor leaders (all dismissed as meddling outsiders), but their own contacts with and firsthand knowledge about miners and steelworkers were actually quite limited. As a consequence, they often found worker responses to their initiatives difficult to predict or comprehend.

Recruitment

Recruitment of an adequate labor supply was no easy task for many employers in the prewar Ruhr, especially in the labor-intensive coal industry. In Ruhr mining, the actual digging of coal remained almost entirely a hand operation prior to 1914. Without substantial mechanization, labor productivity in the ever-deeper mines stagnated or actually declined. In 1888, annual production per worker had peaked at 315 tons. In 1896, miners were producing an average of 277 tons per year and this figure was not surpassed prior to World War I.[1] Given the failure to raise labor productivity, increases in overall output could be achieved only by means of a comparable expansion in the size of the labor force.

The number of miners vastly increased. In 1850, there were only 12,741 miners in the Ruhr. By 1896 the number had increased to 161,870. By 1913 the total was 401,715.[2] Labor shortages were common in the coal industry between 1896 and the war, and industry spokesmen complained that as a consequence production sometimes lagged behind demand.[3] Employers found themselves compelled to hire workers who previously would have been turned away as unacceptable—known union members, for example, or men who had been dismissed elsewhere for strike activity or insubordination.

In contrast, the region's iron and steel industry required fewer workers, both absolutely and relative to the value of output, though individual production units were generally much larger than those in mining. In 1913, when there were 401,715 miners in the Ruhr, there were only 138,326 iron- and steelworkers in the government districts of Düsseldorf, Arnsberg, and Münster, an area that included but also extended beyond the Ruhr coalfield.[4] For the industry as a whole, technological improvements continued to permit marked increases in production without proportional increases in the labor force. As a consequence, iron and steel industrialists were generally less hard-pressed for workers than were employers in the coal industry.

Yet even in metallurgy, it was often difficult to fill the most dangerous and exhausting jobs, especially during the summer when unskilled labor deserted the heat of the blast furnace and steel mill for alternative employment in agriculture and construction.[5] Securing an adequate work force was a particular problem for the huge new primary production facilities such as Krupp's Rheinhausen or Thyssen's Bruckhausen, which were constructed for transport reasons in previously rural areas along the Rhine during the last prewar decades.[6]

Hoping to build a work force as homogeneous and reliable as possible, Ruhr employers made as much use of local labor as they could. It was common practice, especially where a single firm dominated a community, to attempt to hire all boys of the immediate area as soon as they came of working age. A special effort, sometimes involving the threat of sanctions, was made to employ sons of men already working for the firm.[7]

But the indigenous population of the Ruhr could provide only a fraction of the work force needed by the giant corporations of the prewar era. Natural resources and the availability of transportation, rather than the availability of labor, dictated the location of most Ruhr industry. Normally workers had to be attracted from elsewhere after a site of operations had been chosen. The need to compete vigorously for labor with employers in other regions was a major determinant of employment policies.

In the prewar Ruhr, thousands of workers were settled where previously there had been only fields and scattered villages.[8] From 720,000 in 1871, the population of the Ruhr increased to 1,500,000 in 1895 and to 3,100,000 in 1910.[9] The most rapid growth occurred during the tumultuous decade from 1895 to 1905, when the region absorbed an additional million inhabitants. During the five years from 1895 to 1900, many of the region's cities increased in population by 20 to 33 percent. The county of Gelsenkirchen increased the number of its inhabitants by 45 percent during the same five-year period.[10] The population of the Ruhr was increasing much more rapidly than that of the nation as a whole. The demand for labor inherent in the expansion of heavy industry was the driving force behind this dramatic demographic growth.[11]

Only in the mines along the southernmost edge of the coalfield were employers able to recruit most of their workers locally. This was possible because the mines were small and the demand for labor limited. However, the importance of this area, the original center of Ruhr mining, declined precipitously in the second half of the nineteenth century. Whereas at midcentury it still accounted for half of the region's production, by the end of the century it produced only 10 percent. Abandoning the least profitable of these early mines resulted in a local unemployment problem, the disclaimers of employer spokesmen notwithstanding. Young, strong miners could, it is true, migrate northward and easily find employment. But older, less productive workers, wedded to the more traditional work patterns of the oldest mines, were more reluctant to leave and less likely to find other employment to their liking.[12]

North of the Ruhr River, just beyond where the coal dips below layers of secondary rock, was the Hellweg, the most urbanized, densely populated, and economically and socially diverse zone of the Ruhr coalfield.[13] Here the first deep shafts had been sunk, beginning in the 1830s and the 1840s, and the first large iron and steel companies had been established. Industrial development centered around the cities of Duisburg, Mülheim, Essen, Bochum, and Dortmund. From small but long-established towns at midcentury, they had grown to major urban centers with populations in excess of 100,000 before the war. In the 1890s, Essen and Dortmund were the fastest growing cities in Germany.[14] In 1913 Essen was the largest of Ruhr cities with 319,300 inhabitants.[15] A handful of iron and steel concerns predominated in these cities: Krupp in Essen, the Bochumer Verein in Bochum, and Hoesch and the Dortmunder Union in Dortmund. The presence of large, prestigious firms and the availability of what was, for the Ruhr, a wide variety of employment opportunities, especially for skilled workers, made this area a preferred goal for migrating west Germans. As a consequence, major employers here, unlike those in newer areas farther north, were not as troubled by problems of labor recruitment and could meet their needs largely through hiring workers from the three western provinces of Rhineland, Westphalia, and Hesse.[16]

North of the Hellweg lay the Emscher valley, the development of which was initiated in the 1870s. Here, where previously there had been little development of any kind, both industry and population grew rapidly.

Giant mines with labor forces in the thousands were established in an area favored by the abundant presence of good coking coal. The recruitment of labor was, from the beginning, a major problem, one calling for mass importation of workers over long distances, primarily from Prussia's eastern provinces of Silesia, Posen, West Prussia, and East Prussia.[17]

Some hard-pressed Ruhr companies paid recruiters a bounty for every worker sent from the east; others sent their own officials to entice men to migrate westward. For example, in 1912 the Gutehoffnungshütte was paying recruiters a fee of 3 marks per worker plus expenses to procure the labor needed for its mine in Sterkrade. To the workers themselves, the Gutehoffnungshütte would pay neither travel expenses nor salary advances until after three shifts had been worked, but it did offer three months' free rent in company housing and in some instances arranged for the shipment of household goods.[18] For their part, dissatisfied agrarian workers in the east proved more willing to follow the promise of higher wages and better conditions in the Ruhr than to follow the shorter route into the employ of Silesian heavy industry with its justified reputation for long hours and low wages.[19]

The Cologne-Minden railroad provided primary access for workers from the east. Gelsenkirchen, the population of which multiplied tenfold between 1871 and 1910 and which in the process was transformed from a village to a city of over one hundred thousand, was a major port of entry.[20] From there, east German workers might move on to the west or north to such new industrial towns as Wanne, Herne, or Recklinghausen, drawn by the promise of better wages, more congenial working conditions, or the presence of acquaintances from home.

The new towns that mushroomed along the Emscher were less diversified than the older cities to the south. They were typically single-industry, often single-company towns, with almost exclusively working-class populations. Hamborn, an example of particularly mercurial development, was dominated by the Thyssen works. In 1885, when Thyssen employed 700 men in Hamborn, the town's population was 5,270. By 1910, the number of Thyssen employees had risen to 23,979, and Hamborn's population had increased to 102,800.[21] Fully one quarter of the inhabitants in 1910 (25,595) had come from the four eastern provinces. In addition there were in Hamborn at that time almost as many migrants from neighboring countries such as the Netherlands, Austria-Hungary, and Italy (16,500) as individuals who had been born in the city (18,927).[22] Such raw, polyglot proletarian concentrations with their reputations for crime and violence were a matter of grave concern to the Prussian authorities, who proved very reluctant to grant the biggest of these new industrial settlements the right of municipal self-government to which their size otherwise entitled them. Thus, Hamborn's status was that of Prussia's largest rural commune until it was finally given city rights in 1911.[23]

Beyond the Emscher, the iron and steel industry disappeared entirely. The mines, though large, were widely separated. At the northern edges of the Ruhr coalfield, there were no substantial cities at all. All labor had to be imported, either from older Ruhr zones or from elsewhere. The migrants were typically settled in colonies established and maintained by their employers, since other accommodations in this still largely agrarian area were unavailable.[24]

One important consequence of the mass importation of labor into the Ruhr in the late nineteenth and early twentieth centuries was the resulting ethnic diversity of the work force. Particularly significant was the presence of large numbers of non-German-speaking workers from Prussia's eastern provinces. Although these were German citizens and were divided between Polish-speaking Catholics and Masurian-speaking Protestants, inhabitants of the Ruhr typically lumped them together as "Poles."[25]

Such workers were not evenly distributed throughout the industrial region but were concentrated in the newer areas of the north and east, especially in the area bounded by Recklinghausen, Bottrop, Gelsenkirchen, and Herne where more than 20 percent of the prewar population consisted of these so-called Poles, compared to a regional average of less than 10 percent.[26] The coal industry, with its pressing recruitment problems, relied heavily upon Poles. At the beginning of 1912, the *Oberbergamt* Dortmund reported that 36.78 percent of all Ruhr miners were Polish, up from 25.6 percent in 1893. Many mines could not have operated at all without this source of labor. In 1912 twenty-four Ruhr mines and three coking plants employed more Poles and foreigners than native German speakers.[27]

Genuine foreigners were less prevalent in the Ruhr than were so-called Poles. Like the Poles, foreign workers were used primarily in mining, constituting 8.34 percent of the work force of that industry in 1913, up from 2.75 percent in 1893. In iron and steel production, they were used in large numbers only where giant primary production units grew up along the Rhine. Thus, at the beginning of the First World War, every fifth blast-furnace worker in Bruchhausen was a foreigner.[28] Like the Poles, foreign workers were concentrated in certain areas: Russians, Italians, and Austro-Hungarians in the north, the Dutch in the west.[29]

The encouragement Ruhr industrialists gave to the immigration of Poles and foreigners aroused resentment among indigenous workers. Miners, lacking control over entry into their occupation, viewed the poorly trained newcomers as a threat to mine safety. Experienced miners resented being assigned to work the most difficult coal faces so that easier assignments could be given to new recruits. Off the job, the migrants from distant places clustered together and were not readily assimilated into the local population, which typically regarded them as inferior. Not even their German-speaking coreligionists in the religiously divided Ruhr gave the newcomers a very warm welcome. Nor did their employers make a significant effort to hasten their integration into Ruhr society.

Government officials expressed concern about the increasing alien, especially Slavic, population in the Ruhr and pressured employers to favor German-speaking workers when possible.[30] In 1899 the *Oberbergamt* Dortmund issued a regulation limiting employment underground to those who knew enough German to understand directions given in that language and limiting advancement to those who had command of both written and spoken German. But Ruhr employers, hard-pressed for miners, did not always implement the regulation very conscientiously.[31]

Their critics accused Ruhr employers of preferring to hire Polish workers because they were unorganized and made fewer demands than did their west German counterparts.[32] Some managers did indeed value the Poles as willing workers who were grateful for the better housing, wages, and fringe benefits that they found in the west. But the eastern workers did not always remain docile. Being new to industry, they were particularly prone to change jobs frequently. Nor did they remain unorganized. Indeed, after the turn of the century, the Polish miners' union gained ground rapidly on both the socialist and Catholic unions.

Ruhr industrialists, with their strongly nationalist pretensions, must have found embarrassing the charge that their recruitment practices deliberately slighted ethnic Germans in favor of outsiders. The Ruhr elite included within its ranks adherents of the anti-Polish Ostmarkenverein (Society for the Eastern Marches). Among its supporters were Emil Kirdorf and Paul Randebrock of the Gelsenkirchener Bergwerks-AG, Wilhelm Beukenberg of Phoenix, and Friedrich Alfred Krupp.[33]

On the whole, it seems that Ruhr industrialists hired large numbers of migrant workers primarily out of necessity.[34] When possible, they preferred to employ local men in the interest of having a more stable work force and avoiding the hostility of eastern landowners, who resented the loss of much of their labor supply to Ruhr industry. Only when local sources failed to meet the need did most employers resort to migrant workers. In periods of recession and reduced demand for labor, foreigners and Polish workers were often the first to be dismissed. For example, in 1902 the mining director of the Gutehoffnungshütte was instructed, in the interests of furthering the creation of "a sound, stable work force," to fire non-Germans and replace them with German miners who had been dismissed from neighboring mines because of the currently adverse economic conditions.[35] After the turn of the century, more and more firms went over to the policy of hiring no Polish workers.[36]

Retention

If recruiting an adequate labor supply was a major problem for much of Ruhr industry prior to World War I, so was its retention. Because the work was arduous, the coal, iron, and steel industries needed large numbers of strong men. Women were not employed by Ruhr heavy industry. This was in contrast to the situation in Upper Silesia, where women constituted over 5 percent of the work force in mining. Employing women was one means by which that region's employers kept wages low and avoided the kind of active recruitment of migrant labor undertaken by Ruhr industrialists.[37]

The men who worked in the mines and mills of the Ruhr were predominantly young, especially in the newest areas. Of the immigrants pouring into the region at the turn of the century, 48 percent were between the ages of fifteen and twenty-five.[38] In 1893, 44 percent of Westphalian miners were unmarried. Although this figure represented a decline from 53.7 percent twenty years earlier, it nevertheless points to a high potential for geographic mobility on the part of the Ruhr labor force, since young, unmarried workers were more likely to make frequent moves than older men with family responsibilities.[39]

Ruhr corporations competed vigorously among themselves for labor, so much so that at least one of them, the Hibernia mining company, bought up surrounding untapped coalfields, not only as a reserve but also in order to prevent the opening of neighboring mines, which would make it more difficult to recruit and hold an adequate work force.[40] Elsewhere, the thick network of industrial concerns in most of the region, especially in its midsection, meant that alternative employment opportunities were readily available to many workers, often without even a change of residence.

A major complaint of Ruhr employers was that their workers, with more options available to them in this expansive and prosperous era than in times past, were often tempted to act in a manner their superiors regarded as irresponsible. Industrialists complained that employees often failed to show up for work on the appointed day or hour, especially on workdays following Sundays, holidays, and paydays. In Duisburg on such days, 5 to 7 percent of the miners would not appear for work.[41] Employers also complained that workers changed jobs too frequently and capriciously. From 1896 to 1914, in the area of the Knappschaftsverein Bochum, the benevolent society for Ruhr miners, the number of workers leaving their jobs each year in coal mining fluctuated between a low of 34 per 100 in 1905 and a high of 69 per 100 in 1913. During the same period, the number of hirings fluctuated between a low of 38 per 100 employees in 1905 and a high of 78 per 100 employees in 1913.[42] It is important to note, however, that these conditions were neither unique to the prewar Ruhr nor were they uniformly present throughout that region. Comparable high turnover rates were being experienced, for example, by heavy industry in Upper Silesia and in the United States.[43] Within the Ruhr, turnover rates were typically lower than the regional average at the oldest, most established firms. At Krupp in 1912, 59.3 percent of the work force had been employed there for six or more years, and 26.9 percent for more than fifteen years.[44]

The practice of moving from job to job, most marked in the newest industrial areas and among young, unmarried workers, did not abate in the years before the First World War.[45] Ruhr employers complained that rapid turnover compounded the problems inherent in disciplining a work force that was disproportionately young and, more often than not, new to industrial employment. Management perceived this situation as a major obstacle to improving, or even maintaining, existing levels of production and safety. Yet it held significant advantages as well as disadvantages for the employers. Extensive turnover was at least as troublesome to labor organizers as it was to management. And extensive job changing doubtless served as an important safety valve for worker discontent in industries in which provision for grievance settlement was virtually nonexistent.

Strikes and Unionization

Because workers usually came to the direct attention of busy industrial leaders only in conflict situations when they were resisting changes or making demands, they were perceived by their bosses largely as a source of trouble. Employers especially resented strikes and threats of strikes. The entrepreneurial elite invariably interpreted strikes as a contest of wills. To a group attempting to introduce a greater measure of predictability into Ruhr heavy industry, any sign of independence on the part of workers appeared to be willful obstruction.

During most of the Bismarckian era, attempts at labor organization and collective action had suffered from the dual handicaps of unfavorable economic conditions and repressive legislation. Initiatives of the late 1860s and early 1870s, fostered by the transition from state to private direction of Ruhr mines and a lively demand for labor, culminated in the unsuccessful strike of approximately 21,000 Essen miners in 1872. Thereafter, such efforts were cut short by falling prices, unemployment, and a hostile social and political order. For the next decade and a half, there was little large-scale working-class activity in the Ruhr. Such strikes as there were, however, were especially bitter, representing generally unsuccessful protests against reduced wages and longer hours.[46] Then in 1889, the first genuine boom year since 1873, some 87,000 of the 104,000 Ruhr miners struck, an unprecedented event in German history.[47] But the return of depressed economic conditions in the early 1890s crippled efforts to perpetuate large-scale collective action among mine workers.

Yet the massive 1889 strike was not to remain an isolated incident. The general prosperity of the last two prewar decades, the rising cost of living, and pressures for increased productivity sparked more labor initiatives, including two additional mass strikes. In 1905, some 195,706 of the 267,798 miners struck; in 1912, about 235,000 of 365,354 miners did so. These strikes, particularly those of 1889 and 1905, were an impressive demonstration of the potential for solidarity among Ruhr miners, transcending religious, ideological, ethnic, and generational differences.[48]

Following the coal strike of 1889, a socialist-oriented miners' union, the Alter Verband, was formed.[49] It nearly collapsed in the early 1890s but was saved by the prosperity of the second half of the decade. Other miners' unions followed: the Gewerkverein christlicher Bergleute, officially nondenominational but overwhelmingly Catholic, formed in 1894, and the Polish union (ZZP), formed in 1902. There was in addition a miniscule liberal Hirsch-Duncker organization.

Once begun, unionization spread quickly among Ruhr miners. By the 1905 coal strike, the Alter Verband was claiming 62,000 members in the Ruhr, the Catholic Gewerkverein 40,000, the Polish union 12,000, and the Hirsch-Duncker organization 1,000. Total membership claimed by the unions amounted to 42.9 percent of the labor force in Ruhr mining at that time.[50] Union membership surged following the 1905 strike but then stagnated. Because the number of miners employed in the region continued to increase, the percentage who were organized leveled off and then began to decline. By 1912, the Alter Verband was reporting a membership of 69,648 (down from 80,143 in 1908), the Gewerkverein a membership of 40,000, and the Polish union a membership of 30,334, giving a total of 139,932 or 38.2 percent of Ruhr miners then employed.[51] By 1913, only an estimated 31.3 percent of Ruhr miners were organized.[52] Even so, the Ruhr was still far ahead of any other German mining district in unionizing. In 1913, only 15 to 20 percent of Upper Silesian miners were union members.[53]

Although its initial growth had been rapid, buoyed by prosperity and a strong demand for workers, the union movement in the prewar Ruhr failed to enlist the majority of miners, a fact the coal operators used to strengthen their argument against union recognition. The union movement also suffered from being split along confessional, ideological, and ethnic lines, a reflection of the heterogeneity of the work force itself.[54] This allowed the industrialists to argue that negotiation with the unions was impossible because there was no united body with which to negotiate.

Political activity was also divisive. The party involvement of the nominally neutral miners' unions not only handicapped the unions by splitting the labor movement but also served to deepen the schism between organized labor and management by adding another point of contention to the more concrete issues such as wages, hours, and working conditions. According to Krupp director Hanns Jencke, speaking in 1899, the unions served "exclusively as schools of political agitation for Social Democracy."[55] Emil Kirdorf condemned the Catholic unions as being even worse than their socialist counterparts because they pursued their revolutionary goals "behind the mask of Christian love and harmony."[56]

Although Ruhr industrialists characterized the miners' unions as creations of irresponsible troublemakers and subversives, the leaders of those organizations were notable primarily for their caution. This discretion was reflected in a record of attempts to block hasty, locally initiated work stoppages and to avoid unnecessary provocation during labor-management confrontations. Union leaders were aware of the immense economic power of Ruhr corporations and of government sensitivity to the prospect of social upheaval in the densely populated region. Given the unfavorable balance of power the unions faced, they had little hope of even partial success unless they could enlist a measure of sympathy for the miners' cause beyond the ranks of the working class. Excessive militance would leave the miners isolated.

The growth of union membership in Ruhr mines was not matched by comparable developments in the iron and steel industry. Unionization made little headway in metallurgy before the First World War. In the statistics of the metalworkers' union, the Deutscher Metallarbeiter Verband, Ruhr steel mill and blast furnace workers were not even listed until 1907.[57]

And strikes remained virtually unknown in Ruhr metallurgy. As late as 1902, Hanns Jencke could note "with satisfaction" that "among the workers in our iron and steel industry, there has never been even the attempt of a strike movement worth mentioning."[58] And in the remaining prewar years there were no mass strikes either, only an occasional walkout by specialized workers such as boiler makers in Dortmund in 1905 and machinists and stokers in that same city in 1911.

Contrasting patterns of unionization and strike activity in the various branches of Ruhr heavy industry reflected differences in types of workers employed and in their experiences. One factor drawing miners together was their relative isolation, both geographical and social. Unlike the iron and steel industry, mining was widely scattered throughout the region and was more likely to have a rural setting. Working in the mines was considered less desirable than most other occupations in the Ruhr. Nonminers, including many workers in the iron and steel industry, disdained those who made their living in subterranean toil. The low status of miners in the prewar Ruhr contrasted with the relatively privileged position of their predecessors before 1865 when state officials directed the mines. A sense of privileges lost played a continuing role in shaping miners' demands well into the twentieth century.

Miners were drawn together not only by their isolation from other segments of Ruhr society but also by the intensity of their shared experiences of danger underground.[59] Every year, hundreds lost their lives in the mines. Between 1907 and 1914, the lowest annual death toll was 542; the highest was 1,005.[60] In addition, work in the mines was organized around small, loosely supervised groups, a pattern allowing substantial opportunities for agitation. Finally, a sense of solidarity among the coal workers was reinforced by the scarcity of advancement opportunities. There was little in the way of a hierarchy of skills in the mines. There were only three main divisions of work underground: the haulers, the apprentice hewers, and the hewers. Beyond that, there were supervisory positions, but access was restricted. Most miners could not hope for significant advancement except by leaving the industry.[61]

In contrast, a much greater variety of positions and more substantial wage differentials were available in the iron and steel industry.[62] Whereas the highest paid mine workers, the hewers, made less than twice as much as general laborers, the highest paid millworkers such as welders and rollers made more than three times as much as general laborers.[63] In metallurgy, wage differentials were deliberately exaggerated in order to undermine worker solidarity.

Workers in the iron and steel industry had better prospects for advancement than did miners, either through factory apprenticeships or through promotion to lower supervisory positions.[64] Opportunities for intergenerational mobility provided by the rapidly expanding office staffs of Ruhr industry were also more abundant in metallurgy than in mining.[65] After the turn of the century, increased mechanization in metallurgy created opportunities for unskilled laborers to rise into the ranks of the semi-skilled as machine operators. This development contrasted with the late nineteenth-century displacement of many skilled ironworkers—puddlers, for example—as a result of the introduction of mass production techniques.

Ruhr Workers

Long hours, close supervision, and the giant size of metallurgical concerns were additional impediments to the organization of iron- and steelworkers. But even though such workers were less likely than miners to act collectively, their employers were not unaffected by problems arising from labor organization. They considered the possibility that in the future their workers, too, might organize if preventive measures were not taken. Also, with the increasing vertical concentration of heavy industry, iron and steel entrepreneurs were confronted with the presence of organized workers in the mining and the machine and finished products divisions of their concerns. By the end of the period we are considering, all industrialists, even those in the primary iron and steel industries, faced the problem of responding to labor unions.

4
Industry and Government

Relations with Berlin

In their confrontations with the unions and with all individuals and organizations backing labor's demands, Ruhr employers believed they had a natural and pressing claim on government support. Hence they were greatly concerned when such unqualified support was not always forthcoming. The entrepreneurial elite particularly resented sporadic attempts by the state and national governments in Berlin to extend their regulation of working conditions.

During the Wilhelmian era, government efforts to extend greater protection to workers on the job clustered in the early 1890s, when Hans Freiherr von Berlepsch was Prussian minister of commerce, and in the first decade of the twentieth century, when Arthur Graf von Posadowsky-Wehner was Reich secretary of the interior. Berlepsch's appointment reflected Emperor William II's brief flirtation with factory legislation as a means of reconciling workers to the monarchy. During Posadowsky's years in office, social legislation was used as a means of winning Center party support for government programs. Such efforts alternated with periods of renewed repression of the working-class movement. This zigzag course ultimately satisfied neither labor nor management.

Berlepsch and Posadowsky were representative of a number of high-ranking bureaucrats in Berlin who, though very conservative, believed that the state should set limits to the power of employers. Such advocates of factory legislation were motivated in part by a belief in the moral responsibility of the state to protect workers, a theory often propounded by members of the influential Verein für Sozialpolitik (Social Policy Association), and in part by a fear of the potentially revolutionary impact of industrialization.[1] They believed that to secure social harmony, the interests of industrialists had to be weighed against those of other groups in society. Because of fear of the social repercussions of unregulated employer action, many government officials were more willing to make concessions to the industrialists in matters of economic and financial policy than in questions directly involving workers.[2]

To Ruhr industrial leaders, all government efforts to conciliate workers represented an especially pernicious betrayal, more immediately debilitating to industry than the working-class movement itself. They also believed that such efforts to appease the workers were doomed to failure. Emil Kirdorf warned that "ill-considered, excessive worker welfare measures achieve the opposite of that intended; they destroy the best provision for the workers: profitable employment opportunities."[3] Employers complained of the increased costs that government action entailed as a result of direct contributions they were required to make to welfare funds as well as the administrative costs of compliance with a growing number of rules and regulations, plus costs resulting from mandated changes in working conditions and production processes. They repeatedly warned that increased costs not only cut into legitimate and necessary profits but also threatened their ability to compete in the world market against producers who were not similarly burdened.[4]

As much as Ruhr employers fretted about the long-range consequences of increased costs owing to government intervention, they were even more upset by the prospect of government-mandated worker representation of any kind. They argued that any additional opportunities given to employees to organize and vote for representatives only provided occasions for agitators to spread dissatisfaction. In 1909, Eduard Kleine described the danger to a meeting of coal industrialists in lurid terms: "[The government] fosters a danger which is enormous, a danger which can be removed later only with the spilling of much blood. We cannot even be sure that our army will remain intact. If Social Democracy is once successful against heavy industry, it will spread to the countryside and that is a point which we must emphasize to the Conservatives."[5] Such apocalyptic fear mongering survived to 1914 and beyond, at least as far as the most vocal and visible members of the entrepreneurial elite were concerned.

In discussions of their political position vis-à-vis labor, especially in those utterances intended for the public, Ruhr industrialists stressed their weaknesses. Pessimistic Emil Kirdorf claimed that at the beginning of the twentieth century, industry was "without any political influence" in Prussia and Germany.[6] Business leaders in the Ruhr particularly stressed the weakness of their representation in the Reichstag, where universal suffrage and the secret ballot gave an advantage to their adversaries. They were, they claimed, "officers without men" in national politics, lacking the mass constituencies of labor and agriculture.[7]

Party politics were distasteful to the Ruhr entrepreneurial elite. Krupp director Alfred Hugenberg glorified the good old days when leaders in Prussia really led and the masses of the people were untroubled by political theory.[8] Max Roetger, Hugenberg's predecessor at Krupp, spoke for most Ruhr industrialists when he said: "We are not party men but rather independent men of practical affairs and we defend our interests against everyone regardless of the side to which he may belong."[9] But despite their disdain for party politics, determination to use all available means to protect their interests and to promote their social and political as well as economic goals prevented Ruhr industrialists from remaining completely aloof.

In so far as Ruhr employers claimed affiliation with any parliamentary party, it was usually with the right wing of the National Liberals. The long-established but tenuous bonds between the majority of Ruhr industrialists and the National Liberal party rested in part upon that party's tradition of support for the national cause and for Bismarck during the 1870s and 1880s and its advocacy of imperial and naval expansion during the Wilhelmian era. The National Liberal party was also important to Ruhr industrialists because of its key role in the local politics of the two western provinces as chief competitor of the Catholic Center party and the Social Democrats. The party was generally attentive to the material interests of industry. This was especially true of the Prussian Landtag's National Liberal faction, on which the Ruhr entrepreneurial elite exercised considerable influence. They were much less successful in swaying the party's faction in the Imperial Reichstag.[10]

Germany's other major political parties offered few attractions. Given the strongly antidemocratic biases of Ruhr employers, the Social Democratic and Progressive parties were automatically beyond the pale. But close identification with the Conservative party at the other end of the political spectrum was impeded by the dominant role within it of eastern agrarian interests and by its weakness in the western provinces. Less exclusively agrarian than the Conservative party and therefore more congenial to industrial leaders, but with a more restricted electoral base, was the Free Conservative party. F. A. Krupp was linked with this loose coalition of notables, as was Carl Lueg of the Gutehoffnungshütte.

Ruhr coal, iron, and steel industrialists were typically suspicious of the Catholic Center party, especially its populist left wing. Even most of the Catholics in the ranks of the Ruhr elite kept their distance from the Center party. Thus of Matthias Tull, managing director of the Hoerder Verein from 1892 to 1903, the Arnsberg *Regierungspräsident* (the highest civil official in that district) noted with approval that though Tull was a Catholic, he was "not an ultramontanist." Tull's support for the National Liberal party was taken to be proof of this.[11] Most conspicuously Catholic of Ruhr industrial leaders were August Thyssen and Peter Kloeckner, both of whom were associated with the right wing of the Center party.

Industry and Government

Beyond party politics, members of the Ruhr elite showed varying degrees of enthusiasm for the right-wing pressure groups of Wilhelmian Germany, useful for promoting nationalist programs but not always subject to the employers' dictates. Most easily agreed upon was support for officially sanctioned associations such as the Navy League (Flottenverein), established in 1898 with a council that initially included Hanns Jencke and F. A. Krupp.[12] But there were differences of opinion as to whether to support an organization as controversial as the Pan-German League (Alldeutscher Verband). Emil Kirdorf, most rabidly nationalistic and outspoken of all Ruhr industrialists, gave it his support. Alfred Hugenberg had been among its founders in 1890 and was a member of the organization's executive committee from 1894 to 1903. But thereafter, the political isolation that the Pan-German League brought upon itself by its strident rhetoric and attacks upon the government convinced Hugenberg that working behind the scenes would be more effective, and he withdrew from public participation. August Thyssen and Hugo Stinnes, with their international connections, wondered whether the unrestrained imperialistic propaganda of the Pan-German League made economic penetration of foreign areas more difficult.[13]

There were also differences of opinion about the Imperial Association against Social Democracy (Reichsverband gegen die Sozialdemokratie), founded in 1904. The organization's antisocialist premise was one that the Ruhr elite had no difficulty endorsing. Hanns Jencke was a member of the committee that established the organization. Max Roetger joined the organization's executive committee in 1909. As late as 1910, Managing Director Paul Reusch of the Gutehoffnungshütte was insisting that officials of his company should be members. But the Reichsverband, with its base in central and eastern Germany and with its ties to the Conservatives, made little progress in the western provinces.[14]

By 1911, Reusch and his deputies had withdrawn. At the time of his withdrawal, he had already become the chief sponsor of participation by the Ruhr elite in a rival organization, the German Association (Deutsche Vereinigung), formed in 1908. Indeed, so determined was Reusch's advocacy that in 1913 he threatened to resign from the executive committee of the Northwest Group of the Association of German Iron and Steel Industrialists and of its employer association, Arbeitnordwest, if those organizations denied his request for a contribution to the Deutsche Vereinigung.[15] Unlike the Reichsverband, the Deutsche Vereinigung was indigenous to Rhineland-Westphalia, more suited to political conditions there, and more amenable to control by heavy industry. Originally established to combat populist tendencies in the Catholic Center party, it soon became a coalition of the region's antisocialist and antidemocratic forces, Catholic as well as

Protestant, and served increasingly as a front for various political and social initiatives of the Ruhr elite. Ruhr heavy industrialists were joined in support of the Deutsche Vereinigung by their counterparts in the Saar.[16]

In their association with political parties and pressure groups, Ruhr industrialists usually preferred to remain behind the scenes as much as possible.[17] Although they normally demanded a substantial voice in organizations they supported, they preferred to leave public leadership roles to others. In part this simply reflected the many other pressing claims upon their time.[18] But there were other reasons as well. Some industrialists were reluctant to be too closely associated with an organization or position if such association might alienate some other group whose good will was also valuable to Ruhr industry. Ruhr industrialists were also painfully aware that their open advocacy of a cause often did more harm than good with respect to public opinion. Their social and political recommendations were likely to be attacked as merely self-interested schemes to maximize profit.[19]

Usually they were both unwilling and unable to compete personally in the arena of popular politics. One obstacle was their disdain for universal suffrage. Democracy ran counter to their elitist view of society. They believed themselves and other experts better able to judge what was in the best interests of Germany and her people than were the uninformed and easily misled masses. Alfred Hugenberg warned that in an industrialized society, universal suffrage permitted a single large class, the proletariat, to rule over all other classes.[20] An especially pernicious consequence of a democratic franchise, from the point of view of the Ruhr entrepreneurial elite, was that it tempted government and party leaders to seek popular support through the sponsorship of needless social legislation.

In addition to their disdain for the Reichstag and its franchise, there were other obstacles to personal participation by leading Ruhr industrialists. Campaigning and serving necessarily diverted attention from business.[21] And actually sitting in the Reichstag with men representing so many diverse and conflicting interests was much less congenial to industrial leaders than participation in trade associations with other like-minded individuals whom they esteemed for their practical expertise.

There was also the problem of subjection to public scrutiny and possible electoral defeat, especially in light of the rapid increase, beginning in 1890, in the number of Social Democratic votes cast in the region.[22] As late as 1887, Social Democrats had received only a tiny percentage of votes in Ruhr electoral districts: 1.3 percent in the Essen district; 3.3 percent in Duisburg-Mülheim-Ruhrort; 2.1 percent in Bochum-Gelsenkirchen-Hattingen; and 5.7 percent in Dortmund-Hoerde. Nationally, the Social Democrats did better, winning 7.1 percent of the vote in that year. But by 1903, socialist votes in the four Ruhr districts had increased to 28.3 percent, 31.1

percent, 35.5 percent, and 42.8 percent respectively, for a regional average of 34.5 percent as compared to a national average of 31.7 percent. In 1903 the Social Democrats were the largest party in the region, with 118,497 votes, compared to 107,783 for the Catholic Center party and 100,767 for the National Liberals. By 1912 the socialists had increased their lead in the Ruhr, receiving 37.0 percent of the regional vote, compared to 34.8 percent nationally.[23]

The experience of those Ruhr industrialists who did serve in the Reichstag was not very encouraging. Of the thirty-eight members of the prewar entrepreneurial elite, only three served in the Reichstag at any time before 1914: August Servaes of Phoenix from 1880 to 1885, Eduard Kleine from 1887 to 1889, and F. A. Krupp from 1893 to 1898. Servaes and Kleine were elected as National Liberals, Krupp as an independent associated with the Free Conservatives. Both Kleine and Krupp found their electoral practices subject to public censure. Kleine's reelection in 1889 was declared void by an election commission because of improper pressure on working-class voters by his political friends. Kleine subsequently refused to campaign again.[24] As for F. A. Krupp, he first ran in 1887 only to be defeated by the Center party candidate. In 1893, after initially refusing, Krupp reluctantly agreed to run again because Chancellor Leo von Caprivi's army bill was to be resubmitted to the new Reichstag. He won the election on the second ballot in a bizarre situation in which more socialist votes apparently switched to Krupp than to his Center party opponent, much to the horror of Social Democratic leader August Bebel. The Center party challenged the election and accused the Krupp concern of using improper pressure on its workers, including threats of dismissal if they did not vote for their employer. Serving in the Reichstag until defeated in a bid for reelection in 1898, Krupp, unskilled as a speaker and reluctant to alienate any powerful interests that might be of use to his company, was largely inactive.[25]

But even if members of the entrepreneurial elite rarely served, Ruhr industry was not without vocal representatives in the Reichstag, most notably National Liberal deputy Wilhelm Beumer, business manager of the Northwest Group of the Association of German Iron and Steel Industrialists. Despite its numerical weakness and antidemocratic bias, the Ruhr elite had its share of favorable decisions in the national legislature. However, such victories were more often on issues such as the fleet, which could readily be clothed in the mantle of national interest, than on questions relating to the confrontation of labor and management. In the Reichstag, only a minority, namely, the Conservative parties and the right wing of the National Liberals, could be counted on consistently to support the labor policies of the leaders of heavy industry. The major pieces of repressive antilabor legislation introduced into the Reichstag during the Wilhelmian era, measures designed to replace the lapsed antisocialist law and ardently championed by Ruhr industrial leaders, all went down to ignominious defeat.[26]

But the relative weakness of the employers' position in the Reichstag was offset by strength in other spheres. Thus in the House of Deputies of the Prussian Landtag, a majority hostile to organized labor survived on the basis of the three-class system of voting and the open ballot. For Landtag elections, voters in each district were divided into three classes, according to the amount of taxes they paid. Each class, whether it consisted of a wealthy few or an impoverished multitude, chose the same number of electors, who in turn collectively made the final choice of the district's deputy. This plutocratic-conservative franchise for the Prussian parliament strongly favored the interests of the wealthy industrialists. The three-class system of voting produced an overwhelmingly conservative majority—and until 1908, not a single Social Democrat! In the unreformed Prussian Landtag, the political alliance of industrialists and estate owners, representing the greatest vested interests in the state, constituted a formidable combination. For this reason, the coal, iron, and steel entrepreneurs were among the most determined opponents of efforts to reform the franchise of that body.[27]

Despite the plutocratic system of voting in Prussia, industrial leaders in the prewar Ruhr were even less willing personally to campaign for a seat in that state's lower house than they were to campaign for a seat in the Reichstag. Of their number, none served in the Prussian House of Deputies. They preferred, as noted below, appointment to the more prestigious and less time-consuming upper house of the Landtag, the House of Lords.

Ruhr industry was not, to be sure, without representatives in the House of Deputies, but such representatives were typically not members of the entrepreneurial elite itself but less august members of Ruhr management such as Karl Knupe, a director of the Deutsch-Luxemburg concern, Heinrich Althoff, a director of the Rheinische Stahlwerke, and Erwin Hasenclever, a director of the Gelsenkirchener Bergwerks-AG, or they were salaried personnel of industrial federations; such as Wilhelm Beumer, previously mentioned as a member of the Reichstag, and Wilhelm Hirsch, syndic of the Essen chamber of commerce. Supervisory board members of Ruhr corporations such as Theodor Schmieding of the Harpener Bergbau-AG, Ernst von Eynern of Hibernia, and Hermann Mathies of the Gelsenkirchener Bergbau-AG also served as deputies. All were elected as National Liberals. From 1885 to 1898 the county of Moers was represented by a member of the Haniel family, *Landrat* (highest county civil official) Johann Haniel, a Free Conservative.[28]

In the Prussian House of Lords, the Ruhr elite was represented by lifetime members F. A. Krupp, appointed in 1901, Carl Lueg (1903), Franz Haniel (1905), Gustav Krupp von Bohlen und Halbach (1910), and Friedrich Springorum (1912). F. A. Krupp was the personal choice of the emperor. The others were recommended by provincial officials. The men in question were selected not only because they represented established, prestigious family firms but also because they had cultivated close ties with high civil servants and were careful not to criticize the government too harshly in public. Emil Kirdorf and August Thyssen were considered for membership but were found unsuitable because of their outspoken and contentious temperaments. Honoring influential Ruhr industrialists by appointing them to the House of Lords was one means by which the emperor and the ministerial bureaucracy attempted to guarantee the good will of the entrepreneurial elite.[29]

Governing the Ruhr

Administration was an even more important influence, though less publicized, than legislation upon labor relations and working conditions in the Ruhr. And here the balance continued to be weighted heavily in favor of the employers. Despite bureaucratic claims to be impartial and above special interests, the attachment of members of the Prussian bureaucracy to the political and social status quo and their suspicion of organized labor predisposed them to judgments that skewed implementation of the law to the advantage of management. Bureaucratic suspicion of the employers and their profit-making motives was counterbalanced by the force of management's argument that the smooth functioning of industry was essential to maintenance of a stable order in Germany and of German power in the world. The result was, more often than not, exemptions granted to key companies, violations overlooked or only mildly censured, and justice unequally administered, all to the detriment of the working class.

The claim of Ruhr industrial leaders to be a crucial pillar of the status quo, deserving of special protection not granted to competing interests, carried great weight with provincial and local officials in the two western provinces. Directly exposed to the influence of the leaders of Ruhr heavy industry to an extent not possible in the case of their colleagues in Berlin, these men were constantly reminded of the close link between the fortunes of industry and the prosperity and stability of the governmental units under their jurisdiction.[30]

The influence of the Ruhr elite on local and provincial government was deeply entrenched and provided, during the last prewar decades, a most welcome buffer against political and administrative changes initiated in Berlin. The men who held the posts of *Oberpräsident* and *Regierungspräsident* (the highest civil officials at the provincial and district levels) were particularly suited to act as intermediaries between Berlin and the Ruhr entrepreneurial elite because they often came from or moved into the ministerial bureaucracy. The most noteworthy example was Georg Freiherr von Rheinbaben, friend of the powerful Krupps and Haniels, who occupied successively the posts of *Regierungspräsident* in Düsseldorf, Prussian minister of the interior, Prussian minister of finance, and *Oberpräsident* of the Rhine province. It was Rheinbaben who recommended Alfred Hugenberg, his former subordinate, to the Krupps for the highest managerial post at that concern. Also notable were Konrad von Studt, friend of F. A. Krupp, who was *Oberpräsident* of Westphalia and then Prussian minister of culture, and Klemens Freiherr von Schorlemer-Lieser, initial sponsor of the Deutsche Vereinigung, who was *Oberpräsident* of the Rhine province and later Prussian minister of agriculture.[31]

Business leaders were also particularly well served by the institutions of municipal self-government and were among the foremost proponents of the extension of such institutions in the Ruhr.[32] The overwhelming economic power of large Ruhr firms as chief employers and taxpayers in the cities and towns in which they were located was readily converted into equally overwhelming political power through the three-class system of voting that in Prussia was used in local as well as in state elections. Indeed, municipal franchises were even more regressive than the state franchise because a larger percentage of the poor was excluded from electoral participation.[33]

There were glaring inequalities in prospects for political representation for different segments of the voting population in Ruhr municipalities. Thus, in Essen in 1900, the first class of voters, consisting of the wealthiest citizens who collectively paid a third of municipal taxes, was comprised of 3 individuals; the second class, 401; and the third and poorest class of voters, 18,991. In Bochum in the same year, the figures for the three classes were 16; 380; and 8,527.[34]

A typical local election in the prewar Ruhr might find owners, principal stockholders, or directors of the largest corporation or corporations voting in the first class, allied or dependent business and professional men and company officials voting in the second, and workers—by far the largest group—voting in the third class. The use of open ballots in municipal elections meant that even the third class of voters was often directly controlled by the largest firm or firms in the city, with company officials sent to monitor elections to make certain management's candidates were elected.[35]

Whereas in national and state government, most Ruhr industrial leaders preferred to exert their influence indirectly, through propaganda, political contributions, personal contacts, and lobbyists, rather than through office holding, many of them played a more direct and personal role in local government. Of the thirty-eight industrialists we are considering, at least sixteen were at some time city council members. Incumbency of local offices was typically for long periods, sometimes for decades.[36]

In part, participation in local affairs reflected a liberal tradition of communal responsibility that was still cherished in some of the older industrial families with strong ties to a particular city, for example, the Waldthausens and Funkes in Essen.[37] In other instances, entrepreneurial interest in municipal government reflected a determination to have a say in communal taxation. Industrial leaders were also interested in the use of municipal resources for the maintenance of law and order and the protection of property. And they monitored carefully the policies cities adopted for determining terms of labor for the increasing numbers of municipal employees, fearful that concessions to city workers might inspire demands for similar changes in the private sector.

Offices in municipal government for leading Ruhr entrepreneurs were almost automatic if they chose to claim them. However, over time there was a tendency for industrial leaders to withdraw from personal participation even in communal affairs and to delegate this task, too, to their deputies or to the salaried personnel of industrial interest groups.[38] One reason for this trend was the growing size of Ruhr corporations, which often expanded to include works in or near a number of different towns and cities. In addition, the imperious leaders of Ruhr industry did not react gracefully to having their will thwarted in public. Thus, August Thyssen's appearances in the Mülheim city council came to an end in 1910 when that body, over his protests, approved a canal project that favored Hugo Stinnes's interests over his own.[39]

Prejudicial as the system of local elections was to working-class claims to any meaningful say in local affairs, some tentative changes were underway before the war, much to the dismay of the region's business elite. Workers, as representatives of either the Catholic Center or the Social Democratic party, began to appear in the communal councils of the Ruhr after the turn of the century. Working-class candidates had their best chance of being elected in new industrial towns or in industrial suburbs of established cities where the population might be almost exclusively working class.[40] For example, in 1902 in proletarian Altendorf, incorporated into Essen the previous year, payment of 156 marks in taxes placed an individual in the first class of voters. In the central city, the comparable amount was 79,377 marks. All of Altendorf's first representatives in the Essen city council were members of the Center party. By 1909, Altendorf provided four of the seven workers in the Essen city council.[41]

In 1907, there were seventy-eight Social Democratic communal deputies in the Ruhr, though none in the major cities.[42] The first Social Democratic deputy in the Essen city council was elected in 1908.[43] Ruhr employers railed against what they termed the "politicization" of municipal government, by which they meant the representation of political parties rather than local interests, especially their own, but they could not entirely exorcise the proponents of change even in their own immediate neighborhood. In addition, since the 1890s the municipal three-class system itself was being subjected to increased challenge not only from working-class spokesmen but from bourgeois reformers as well.[44]

To leaders of Ruhr heavy industry, the proponents of change seemed to be penetrating all spheres relevant to industrial activity, constituting an unaccustomed challenge in some very sensitive areas. Given the highly favored position of Ruhr employers in Imperial Germany, their consciousness of indispensability to the established order, and the still largely unlimited power that they exercised within their own domains, it is not surprising that they viewed with intense suspicion and hostility all proponents of social and political change wherever they encountered them—in the national arena, in local government, or on the job.

5
Initial Challenges

Before examining employer policies and their implementation between 1896 and 1914, we need to place them in the context of the events of the immediately preceding years. The attitudes and expectations of Ruhr employers in 1896 strongly reflected their unsettling experience of labor unrest and unwelcome government intervention from the time of the massive coal strike of 1889 through the early 1890s. Nothing of significance was settled in those confrontations and the issues they highlighted constituted much of the agenda of prewar disputes in the Ruhr. Although falling outside the chronological limits of this study, these early challenges to employer authority and their repercussions will be briefly summarized here to indicate the labor-related problems and prospects that influenced the employers' choice of tactics as the nineteenth century drew to a close.

The 1889 Coal Strike

The first mass strike in German history, the Ruhr miners' walkout of 3–20 May 1889, was partly an expression of resentment against the stricter discipline mine operators had imposed during the years after 1873 in an effort to master economic difficulties.[1] During the economic upturn that began in 1887, longer hours and the failure of wages to keep pace with rising prices and corporate profits heightened employee dissatisfaction. Early in 1889, a series of miners' meetings and local strikes escalated until 84 percent of Ruhr miners were absent from their jobs.[2] Within days, strikes broke out in Germany's other mining districts as well, though events in the Ruhr overshadowed other disruptions.

In the Ruhr, complaints about arbitrary determination of wage rates and penalties, forced overtime, the increasing length of unpaid time required for descent into and ascent out of the mine, and rough and capricious treatment by supervisors—grievances heard frequently throughout the prewar era—played as great a role in mobilizing the miners, or greater, than did demands for increased pay. But the employers were initially willing to address only the money issue, some of them admitting that recently improved prices justified higher wage demands. In the first few days, certain employers promised higher pay in an attempt to entice miners back to work; others insisted that work be resumed before the wage issue would be considered. In either case, coal industrialists insisted that wage rates should continue to be determined for the individual mine, not for the industry as a whole. On 11 May, in its first public response to the strike, the executive committee (*Vorstand*) of the Bergbau Verein adamantly rejected any industry-wide negotiation with worker representatives as constituting a dangerous precedent irrevocably undermining the authority of employers. Foremost spokesman for this uncompromising position was Hanns Jencke of Krupp.[3]

Ruhr coal industrialists initially felt secure in their expectation of government support. The unruliness of some of the instigators of strike action—young, poorly paid haulers and horse drivers—had caused local police and regional authorities in the government districts of Arnsberg and Münster to join mine owners in demanding and obtaining the immediate dispatch of the military to the Westphalian part of the coalfield. Military intervention, however, merely served to heighten the confrontation and resulted in the deaths of several miners and innocent bystanders. In the Rhenish part of the coalfield, located in the government district of Düsseldorf, *Regierungspräsident* Hans Freiherr von Berlepsch refrained from calling for military assistance, and there the strike took a more peaceful course.[4]

As the young strikers were joined after the first few days by the majority of their older work mates, strikers' tactics changed. Most important was the miners' decision, drawing upon traditional expectations from the era when the Prussian state directly administered the mines, to send a delegation to William II. The new emperor, inspired for the moment by visions of winning popular support for his reign and perceiving corporate greed rather than socialist agitation as the primary cause of the strike, proved receptive.[5]

The mine operators were infuriated. They took no comfort from the government's invitation to the Bergbau Verein to send its own delegation to Berlin, even though they decided to do so.[6] The employers were joined in their displeasure by Bismarck. Unlike William II, who wanted the fastest possible settlement of the strike, his aged chancellor, interested in preparing bourgeois public opinion for new antisocialist initiatives, was not averse to a prolonged struggle in the Ruhr.[7]

Already feeling betrayed by the emperor's intervention, the employers' delegation discovered upon arriving in Berlin that Friedrich Hammacher, the long-time chairman of the Bergbau Verein and National Liberal deputy in the Reichstag and in the lower house of the Prussian Landtag, had actually entered into negotiations with the miners' representatives at the urging of some fellow members of the Reichstag and in the interest of the restoration of social peace in the Ruhr.[8] In view of these developments, the executive committee of the Bergbau Verein felt compelled, though grudgingly, to accept the bulk of the settlement Hammacher had negotiated. Although omitting from their version of the agreement any reference to the establishment of worker committees (*Arbeiterausschüsse*) in the mines, a proposal Hammacher had accepted and even welcomed, the Bergbau Verein did agree to the principle of voluntary overtime and to wage increases for returning workers, though no exact amount or percentage was specified. The mine owners' association also stated that workers would not be punished for strike participation. But on the important issue of regulating the length of time miners must spend in unpaid descent and ascent in the mines, the Bergbau Verein's statement, which claimed up to an hour of the workers' time for that purpose, was a serious disappointment to the strikers, who wanted the trip between the surface and the coal face included in the normal eight-hour shift. This problem, which became more pressing as mines became deeper and work forces larger, was to be a source of disagreement between miners and their employers into the new century.[9]

This was the first and last "negotiated" settlement of a regional strike in Ruhr heavy industry before the First World War. Mine operators, convinced that they could have completely crushed the strike if there had been no government interference, bitterly resented the forced settlement. Much bitterness was felt toward the conciliatory Hammacher, who was unceremoniously dropped from the chairmanship of the Bergbau Verein in 1890 and replaced by hard-liner Hanns Jencke.[10] The mine operators never acknowledged the legitimacy of the strike and that year's agreements were kept poorly if at all.[11]

Berlin's hesistant intervention in the 1889 strike marked a departure from the government's unquestioning endorsement of employer authority that had prevailed during the previous quarter century. High-ranking administrative personnel in Rhineland and Westphalia were reshuffled in the aftermath of the strike. The Arnsberg *Regierungspräsident* and the Westphalian *Oberpräsident* were both removed after they proposed that a threatened renewal of the strike be countered by declaring a state of siege. Their successors were instructed to adopt a more positive approach toward the miners in the interest of restoring social peace in the Ruhr. In contrast, Düsseldorf *Regierungspräsident* von Berlepsch, who had refrained from calling in the military during the strike, was promoted to the post of *Oberpräsident* of the Rhine province and then in January 1890 was made

Prussian minister of commerce.[12] For their part, the miners, encouraged by the reception their delegation had received from the kaiser in 1889, addressed increasing numbers of petitions to the *Oberbergamt* Dortmund during the next few years, and that agency showed itself more receptive to such appeals than it had been in the past.[13]

Bismarck disapproved of these changes, but his days in power were numbered. The political events of the year following the strike, especially the successes of the Social Democrats in the Reichstag election of February 1890, in which they received 19.7 percent of the national vote compared to 7.1 percent in 1887, and the dismissal of Bismarck in March, were upsetting to the Ruhr elite. Even after Bismarck left office, Ruhr industrialists remained his enthusiastic supporters, making him an honorary member of the Bergbau Verein in 1895.[14] It should be noted, however, that the mine owners' association cautiously refrained from taking that step until after the public reconciliation of the emperor and his former chancellor in 1894, an event that Friedrich Alfred Krupp, anxious to be on good terms with both men, commemorated with a special bequest.[15]

Ruhr business leaders continued to regard government-business relations under Bismarck and the rigidly authoritarian political and social order that he represented as the norm against which all subsequent governments were to be judged, usually negatively as it turned out. Among members of the Ruhr elite, there was a tendency to look back nostalgically to the Bismarckian era, despite its economic upheavals and tribulations, as a time when the employers' authority seemed more secure and the exercise of industrial command less complicated, less constrained by political and social impediments.[16]

After Bismarck

In addition to the 1889 coal strike and the dismissal of Bismarck, other developments were upsetting to the Ruhr elite. A spate of legislative activity in the early 1890s reflected the initiative of the emperor and the new Prussian minister of commerce, Freiherr von Berlepsch, whose program aimed at the reconciliation of the working class to the existing order. New measures included the Supplementary Imperial Trade Regulations (Novelle zur Reichsgewerbeordnung) of 1891 and the Supplementary Prussian Mining Act (Novelle zum preussischen Berggesetz) of 1892. One of the goals of this legislation was to encourage the creation of avenues for the representation of employee interests, but this was made contingent on voluntary employer cooperation, which was not forthcoming. In the Ruhr mines, not a single

Initial Challenges

worker committee of the kind encouraged by the legislation was formed.[17] But even though the factory legislation of the early 1890s was largely ineffective, the coal, iron, and steel industrialists saw these efforts at state intervention as ominous portents. In particular, the Prussian Mining Act of 1892 raised an agonized protest from the representatives of the coal industry. The Bergbau Verein accused the Prussian government of showing an unwarranted lack of trust in employers.[18]

The bitterness Ruhr coal industrialists felt about the outcome of the 1889 strike and its immediate aftermath stiffened their resistance to future labor protests. They would not again be so easily forced into concessions to the workers.[19] This was amply demonstrated by their rigid posture during the continuing labor unrest of the early 1890s. During the Ruhr coal strikes of 1890, 1891, and 1893, each enlisting the support of about twenty thousand miners, large numbers of strikers were summarily dismissed when they failed to heed a call to return to work.[20] Reporting on the 1893 coal strike, Hanns Jencke urged F. A. Krupp to purge all Social Democrats from his employ.[21] Use of this tactic was facilitated by the economic slump of the early 1890s, which temporarily eased the demand for labor. In all, 828 Ruhr miners lost their jobs as a consequence of the 1893 strike. The rest were taken back, but only after a waiting period, in order to teach them a lesson. In addition, those who were hired again were listed as new workers. As a consequence, they lost all accumulated benefit claims.[22]

Continued strike activity in the early 1890s and further successes by the Social Democrats in the Reichstag election of 1893, in which they received 23.3 percent of the vote nationally, were instrumental in moving the impulsive emperor from flirtation with social reform to advocating harsh repression. From 1892 to 1896, William's thinking was influenced by his association with the reactionary and outspoken Saar iron and steel industrialist and Free Conservative Reichstag deputy Carl Ferdinand Freiherr von Stumm-Halberg, who claimed that all working-class organizations were a threat to the established order and who practiced at his steelworks an authoritarian paternalism more extreme than anything known in the Ruhr. Stumm employees, for example, were expected to secure company approval before marrying.[23]

The Ruhr coal strike of 1893 had been called in sympathy with the December 1892 walkout of over 25,000 Saar miners. The Saar strike had a particular impact on the emperor because most of that region's mines were state owned (in contrast to Ruhr mining, in which private enterprise reigned supreme). The Prussian state as employer proved no more willing to tolerate union activities in its mines than were Ruhr corporations, and the 1892 strike in the Saar was sternly suppressed.[24]

After the unqualified failure of strikes in the early 1890s, only occasional local strikes took place during the next decade. Largest and most commented on of such walkouts was the 1899 strike of poorly paid unskilled workers in mines centering on the city of Herne. In June, protests by young haulers, mostly migrants from the east, against withholding increased pension contributions from their meager pay escalated into a strike involving approximately thirty-five hundred out of 18,000 miners employed in eleven large mines. Clashes between strikers and local police strengthened the employers' demand for military intervention, resulting in the sending of some two thousand troops to Herne. In their harsh suppression of the strike, Herne's coal industrialists, foremost among them Karl Behrens, managing director of the Hibernia mining company, could capitalize on widespread public suspicion of Polish workers. The only concession Behrens was willing to make in the interests of restoring industrial peace was to agree not to fine returning workers six days' pay for breach of contract, as the law allowed, instead limiting the fine to those permanently dismissed.[25]

The *Zuchthausvorlage*

In the mid- and late 1890s, employers in Ruhr heavy industry were encouraged not only by the failure of miners to consolidate the gains of 1889 but also by Berlin's turn away from recent efforts to extend factory legislation. Early demise of the so-called New Course was accompanied by renewed governmental preoccupation with repressive measures, among them the *Umsturzvorlage* (Bill against Subversion), which proposed severely punishing those who attacked the institutions of religion, marriage, and the family as well as the monarchy and private property. Introduced in the Reichstag in 1894 against a background of anarchist assassinations elsewhere in Europe, it was voted down the following year[26]

To Ruhr industrialists, a welcome confirmation of the government's reorientation was the 1896 resignation of Berlepsch and his replacement as minister of commerce by Ludwig Brefeld, a confidant of the heavy industrialist-dominated Centralverband.[27] As of 1897, the constellation of personalities in Berlin, especially Bernhard von Bülow, Alfred von Tirpitz, and Johannes Miquel, and the foreign and domestic policies they represented, could hardly have been more congenial to the wishes of Ruhr industrialists. In particular, the entrepreneurial elite warmly supported Foreign Minister Bülow and Secretary of the Navy Tirpitz in their advocacy of naval expansion as an instrument of national integration.[28]

The avowed aim of Finance Minister Miquel was to rally the propertied interests, both agrarian and industrial, to the government. This approach had the support of members of the Ruhr elite, who were ready to pay the price of acquiescing in increased grain tariffs as part of a trade-off for Conservative support for naval expansion.[29] High agricultural tariffs, of course, cost industrial employers money in the form of higher wages. But though they might complain privately about the excesses of the agrarians' Bund der Landwirte, formed in 1893, they unleased no agitation against it but rather sought to make adjustments by the use of expedients such as company stores to secure cheaper produce for their workers.

In the late 1890s, the favor of industrialists was actively courted by Berlin. The government's intensified antisocialist campaign contributed to this end. The emperor had become increasingly aware of the weighty arguments in favor of conciliating his wealthiest subjects, suppliers of the hardware for Germany's army and fleet, and at the same time striking a blow against those disagreeable and ungrateful socialists. In 1898, William II promised the industrialists what they had sought since the lapsing of the antisocialist law in October 1890, repressive legislation designed to limit the freedom of striking workers. The kaiser promised to use the power of the state to shield "Westphalian industry" against economic difficulty.[30] This promise was embodied in one of the most extreme legislative proposals of his reign, the *Zuchthausvorlage* (Penitentiary Bill). The stated purpose of the *Zuchthausvorlage* was to protect strikebreakers by providing harsh penalties, beyond those already existing in criminal law, for anyone attempting to dissuade men from working, not only by violence and threats but even by argument or social pressure of the kind associated with peaceful picketing.[31] The object was to undermine organized labor by weakening the effectiveness of its ultimate weapon, the strike.

The proposal was extremely unpopular, not only with workers but also with almost the entire urban population of Germany, including many employers, though none of them were from heavy industry. There was even a marked difference of opinion within the Centralverband. Within that group, the chief opposition came from south German textile manufacturers. Their spokesman, *Kommerzienrat* Karl Krafft, argued that such a law was unnecessary because adequate legal safeguards already existed. Also, in his opinion, the working-class movement did not constitute the grave threat to the established order that it was alleged to be by men such as Bueck, Kirdorf, and Jencke.[32]

The enthusiasm of the leaders of heavy industry for the *Zuchthausvorlage* and their arguments in its favor exemplify their approach to labor problems at the end of the nineteenth century. Their main argument, as articulated by Hanns Jencke, was that attempts to reconcile workers to the state by means of social legislation and other concessions had been a dismal failure, as attested by the continued increase in socialist votes and union membership. The goal of preserving industrial peace could not be achieved by governmental wooing of labor. Only a serious show of strength and community of interest on the part of the propertied classes had a chance of limiting the spread of dangerous ideas and practices. Only with such firm policies could German industry remain competitive in the world market and thus continue to provide for the livelihood of the workers.[33]

Even with government sponsorship and industrial backing, legislation as patently reactionary as the *Zuchthausvorlage* was predestined to resounding defeat in the Reichstag, where only the Conservative parties and the right wing of the National Liberals favored it. The majority of the National Liberals joined the Social Democrats, the Progressives, and the Catholic Center party in voting against the bill. This so infuriated Jencke that he recommended the Ruhr elite sever all ties with the National Liberal party.[34] This proposal was hardly feasible, but it exemplified the tensions that in the new century would characterize their relations with all but the most right-wing National Liberal leaders.

The ignominious defeat of the *Zuchthausvorlage* reflected widespread opposition to the reactionary and repressive course advocated by the heavy industrialists. The employers and their ministerial allies needed legislative backing for their antilabor proposals, but they were hindered by an almost constant majority opposition in the Reichstag, a resistance that was to prove particularly forceful during most of the first decade of the twentieth century.

The erratic nature of the government's social policies and the ineffectiveness of most state efforts for or against labor made the entrepreneurial elite increasingly skeptical of the ability of government authorities to cope with problems posed by political and economic organization of the working class. As a result, after the failure of the *Zuchthausvorlage* in 1899, Ruhr employers abandoned for the time being much of their dependence on government initiative and concentrated on finding their own solutions. All they asked of the state in most instances was that it not intervene except to maintain order. They concentrated most of their attention on their own firms and on maintaining control over their own employees.

6
Company Welfare Programs

The efforts of Ruhr coal, iron, and steel producers to cope with the labor problems facing them at the end of the nineteenth century took two main forms. Neither of them was new, but both now received more attention. One was the expansion of employer-sponsored welfare services to faithful workers, in effect an attempt to buy employee loyalty and good will by the provision of increasingly elaborate fringe benefits. The other area of employer initiative was the effort to increase worker productivity and to improve predictability of job performance through changes in wages, hours, disciplinary procedures, and supervision. Ruhr industrialists proceeded simultaneously on both fronts.

Employer Motives

Ostensibly, voluntary employer contributions to welfare funds, such as those providing housing, insurance, pensions, educational and recreational facilities, and health care, were motivated by concern for the well-being of workers and their dependents. Yet in the more private statements industrial leaders made regarding the provision of social services, altruistic concern invariably received less emphasis than did more practical considerations. The earliest of these practical considerations to be addressed, and one constituting a primary motivation for the initial development of large-scale social institutions by private industry in the Ruhr, was the need to attract workers to isolated areas and to hold them there. This need was particularly great during the first significant expansion of heavy industry in the 1850s.[1] By the end of the century, fewer of the region's major heavy industrial enterprises were still isolated in the countryside, but the need for the employer to provide some of the basic necessities of life in addition to wages did not completely disappear even in urban areas. Because of the continued rapid growth of the industrial population, many communities were unable to keep pace with the growing demand for services and accommodations, and employers might still find themselves compelled to provide what hard-pressed towns and cities could not.[2]

The extensive employee welfare programs for which Ruhr industrialists became noted were devised not only to attract and hold an adequate labor force but also to deflect criticism, especially bureaucratic criticism. In the early and mid-nineteenth century, the Prussian state bureaucracy, given its service ideology and its claim to be immune to special interests, bolstered its sense of superiority over parvenu entrepreneurs by expressing disdain for the unenlightened and socially reckless pursuit of profit. Ruhr industrialists, to a significant degree, accommodated themselves to this critique. They were reluctant to posit profit as the goal of their efforts, except as it was deemed necessary to guarantee a fair return to investors and ensure the continued financial health and survival of the enterprise. Sharing the concern of state officials that rapid economic development might spawn revolutionary upheaval, Ruhr employers argued that their contributions to worker welfare demonstrated their sense of social responsibility.

Ruhr entrepreneurs also saw voluntary social expenditures as a means of blocking expanded government social legislation, which would entail not only increased costs but also increased bureaucratic interference. Industrial spokesmen maintained that the necessary minimum of state welfare had been provided by Bismarck's social legislation of the 1880s. Ruhr industrialists, notably Louis Baare of the Bochumer Verein, had initially supported a limited amount of such legislation. In particular, they had advocated state-mandated accident insurance, at least in part as a means of spreading the costs of heavy industry's high accident rates over a broader base.[3] This accomplished, Ruhr employers argued that remaining needs should be met by private initiative.[4]

Employers and employees developed contrasting interpretations of company welfare programs. Employees came to regard so-called welfare benefits, especially premiums, bonuses, and pensions, as part of their earned income, an essential supplement to their regular money wages. Employers regarded the benefits conferred as free gifts to which the worker had no legal or moral claim.[5] They also saw welfare benefits as a reward for absolute loyalty. This attitude was reflected in a speech that Emil Krabler, managing director of the Kölner Bergwerksverein, gave in 1898, honoring those workers who had been employed by that company for twenty-five years. Krabler explained that the gift made to such workers on that occasion was not a reward for their services, since those had been paid for in wages, but for their loyalty. All workers were excluded from receiving the gift who at any time during the past twenty-five years had participated in a strike and had thus broken faith with the company.[6]

Company Housing

After 1896, as in earlier stages of industrialization, one of the most conspicuous forms of voluntary expenditure on the workers continued to be for housing. The second half of the 1890s saw rapid construction of company dwellings. In the area under the jurisdiction of the *Oberbergamt* Dortmund, the number of housing units owned by the mines increased from 10,255 in 1893 to 26,245 in 1900. As a consequence, despite the rapid growth of the work force during those years, the percentage of workers living in company housing increased from an estimated 11.2 percent in 1893 to 18.5 percent in 1900. During the same period, the percentage of miners with their own households living in company houses climbed from 12.5 percent in 1893 to 21.5 percent in 1900. And the renewed spurt of building made possible not only the housing of many more workers, especially in the newer areas of the north but also alleviation of some of the worst overcrowding of earlier years.[7]

In the most recently developed and therefore isolated areas, workers had little choice but to live in the housing provided by the firms employing them. This circumstance rendered specious the industrialists' claim that companies should be allowed to do as they liked with their houses because workers were not "forced" to live in them.[8] Even in urban areas where other accommodations were available, the rapid growth of population meant that private rentals were often scarce, expensive, and far from the place of employment. The advent of streetcars did introduce an element of greater choice for the better paid workers who could afford the cost of transport. Thus, metallurgical workers at Thyssen's Deutscher Kaiser company reportedly preferred commuting from dwellings in nearby towns to living in company housing.[9] But many other workers in Ruhr cities found it either necessary or desirable to request housing from their employers. At Krupp in Essen, workers were said to put their names on lists and wait for years for their turn to move into the firm's colonies, especially the newer ones with more commodious houses.[10]

Company housing and related privileges offered a considerable economic advantage to workers. Company housing usually had better quality and more living space for the price than did private rentals. Comparable dwellings on the open market often rented for half again as much as Ruhr employers charged.[11] Also, there was often a provision that at the end of the year, a half or whole month's rent would be remitted if the dwelling had been kept in good condition.[12] Usually included along with company housing, especially for miners, were stalls for animals and land for gardens. Mining corporations were in a position to offer their workers relatively low-density housing because they typically owned substantial amounts of land, acquired in the interest of guaranteeing future coal reserves and of protecting themselves against claims that their activities underground resulted in structural damages to buildings in the surrounding area.[13] The decision to make some of this land available to the miners reflected not only a traditional pattern of tenancy among such workers but also their employers' hope that contact with the land would prevent the complete "proletarianization" of working-class families.[14]

In return for these benefits, the industrialists protected their own interests by imposing restrictions. The most important was that occupancy of the house was limited to the term of employment. According to the rental contracts of a majority of the firms providing housing, a worker who gave notice or was fired had to vacate his quarters by the last day of work.[15] A worker who quit or was fired was therefore confronted with the necessity of finding both a new job and new housing.

Workers living in company housing had a much lower rate of job turnover than other employees. A 1902 study revealed an annual job departure rate of 53.8 percent among Ruhr miners generally but of only 7.9 percent among those living in company housing.[16] The striking difference in turnover rates can be explained in part by the industrialists' selective policy for distributing rentals. The workers occupying such housing were married and usually older and more reliable than other employees. But these factors are not enough to explain the whole difference. The binding effect of company housing must have been considerable. Although the firms with housing usually realized only 1 to 3 percent on their money because of the low rents, the investment more than justified itself in the greater stability of trained personnel.[17]

Although company housing was intended primarily to reduce turnover of personnel, it was also a potential weapon against strikes. According to the work orders of 1892, workers who were absent without permission for three days might be struck from the list of employees. Participation in a strike was hardly considered an acceptable excuse for absence. Yet the oft-threatened eviction of striking workers, unlike that of workers permanently dismissed, was not always carried out and never on a mass scale. In each of the major coal strikes prior to World War I, striking workers were threatened with eviction, but implementation of the threat was prevented by adverse public opinion and the refusal of government officials to provide the necessary force to carry out mass dispossession.[18]

Industrialists also used company housing as a means of observing and regulating worker activities during leisure hours. Employers viewed company-owned workers' colonies, especially the newer ones that generally had more amenities than did those built during the first great surge of industrialization, not only as the provision of a physical necessity but also as a means of establishing an orderly and controlled environment conducive to the molding of orderly and controlled lives. In the most carefully planned colonies, the intent was that workers would live in proximity to parks and libraries rather than taverns.[19] They would also live under the watchful eyes of company officials. In almost every rental contract, company officials in charge of housing, sometimes *any* company official, had the right to enter and inspect the worker's home at any time. In this manner, the company could not only inspect the condition of the dwelling but could regulate such personal matters as the newspapers subscribed to and the character of guests.[20] Sons of the family employed by a rival firm, for example, were not allowed to stay the night without special permission. Upon reaching a suitable age for employment a boy either had to go to work for the company employing his father or else leave home.[21]

Company disapproval of certain private activities of workers could lead not only to eviction from their dwellings but also to dismissal from their jobs.[22] At the end of the nineteenth century, most Ruhr employers still believed that it was possible to avoid labor trouble by observing and dismissing those employees who were involved in or influenced by organizations or movements the industrialists considered subversive. Yet their own efforts to herd workers together into company housing often facilitated growth of the very sense of employee solidarity that they sought to avoid.[23]

Other Benefits

The effectiveness of company housing as an instrument for controlling the actions of employees, great as it was, was limited to the minority of workers who lived in it or hoped to do so. Of more general significance, as measured by the number of potential recipients, were various kinds of employer plans to provide workers with protection against misfortune. Despite the institution in the 1880s of state social insurance for sickness, accident, and old age, private employer-sponsored insurance plans continued to thrive and even expand, either in areas not yet provided for by the Reich, such as family health insurance or survivors' benefits, or in areas where there was a choice between private and state coverage, such as workers' health insurance or old-age pensions. Like housing, insurance could be used to reward or punish workers and to bind them to their jobs. In general, insurance in coal mining was less subject to abuse than it was in the iron and steel industry because in mining the most important types of insurance were controlled not by the individual firms but by the *Knapp-*

schaften, the miners' benevolent societies, which included representatives of both employers and miners.

By the second half of the nineteenth century, most private industrial insurance plans had written statutes and some provision for the representation of workers in their administration. But worker representation did not necessarily insure any significant measure of worker control. It was common for workers to elect half the members of an administrative committee and the employer to appoint the other half, with the deciding vote in case of a tie being cast by the chairman, an appointee of management. Even such representation as the workers had for their interests under such a system was sometimes negated by the election procedure, as was the case at Krupp, where worker representatives were "elected" by acclamation. A secret ballot was granted only if demanded by one of the assembled workers. But no one ever made that demand.[24]

Control over the administration of insurance funds was important not only because it might save the firm money but also because it permitted management to decide who was "worthy" of receiving benefits. This was a possible means of punishing employees who failed to follow company dictates. Among some of the more old-fashioned entrepreneurs, this type of control also reflected the remnants of a self-imposed duty to regulate the morals of workers and their families. Some employers still imbued with this notion even retained the right to review pensions already granted. For example, not until 1907 was a new statute devised for the Gutehoffnungshütte's pension fund omitting the provision that a pension might be revoked if a retired worker or former employee's widow was judged to be leading an immoral or drunken life.[25] Such provisions were curiosities after the turn of the century, but they demonstrate the extent to which older industrialists had felt justified, even duty-bound, in regulating the personal lives of workers.

In heavy industry, the worker was insured, however inadequately, either by the state or by his employer, against all the major misfortunes that might befall him in normal life—except unemployment. Before the First World War, only one firm in Ruhr heavy industry, the Hoerder Verein in 1895, had established voluntary unemployment insurance for its employees.[26] None of the other firms followed suit. Not only did most Ruhr industrialists decline to provide their own unemployment aid for workers, but they also opposed the introduction of unemployment insurance by state or local government. Employers objected to the added costs of state unemployment insurance and feared that in the event of a strike it would remove a major burden from the strike funds of the unions.[27] In addition, they believed that payment of unemployment compensation would encourage laziness and irresponsibility on the part of workers.

Company Welfare Programs

Ruhr industrialists were not indifferent to the problem of unemployment. They saw any concentration of idle men as a potential threat to order. However, they believed that the answer was not insurance but a prosperous and expanding industry. Actually, from the mid-1890s to the war, unemployment was not a major problem in Ruhr heavy industry, at least as far as established workers were concerned. To be sure, even the regular work force experienced seasonal and cyclical fluctuations in employment hours from short time to overtime. Nevertheless, the prospect of relatively stable employment was one of the most important recruiting features of Ruhr industry.

Given the scarcity of reliable employees, it was in the interest of Ruhr industrialists to keep them employed during hard times to prevent their dispersion and thereby insure the presence of an adequate work force when the situation improved. During short recessions, large firms usually produced for inventory, carried out repairs, or operated part-time rather than dismiss valuable workers.[28] Spokesmen for heavy industry exhibited this practice as evidence of the alleged moral superiority of employment practices in that region over those they claimed prevailed in England and America. In the English-speaking countries, they asserted, only money, not social responsibility, counted and masses of workers were dismissed at the first sign of an economic downturn.[29]

The development in the Ruhr of giant corporations with large capital reserves favored comparatively steady employment policies. Leaders of Ruhr heavy industry such as Emil Kirdorf claimed, with some justification, that the development of cartels facilitated the maintenance of steadier employment and wage rates for the workers.[30] Yet it should be noted that though Ruhr employers attempted to provide continuous employment for the core of their work force even when demand temporarily slackened, they alone determined who should be retained and hastened to use such occasions to dismiss troublesome workers or agitators as well as less productive employees without incurring too much public censure.[31]

In the late 1890s, the most widespread and important forms of insurance voluntarily supplied by private industry were family health plans, pensions for widows and orphans, and pensions for superannuated workers. Of these, old-age pensions were most subject to abuse. The iron and steel magnates were the worst offenders. Pension funds were a useful means of binding experienced workers to the job. The crux of the problem of pension funds was the question of what should happen to the worker's accumulated contributions if he resigned or was dismissed. Almost universally, he forfeited his benefits. At the Hoerder Verein, deductions were even made from the pay of departing workers for funds from which they could never expect to collect.[32]

Public controversy over the loss of pension benefits focused on Krupp. Statutes of the Krupp pension fund specified that workers leaving Krupp would have no claim to accumulated benefits.[33] A contemporary observer calculated that in the period from 1894 to 1907, some sixty thousand Krupp workers lost their pension contributions.[34] The question was tested in the courts at the instigation of the unions. In 1911 the Reichsgericht declared the provision legal.

At the end of the nineteenth century, perhaps the most rapidly expanding area of employer welfare activity involved the provision of services for the families of employees, especially health services. One reason for this extension of aid to the family was simply that a very real need existed. When Emil Krabler established the first family health service in Ruhr coal mining in 1880, 114 of the 215 children who died in Altenessen in that year had received no doctor's care.[35] Another reason was that this type of private welfare was as yet little subject to regulation. In 1906, for example, the executive committee of the Bergbau Verein advised employers to make contributions to family health plans rather than to other funds more closely regulated by the state.[36] A third reason for the extension of family welfare benefits was that once a new institution became established in a few leading firms, the others usually had to follow suit. It was expected of them. Before the First World War, two-thirds of the mines in the Ruhr coalfield had established family health services modeled after that initiated by Krabler in 1880.[37] A fourth reason was that the employers wished to foster a healthy family life as a means of making the workers settled and stable. A final reason was the desire to create a sense of community that had been lost or had never existed. The Ruhr employers' image of the factory community as an extended family, though absurd in light of real conditions, did not fade away completely prior to World War I.

In the large corporations of the prewar Ruhr, paternalistic concern for company employees remained a frequently invoked ideal. Such concern continued to be one of the factors motivating the establishment of elaborate systems of industrial welfare designed simultaneously to reward faithful workers and to restrict their freedom of movement. Thus, it was reported of Wilhelm Liebrich, managing director of the Concordia mining company from 1890 to 1920, that he maintained a personal fund from which he granted at his own discretion aid to workers in need, such aid being delivered by the director's wife on her visits to employees' families.[38] At the celebration of the centenary of the Krupp concern in 1912, public statements emphasized the image of the company as an extended family, bound together by a community of interests.[39]

Welfare benefits were useful not only as instruments of control but also as instruments of integration, especially at those companies such as

Company Welfare Programs

Krupp, the Gutehoffnungshütte, and the Bochumer Verein that were most successful in establishing reputations for relative generosity in such matters.[40] But employer endowments did not always have the intended results. The spirit in which they were administered often increased rather than lessened tensions between workers and employers. Employers expected gratitude and loyalty but often reaped resentment for programs whose overt purpose was to serve the well-being of workers but whose covert purpose was, more often than not, to limit their freedom. Given with an eye to publicity, allocations for worker welfare often benefited only selected employees and their dependents or remained invested in the firm at low rates of interest while actual benefits were paid for by contributions of the workers themselves. Above all, it did not escape notice that where so-called welfare institutions were most extensive and comprehensive, working conditions were often harshest and discipline the most authoritarian.[41]

7
The Terms of Labor

Wages

Compared to employer-sponsored social services such as pensions and housing, with their high potential for abuse and their deceptive publicity, entrepreneurial wage policies were a more accurate measure of the industrialist's contribution to his workers' well-being. In general, wage policies reflected the same underlying characteristics that determined the administration and distribution of welfare benefits. As they did with social services, apologists for Ruhr heavy industry emphasized the "generosity" of wage payments. Employee earnings were invariably described as being as high as was consistent with the continued prosperity of industry. Employers pointed to the rapid rise in money wages after 1896. Consumer prices, however, also increased, especially during the last prewar decade, and on balance, real earnings per shift of coal, iron, and steel workers were little higher in 1913 than they had been in 1896, and not as high as in 1900. The increase in real wages during the boom of the late 1890s, when competition for workers had been particularly intense, was reversed by cuts in nominal and real wages during the recession of 1901–1902. Those losses were not made good, in many cases, until 1907. The recession of 1908–1909 brought renewed cuts. Nominal wages surged again during the last prewar boom but most of these gains were eaten up by the rising cost of living.[1]

Ruhr employers liked to stress that their workers were among the best paid in Germany. Was that claim justified? Information on industrial wage differentials prior to 1913 is scanty. However, a study by the Imperial Statistical Bureau of wages paid in 370 establishments in March 1914 listed average daily earnings of male and female workers in twelve basic industries. Only the earnings of male workers will be used for comparison, as Ruhr heavy industry did not employ women. Of the twelve industries reported, printing, with its highly skilled labor force, ranked highest with male workers earning a daily average of 6.50 marks. The next three highest paying industries listed, namely, metal, machine building, and chemicals, paid 5.54 marks, 5.32 marks, and 5.16 marks, respectively. Compared to these average daily earnings, hewers and haulers in coal mines in the area under the jurisdiction of the *Oberbergamt* Dortmund earned an average of 6.25 marks per shift in the first quarter of 1914. In the same period, a skilled metal worker at Krupp in Essen earned an average of 6.67 marks per shift. An unskilled male worker at Krupp earned an average of 5.42 marks.[2]

Ruhr heavy industry paid higher wages, both in nominal and to a lesser extent in real terms, than did heavy industry in other areas of Germany. This regional differential was most important with reference to Silesia, since Prussia's eastern provinces formed an important source of recruits for Ruhr industry. The average earnings per shift of hewers and haulers in the *Oberbergamtsbezirk* in 1896 was 3.60 marks and in 1913 was 6.47 marks. A similar worker in Upper Silesia earned an average of 2.82 marks per shift in 1896 and 4.71 marks in 1913.[3] But workers who came to the Ruhr during the Wilhelmian era found that their higher money wages were in part eaten up by the higher cost of living. A British investigating team calculated that if the cost of living in Berlin (food, fuel, and rent) in 1905 were taken as index base 100, then the comparative index numbers for Bochum, Dortmund, and Essen would be 88, 90, and 92, respectively, whereas the comparative index number for Königshütte, a city located in the center of the Upper Silesian industrial area, would be only 78.[4]

There were also local differences in nominal wages paid within the Ruhr industrial area itself. In 1905, miners in the southern Ruhr earned an average of 3.90 marks per shift whereas miners in the northern Ruhr averaged 4.07 marks. In 1913 the figures were 5.18 marks in the south and 5.42 marks in the north.[5] The higher wages paid by the newer, larger, more prosperous, and more technically advanced mines of the north enabled them to lure young workers from the south, just as the Ruhr as a whole attracted workers from the east. In the competition for workers, the largest and most prosperous firms enjoyed the advantage of lower labor costs per unit of production and larger profit margins that enabled them to pay higher wages and to offer more benefits and greater security than their less prosperous competitors. Krupp and similar giant firms never had to worry about securing enough workers, not even during periods of the greatest scarcity of labor. They always had more than enough applicants to cover their needs without having to engage in the active recruiting to which less fortunate companies resorted.[6]

As was the case with voluntary social services, the benefits of entrepreneurial wage policies were not distributed equally to all workers. Chief beneficiaries were the experienced, reliable, and docile workers. Especially during periods of rapid industrial expansion, the competition for such workers contributed to increases in wage differentials.[7] For instance, in the first quarter of 1896, the average wage of surface workers in the Dortmund coal industry was 72.5 percent that of underground miners. By the first quarter of 1900, in the wake of the hectic industrial boom years following 1896, the wage of workers above ground was only 64.7 percent that of the hewers and haulers.[8]

Also like voluntary social services, wage policies were administered in a highly arbitrary fashion. Both were designed to emphasize the absolute power of the employer, limited only by competition for workers. At a time when English coal, iron, and steel industrialists had already experimented with sliding scales that tied wages to the selling price of the product, and with collective bargaining, the leaders of Ruhr heavy industry adamantly refused to recognize any right of organized labor to participate in the determination of wage rates.[9] An extensive study of wage policies of the region's largest iron and steel companies, published in 1907, indicated that not a single negotiated wage settlement existed.[10] The same was true of mining. Otto Heinemann, head of the Krupp Bureau for Worker Affairs (Büro für Arbeiterangelegenheiten), noted in his autobiography that at that company before the war, wages were not even discussed with new employees when they were hired. A worker found out what he was being paid only at the end of the first pay period when he actually had the money in hand.[11]

Dissatisfaction with wage rate determination and administration caused as much or more bad feeling between labor and management in the Ruhr as did dissatisfaction with the amount actually paid.[12] This was particularly true in coal mining and in the manufacture of finished iron and steel products, industries in which wage rates were subject to frequent adjustment. In contrast, rates for metallurgical workers once set were likely to remain in force for relatively long periods, and thus were less likely to be a source of recurrent disputes. Also, since metallurgy was less labor intensive than mining and finished metal goods manufacture, employers in that industry had less incentive to look constantly for ways to cut labor costs.

In mining, given the difficulties of supervising workers dispersed underground, piece rates for the majority of the work force had been introduced early in an attempt to guarantee at least a minimal level of effort. Because working conditions and ease of operations varied substantially even within the same mine, separate piece rates were set for each coal face. The *Steiger*, the miner's immediate supervisor and often the only member of the company bureaucracy with whom he had regular contact, estimated how much coal each team of workers could be expected to produce under the conditions prevailing where they worked and set the rate accordingly. Members of the work team shared the total sum earned in proportion to their qualifications. Piece rates were set for an indefinite time, but since conditions changed as work progressed, the rates were typically altered at least once a month.[13]

This traditional system of setting pay rates was a recognized source of enmity in labor-management relations. Within the same mine, the pay of hewers might vary as much as 30 or 40 percent or more. The highest pay did not necessarily go to those who were most skilled or hardest working. The resulting dissatisfaction was one cause of frequent job changes.

Among possible alternatives to the existing system, any wage scale established by negotiation between the region's organized workers and management was rejected as unworkable by Ruhr employers. Coal industrialists had two arguments to explain why such a system might be feasible in British mining but not in the Ruhr. First, they claimed that worker organizations of the Ruhr were neither as representative nor as reliable as those in England and were totally unsuitable as partners for negotiation. Second, they argued that geologic conditions were much more complex in the Ruhr than in England and precluded any general settlement of the wage issue.[14]

But if Ruhr coal industrialists rejected negotiated wage settlements, they were by no means satisfied with existing procedures. Greater uniformity and predictability were desired not only for smoother operation but also for more accurate cost accounting. To this end, the discretionary power of the *Steiger* in setting and calculating wages had to be curbed. A first step was to subject the lowest ranking supervisors to increasing supervision by new intermediary levels of industrial bureaucracy, while emphasizing the keeping of more accurate records of piece rates guaranteed to each team of miners.

A *Steiger* employed by the massive Haniel-owned Neumühl mine in 1903 described the efforts being made there to counteract some of the abuses still prevalent elsewhere in the Ruhr. At Neumühl, the *Steiger* were instructed to put all wage agreements in writing as they were made and not to depart therefrom no matter how much or how little was owing to individual workers at the end of the month. Workers should always know exactly what was due them. This procedure was intended to eliminate the practice whereby supervisors set unrealistically low piece rates and then adjusted the final wage upward to a more realistic level, at least for those miners who had not subsequently incurred their wrath.[15]

Some of the same problems and attempted solutions that developed in coal mining also emerged in the determination of wage policies in the iron and steel industry. The setting of piece rates was again the central issue. Whereas the general use of piece rates in mining was long established, a legacy of the period of state direction, their widespread adoption in the iron and steel industry was of more recent origin. In the later part of the nineteenth century, more and more iron- and steelworkers were made subject to piece rates. The largest and most modern companies took the lead. Thus, in 1871, company officials of the Gutehoffnungshütte were instructed that piece rates should be used as much as possible.[16] During the depression years that predominated in the 1870s, employers looked increasingly to piece rates as a means of lowering wages while generating the least resistance. Employers found that piece rates were easier to revise downward when times were bad than were hourly or daily wages. Some workers could make up at least part of the loss through increasing productivity. This in turn facilitated a reduction in the work force. During the boom years of the late 1890s, the use of piece rates was again extended, but more as a means of raising total productivity than as a means of reducing wage levels.[17]

During the last prewar decades, the use of piece rates to increase the pace of work was a frequent grievance among the workers affected. Workers often found that improved productivity as a result of greater effort on their part resulted in only a temporary increase in their take-home pay, followed by a downward revision of piece rates. This practice was particularly prevalent at the largest, most modern companies with the most sophisticated cost accounting systems.[18] Workers often complained that high piece rates were awarded only to a few privileged members of a work team and the other members of the team, paid by the hour or the day, were forced to keep pace with their more highly motivated associates without sharing in the rewards.[19] However, as employers well knew, workers were not defenseless in such matters and could, through peer pressure and even intimidation, seek to prevent their colleagues from exceeding customary levels of production. But such resistance was inherently more effective in coal mining, where the work force was more cohesive and where close supervision was especially difficult, than it was in the iron and steel industry.

As Ruhr iron and steel producers turned increased attention to the careful setting and manipulation of piece rates, they inevitably focused more attention on the actions of the personnel responsible for this task. In the initial stages of the industry's development, there had been little uniformity in the determining of wages. Emphasis was typically on the judgment and authority of the *Werkmeister,* counterpart to the *Steiger* in coal mining. The *Meister* determined the worth of each worker he hired and calculated the wages due him.[20] Under the circumstances, the same charges of caprice and favoritism were heard as in mining. However, in the period we are examining, the trend in the largest and most modern firms was to limit the *Meister* to an advisory role in the setting of wage rates. Increasingly, the actual determination of wages passed to men more remote from the individual worker—to engineers, who were being employed in ever greater numbers, and to centralized accounting offices.[21] In addition, efforts were made to insure that the *Meister* abided by decisions made by those above them in the industrial hierarchy. Thus, in the Krupp machine shops, fifteen men maintained constant surveillance of the record books kept by the *Meister* to make certain they were actually calculating the pay of individual workers at the rates stipulated by the company.[22]

Newer methods of determining wages insured greater uniformity both within and among companies. Wishing to abandon existing wage policies on the grounds they were too erratic and too unsystematic, Ruhr employers instructed their lieutenants to search for more effective alternatives. In attempting to come up with such alternatives, managerial personnel drew not only upon their training and experience but also increasingly upon the experience of other industries, even other countries. For instance, Otto Heinemann, head of the Krupp Bureau of Worker Affairs, reported that he and a colleague were sent to study prevailing methods at other large German firms, including Siemens and the Allgemeine Elektrizitäts-gesellschaft (AEG) in Berlin.[23] Karl Wilke, who became head of the central accounting office of the Gelsenkirchener Bergwerks-AG in 1902, recounted how Emil Kirdorf stressed the importance of framing such policies for the firm as could be applied elsewhere in Ruhr mining. The reasoning was that given the immense size of the firm and the prominence of its leader, its managerial practices should properly serve as models for other companies. Wilke also noted the importance Kirdorf attached to uniformity of practice within the giant Gelsenkirchen combine, often precipitating protests from individual mine directors under his command who were used to doing things in their own way.[24]

In both mining and metallurgy, setting basic wage rates for individual workers only partly determined their actual earnings. Premiums and fines also had a substantial impact, and their distribution was a frequent source of dissatisfaction among workers. Premiums were awarded either for attaining certain production goals or for reliability. Workers complained that production premiums encouraged those who sought them to take chances, leading to increased accident rates. Particularly resented were the high production premiums paid to supervisory personnel, to the *Steiger* in the mines and to the *Werkmeister* in the steel mills. For example, in the largest Ruhr rolling mills, the premiums earned by the *Meister* typically amounted to as much as their base pay. Where production premiums formed such a crucial component of their earnings, *Meister* were often viewed by their subordinates as drivers rather than leaders of men.[25]

Fines were the negative, punitive counterpart of premiums and were widely used in Ruhr heavy industry. Their arbitrary imposition was often a source of friction between workers and supervisors. Among the most common reasons for levying fines were unexcused absence and tardiness.[26] Harshest of the fines in use in the prewar Ruhr was one intended to impede abrupt work stoppages or job changes by workers, either individually or collectively. Ruhr work orders drawn up in 1892, in compliance with a law requiring such orders in plants employing more than twenty workers, stipulated that unexcused absence for three days was grounds not only for dismissal but also for a fine of up to six days' wages.[27] Such a fine could be levied against strikers or against employees who quit without giving the required two weeks' notice. Yet it was not always applied in either case. In practice, allowances had to be made. At Krupp, for example, the fine was not used during the last prewar decade because of the bad publicity and litigation that it involved.[28]

More important and more resented than fines for transgressions against company rules were penalties levied for work judged to be unacceptable. In mining, the long-standing practice of *Wagennullen* consisted of refusing payment to miners for loads of coal mixed with an unacceptable quantity of rock. This practice appears particularly harsh when contrasted with the procedure used in British mining of merely subtracting from wages a sum proportional to the amount of rock present and paying for the remaining quantity of coal.[29] *Wagennullen* had been an important issue in the 1889 coal strike. Subsequently there had been a modification in its use. Some Ruhr mines dropped the practice entirely. Others agreed to partial payment. But in many mines the practice continued as before. For example, in 1898, in the East Dortmund mining district, 13,348 miners lost a total of 54,933 marks because of *Wagennullen*, as compared to only 16,175 marks lost as a result of other kinds of fines.[30] *Wagennullen* was to be a major issue in the 1905 coal strike.

In the iron and steel industry, a similar problem was whether workers in rolling mills would be paid for sheet metal that was not up to specifications. As in the case of *Wagennullen*, policies were not uniform from company to company. Some employers refused to make any payment, some paid but levied a stiff fine, and others paid for all production at contracted rates except for sheets so bad they were fit only for scrap. The first and harshest of these options was typically used where workers were most defenseless, where many migrant Polish laborers were employed, or where plants were most isolated.[31]

Supervision

Wages served, then, not just to attract and hold workers and provide for their sustenance but also to motivate and discipline. These latter purposes assumed increasing importance in the wage schemes introduced or modified in the last prewar decades. Elaborate piece rate and premium schedules were intended to ease the problems and uncertainties of supervising large numbers of men, unknown to their ultimate employers, by providing carefully calculated incentives for worker diligence that did not depend on traditional expectations or on the whims of individual overseers. But changes in wage policies were only one aspect of efforts to introduce greater uniformity into on-the-job relations.

In the pursuit of more uniform and centralized control of production, one problem area needing attention was the practice of subcontracting. Since the 1880s, Ruhr mine operators had made increasing use of subcontractors to carry out specific tasks, particularly for boring shafts through rock in locations where special machinery or skills were needed.[32] Subcontractors hired, paid, and supervised their own workers. The numbers involved were relatively small, for instance only 895 men employed by twelve Ruhr mining subcontractors in June 1895.[33] But since they moved about from one assignment to the next, they attracted a disproportionate amount of attention. In the mid-1890s, complaints in working-class newspapers spurred government inquiry into the matter.

Employers, for their part, found the practice increasingly unsatisfactory, not only because it attracted outside criticism but also because it infringed upon their desire for complete control over what happened in the mines. The consequences of such lack of control could be embarrassing. For example, in October 1897, a working-class newspaper reported the use of convict labor at a mine belonging to the Gelsenkirchener Bergwerks-AG. Managing Director Kirdorf felt called upon to answer in a bourgeois paper that the convicts had been hired without his knowledge by a subcontractor employed by the mine to help construct a new railway station.[34] By 1898, the Bergbau Verein had reached agreement with the *Oberbergamt* that workers employed by contractors were to be considered employees of the mine for the period of the contract and to be subject to its discipline. But the real answer to the problem, at least as far as the larger companies were concerned, was to procure for themselves the specialized machinery and workers that would eliminate the need to use subcontractors.[35]

Although subcontractors could increasingly be dispensed with in the interest of more centralized control, the same was not true of a company's own supervisory personnel, the indispensable intermediaries between the managerial elite and workers. Crucial to achieving more rationalized, centralized direction of huge concerns was the need for increased regulation of the relationships between workers and their supervisors. Only if Ruhr employers could control and reshape these relationships could their hopes for more effective management of labor be realized. No other problem of labor relations was as difficult or as sensitive as this one.

In the large-scale industries that developed in the Ruhr in the second half of the nineteenth century, lower supervisory personnel, the *Werkmeister* in metallurgy and the *Steiger* in mining, among the oldest and most traditional elements of the industrial bureaucracy of the region, often exercised authority within their assigned domains virtually unchecked by interference from above. Much of their power and influence rested upon their unparalleled familiarity with workers and working conditions gained through close daily contact. In rapidly expanding industrial combines, this precious knowledge made them invaluable to company leaders who had become far removed from actual production. Often the easiest and most immediate, and therefore earliest, response to the complex managerial problems created by the expanding scale of operations was to leave decisions affecting individual production units to the discretion of supervisory personnel.

This was especially true of matters relating to workers. For an individual worker of a large company, the character and temperament of his immediate supervisor was often more important in determining the conditions under which he labored than any other factor. Among the functions commonly delegated to lower supervisory personnel were hiring and firing, the determination of wage rates for individual laborers, the imposition of fines and other forms of punishment, the making of work assignments, and the supervision of their implementation. Workers might find their supervisors petty tyrants in some instances, indulgent comrades in others. Frequently heard were complaints of favoritism, nepotism, and capriciousness.[36]

As the century drew to a close, increased demand for the products of Ruhr heavy industry put a premium upon increased production. At the same time, the managerial elite was seeking increasingly centralized control and accountability. As a consequence of both developments, there was less and less inclination at the top of Ruhr industry to rest content with existing modes of supervision in mine and mill. In the interests of increased uniformity and predictability of on-the-job discipline and productivity, employers sought, on the one hand, to limit personal contacts between workers and supervisors and, on the other, to limit the discretionary powers of overseers, rewarding and promoting those who conformed most closely to new expectations.

Attempts to reduce unregulated personal contacts between workers and their immediate superiors included changes in the status of supervisors as well as changes in their recruitment, training, and leisure activities. Simplest of the cluster of changes affecting *Meister* and *Steiger* was the reformulation of their roles in company work orders. The work orders drawn up in 1892 reflected a growing concern with this problem. For example, the work order formulated by the Gutehoffnungshütte explicitly forbade "friendly contacts" between workers and supervisors. Supervisors were forbidden to accept gifts of any kind from subordinates.[37] At Krupp the work order of 1892 for the first time sharply distinguished between the status of worker and that of *Meister*. *Meister* were no longer to perform manual labor. Their role was to be exclusively supervisory. And they were no longer to be paid by the hour or by the piece, like workers but, rather, were to receive a salary plus premiums.[38] To be raised to the ranks of the salaried not only improved the status of *Meister* but also helped shield their income from those fluctuations caused by trade cycles and increasing age that were the lot of ordinary wage earners in heavy industry.[39]

With the rise of an independent labor movement, employers worried that personal contact between workers and supervisors might lead not only to indulgent supervision but also to the contamination of overseers with trade unionist and socialist attitudes. For this reason, loyalty to the employers' cause was a crucial prerequisite for admission to the ranks of lower management. Thus, a number of large Ruhr concerns hired only Protestant supervisors. Catholics were suspect because they might sympathize with the Center party.[40] Needless to say, anyone even suspected of unionist or socialist sympathies was automatically excluded from consideration.

In the iron and steel industry, *Meister* still were typically drawn directly from the ranks of the workers they were to supervise—whether skilled, semiskilled, or unskilled. Depending upon the aspect of production involved, the necessary specialized knowledge might be acquired through on-the-job experience, artisanal or factory apprenticeships, or trade school courses.[41] The Ruhr elite favored keeping formal education for future *Meister* to a minimum determined by the technical requirements of the job, fearing that any more would make such persons demanding and dissatisfied with their lot. As much as possible, practical experience was favored over theoretical preparation.[42] Whichever avenue of advancement an aspirant followed, the success of his quest depended in large measure upon his superiors' evaluation of his social and political attitudes and his reliability.

In general, the transition from worker to supervisor was more arduous in coal mining than in the iron and steel industry. The greater formal rigor in the training of *Steiger* as compared to the training of *Meister* stemmed primarily from the long tradition of state regulation in mining, which had fostered extensive bureaucratization from an early date. Special schools known as *Bergschulen*, supported and controlled by the Ruhr elite, trained supervisory personnel for the mines. The lower class of the *Berg-*

schule provided training for those who hoped to become *Steiger*. By the beginning of the twentieth century, the *Steiger* without *Bergschule* training and accreditation, the kind of official most likely to fraternize with workers, was becoming a rarity. A 1907 survey revealed that of 3,331 *Revier-* and *Hilfssteiger* (divisional and assistant *Steiger*) in the Ruhr, only 319 were without such training.[43]

The training of miners' sons to become *Steiger* was possible because pupils in the lower class of the *Bergschule*, where half-day sessions prevailed, could support themselves by working in nearby mines. In 1913, for example, 62 percent of those being trained in Bochum as *Steiger* were sons of miners, while only 14 percent were sons of mine officials and 24 percent were from families unconnected with mining.[44] Nevertheless, the two grueling years at the *Bergschule*, often requiring change of residence for that period, were an insurmountable obstacle for all but the most dedicated and compliant miners, especially since several years of mining experience, preparatory classes, and currying favor with company bosses were necessary just to gain admission.[45]

Regardless of whether *Meister* or *Steiger* came from the ranks of upwardly mobile workers or were recruits from other classes, Ruhr employers sought to guarantee that in the future their primary identification would be with management. To this end, overseers were comparatively well paid, permitting them to adopt a life style different from that of most workers. In the 1890s the earnings of supervisors in the mines ranged from 50 to 80 percent higher than those of ordinary miners.[46] In 1910, when the average annual income of Ruhr miners was 1,494 marks, the average income of mine supervisors was 2,516 marks. *Meister* in the iron and steel industry earned at least as much.[47] Supervisors were typically better paid than other large groups within the industrial bureaucracy such as clerical workers, draftsmen, and technicians who, though they might have more formal education than the overseers, did not share with them the responsibility for the direct exercise of authority over the workers.[48]

Supervisors also enjoyed a number of privileges that further distinguished them from workers. Many companies provided rent-free housing for their officials, reserving the largest and most comfortable dwellings for their use. Paid vacations were another benefit granted company officials but denied to workers. On the job, the bourgeois dress of the overseers visibly separated them from the workers. Off the job, large companies attempted to prevent social contact between workers and supervisors by organizing separate leisure activities for the two groups.

In order to make lower supervisory personnel into more dependable and effective instruments of discipline in mine and mill, employers sought to guarantee to themselves not only the unquestioning loyalty of these men but also, and this proved more difficult, their strict compliance with company rules and policies. On the simplest level, this meant ending company toleration of certain traditional privileges of supervisory personnel. Among these was the use by *Meister* or *Steiger* of the company's men and materials for his own purposes. For instance, a supervisor might assign one of the crew under his authority to spend time working on his garden plot. This was now rigorously prohibited. Increasingly elaborate systems of passes were devised, in part to prevent such misuse of company employees.[49]

More rigorous and explicit standards were set for the job performance of supervisors. Administrative details became ever more important. There were complaints if reports were not signed by the proper official or not drawn up according to the prescribed formula. Actions taken were to be carefully recorded and the resulting records made available for inspection at any time.[50] In large multiplant concerns, production quotas for individual units were set by the central office. Lower supervisory personnel were made increasingly aware by their superiors that certain minimal levels of daily production had to be met if they were to have any hope of advancement or even continued employment. This was the stick that was paired with the carrot of production premiums.

In the coal industry, by the end of the nineteenth century, *Steiger* were expected to descend into the mine at the same time as the workers, rather than follow later. This change had been initiated by Emil Krabler and other employers had followed suit.[51] In the mines of the Gutehoffnungshütte, *Steiger* who failed to see to the loading of coal of adequate purity were required to spend extra shifts supervising the sorting of coal, to convince them to exercise greater vigilance in the mine.[52]

The managerial elite increasingly resorted to other segments of the expanding industrial bureaucracy both to monitor the functions of supervisors and to limit their discretionary powers. The number of administrative and technical specialists increased at a rate much faster than that of either workers or supervisory personnel. For example, in Ruhr mining in 1893, the ratio of specialized to supervisory officials was 1:6. By 1907, the ratio was 1:2.[53] As the number of specialists in the industrial hierarchy increased, functions previously performed by supervisory personnel were transferred to them.[54] More and more, the organization of labor passed to technical experts, especially the increasingly numerous engineers in the iron and steel industry.[55] In addition, centralized bureaus took over responsibility for hiring and firing as well as for determining wages. The role of the *Meister* or *Steiger* in such matters was increasingly confined to an advisory function. By 1914, the Bureau of Worker Affairs at Krupp employed as many as 350 men. The specialists who guided this bureau were products not of the workshop but primarily of state and municipal bureaucracies.[56]

One important purpose of such centralized bureaus was to limit opportunities of lower supervisory personnel for practicing the most blatant kinds of nepotism and favoritism that earlier had been tolerated or even encouraged.[57]

As the number and variety of company officials increased, so too did the number of ranks separating the *Meister* or *Steiger* from the managerial elite.[58] Those who occupied the ranks of middle management were of crucial importance for implementing new policies and were increasingly chosen for their readiness to impose rigorous and uniform discipline on all those subject to their authority, supervisors as well as workers. *Steiger* Georg Werner, who was to form in 1907 the independent Steigerverband that Ruhr employers would find so intolerable, pointed to Hugo Stinnes as a leader in this development. According to Werner, in the years 1903–1905 Stinnes promoted a number of energetic works managers (*Betriebsführer*), who were charged with the task of increasing productivity and lowering costs in any way possible. The Stinnes mines were located in the older area of the southern Ruhr coalfield and were at a disadvantage compared to the newer mines of the north with their rich deposits of valuable coking coal. Only strict attention to both organization and technical detail and constant reevaluation of all policies and procedures could insure profitability for these mines. There was little margin for waste and inefficiency. According to Werner, the Stinnes system meant harsher discipline, disregard for established practices, limitations on the authority of the *Steiger*, and increased reliance upon newer elements of the industrial hierarchy. In short order, this approach was being held up as a model for students at the *Bergschule* in Bochum and imitated by other Ruhr employers.[59]

Work Rules

Disciplined and reliable supervisors of all ranks were crucial to successful implementation of reformulated work rules. In the last prewar decades, work rules were changed or reinterpreted with particular frequency as they related to hours of labor, that is, to the extent of the employer's claim on his employees' time. At issue in some instances might be the total number of hours to be spent at the work site and in others the number, duration, and distribution of pauses. Sometimes the practices being changed were of relatively recent vintage. For example, in 1896 the otherwise ostentatiously nationalistic Krupp steelworks announced that henceforth there would be no holiday in honor of the anniversary of the Sedan victory of 1870.[60] Often, however, the practices being changed were time-honored. For example, Gustav Knepper, commissioned by Stinnes in 1903 to turn some of his mines in the southern Ruhr into profitable operations, ended the traditional practice of the miners' eating their morning bread and butter on company time before starting work.[61] This sharing of refreshment and conversation after the descent into the mine but before dispersal underground was a cherished institution to the miners. To the employers, however, it meant not only lost time but also an opportunity for malcontents to engage in political and union agitation among their fellows.[62]

Changes in the work rules were simply dictated to the workers, typically through notices posted in the washrooms. To be sure, the law mandating written work orders for industrial concerns employing more than twenty persons also stipulated that changes could be made only after members of the work force had been given an opportunity to express their views. But there was no provision that workers' views, once heard, would be given any weight, and often even the empty formalities were dispensed with by Ruhr employers.

Workers did on occasion protest the weakening of what they perceived as their rights on the job. One such encounter occurred at Krupp in 1902. In the spring of that year, changes in the regulation of the lunch break of some employees roused such dissatisfaction that there was a possibility of a strike. The workers most directly involved were smiths, skilled workers noted for their sensitivity to job control issues. Efforts of workers to organize and negotiate through representatives were summarily rejected by the company. Instead, in a grand gesture, F. A. Krupp had four laborers selected and escorted to his villa, where they, in dirty work clothes, could hardly have been anything but awed. When the workers presented their grievances about the new regulation, Krupp replied that it would be impossible to comply with their wishes. He knew, Krupp continued, that this would not make them happy, but he had to ask them to accept the situation *for his sake*. He could not go into details with them. They would have to believe him that the regulation was good, fitting, and necessary. According to newspaper reports of the incident, the workers not only accepted Krupp's declaration but even built bonfires that evening in his honor.[63] That this confrontation of 1902 did not turn into a strike, whereas similar incidents in the Ruhr coal industry in 1904 led to the massive coal strike of the following year, can be charged to two factors: first, the lack of solidarity among iron- and steelworkers; second, the ability of the Krupp firm to call upon a tradition of loyalty and obedience. That tradition was the product of the company's commitment to providing reliable and docile employees with both lifetime security and benefits as good as or better than those available from other Ruhr concerns. Even so, the dangers to industrial peace that were inherent in the situation had not been lost on Krupp, who cautioned his *Direktorium* in the aftermath of the affair to exercise utmost care when making any future changes affecting "the traditional usages of the workers."[64]

Hours were a sensitive issue in the iron and steel industry. That cruelly long work weeks still prevailed for metallurgical workers was highlighted by government, union, and industry investigations in the last decade before the war. The twelve-hour shifts for those employed in units with continuous production, combined with twenty-four hour shifts on Sundays when those who worked days and those who worked nights changed places, stood out as among the most exhausting in German industry. This problem will be discussed in chapters 9 and 10.

But before the 1905 coal strike, the focus of concern regarding work schedules was on mining. Ruhr miners were especially sensitive to any efforts to extend the number of hours they had to spend below ground, both because of the arduous and dangerous nature of their employment and because the eight-hour shift was widely regarded as one of the few remnants of an earlier privileged status.

In mining, the problem of hours was linked to the problem of labor productivity. As noted in chapter 3, annual output per miner failed to show any improvement during the years from 1896 to 1914. Continued reliance on hand labor was at the root of the difficulty, though worker resistance to speed up incentives doubtless also played a role. Leaders of the Ruhr coal industry were conscious of the need to mechanize. Coal-cutting and -hauling machines would not only boost output but also make supervision easier underground. A 1900 Bergbau Verein report noted with envy that in the previous year 23 percent of total United States coal production was cut with machines. In the Ruhr, on the other hand, where geological conditions hampered their use, machines were only then being introduced on an experimental basis in a few mines.[65] A significant break-through was not to be achieved until after the First World War.

With labor productivity stagnant or even declining, Ruhr coal industrialists were hard-pressed to meet demand during peak periods. They could and did hire more miners but at times there were too few available and at other times employers hesitated to add substantially to their work forces to meet a demand surge that might be only temporary. Recourse to longer hours, even if they had to be forced upon reluctant employees, was a tempting short-term solution to the problem.

Forced overtime had been an important issue in the 1889 coal strike. The Essen Protocol, the agreement reached between the Bergbau Verein and the worker representatives in that year, had contained a statement specifying that miners should be free to leave at the end of their regular eight-hour shifts if they chose not to participate in planned overtime. There was some decline in the frequency with which overtime was scheduled in the years immediately following the strike, but probably more because the early 1890s were recession years than because of the agreement. By the middle of the decade, however, as demand surged, overtime shifts were again frequent. And it was not common to give miners a choice in the matter.[66]

Much more resented than forced overtime, for which the miners were at least paid, were efforts by the coal industrialists to extend their claims on the miners' time by lengthening the time required for the unpaid descent into and ascent out of the mine, the *Seilfahrt*. As mines became deeper and work forces larger, getting miners into and out of the pits became increasingly complicated and time-consuming. The length of the *Seilfahrt* had been an important issue in the Ruhr coal strike of 1889 and was one of a number of issues not satisfactorily resolved in that confrontation; it continued to be a source of tension into the new century.

The issue flared into prominence in 1904. In January, the new director of the mine Oberhausen, which belonged to the Gutehoffnungshütte, announced a lengthening of the *Seilfahrt* from forty-five minutes to a full hour each way. The miners resisted, assuming the role of defenders of the status quo. They appealed to the *Oberbergamt* Dortmund, which in turn tried to persuade management to reach a settlement on the regulation of hours. The leadership of the Gutehoffnungshütte refused to respond directly to the workers' demands, arguing not only the technical merits of the company's case but also arguing that concessions would undermine the employer's authority and encourage similar protests elsewhere. Management finally did agree, however, to shorten the time for the *Seilfahrt* in return for permission from the *Oberbergamt* Dortmund to increase the number of miners who could be carried up or down at one time.[67]

Throughout the confrontation at the Oberhausen mine, union leaders had urged caution. They did not believe the time was yet right for a major strike. But though the conflict could be contained in that particular instance, the problem did not disappear. What had happened at the Oberhausen mine was not an isolated incident. Other Ruhr managers responded to the problems of deeper mines and larger work forces by making workers come earlier and stay longer rather than cutting into the regular work shift.

Dissatisfaction among Ruhr miners was mounting. To the unresolved issues of the 1889 strike, such as forced overtime, length of *Seilfahrt*, and the regulation of *Wagennullen*, were added disaffection over stricter work rules and the constant recalculation of wage rates, dissatisfaction with safety precautions in the ever-deeper and more dangerous mines, and the threat of ancylostomiasis, a severe anemia caused by hookworms.

The last of these irritants allegedly had been introduced by migrant workers into the Ruhr toward the end of the 1890s. The rapid spread of the disease bore witness to the unsanitary conditions in the mines.[68]

In this unstable situation, two local incidents escalated into the massive Ruhr coal strike of 1905. Significantly, both of these incidents involved new, young managers at older, marginally profitable mines of the southern Ruhr. One of these incidents took place at the mine Herkules, owned by Carl Funke. In 1898, Funke placed Herkules under the direction of Ernst Tengelmann, the man who in 1913 would be his successor as the dominant personality of the Essener Steinkohlenbergwerke AG. Tengelmann's task was to make the faltering mine more efficient. In December 1904 a strike threatened at Herkules over management's refusal to rehire a miner fired because he had criticized Tengelmann in a public meeting.[69]

More significance attached to the other December incident, which took place at the Stinnes-controlled Bruchstrasse mine. The mine director at Bruchstrasse since 1903 was Gustav Knepper, one of Stinnes's bright young men, the man who in 1905 was to become the head of all mining operations for Stinnes's giant Deutsch-Luxemburg concern. As in the case of Tengelmann, Knepper's assignment was to reorganize a marginal mine. As already noted, one of his first acts had been to abolish the practice of the miners pausing for breakfast at the beginning of their shift before dispersing for work, a practice that had subtracted almost half an hour from work time. Then at the end of 1904, Knepper decided that the increased size of the work force necessitated an increase in the length of the *Seilfahrt* from one-half hour to a full hour, and a notice to that effect was posted.[70] The miners resisted and appealed to the *Oberbergamt* Dortmund to intervene.

It should be noted that the decision to extend the *Seilfahrt* came from Knepper, not Stinnes. Stinnes expected his lieutenants to operate independently on virtually everything not involving major financial decisions. Stinnes only learned of the trouble brewing at Bruchstrasse after the notice had been made public. This incident illustrates the difficulties the leader of a large concern faced in keeping properly informed about what was happening throughout his empire. Although in general agreement with the proposed change, Stinnes believed that the timing was wrong and that it would have been preferable to wait. He encouraged Knepper to avoid further ill will by treating the workers "calmly, not harshly."[71] But since the announcement had already been made, Stinnes believed it should not be withdrawn, even though during the same month a similar pronouncement at the mine Westend, controlled by the Phoenix steelworks, was withdrawn in the interests of preventing a strike.[72] Stinnes assured Knepper that he would not "leave him in the lurch."[73] The appearance of a strong and united administration had to be preserved at all costs.

The Terms of Labor

From the beginning, the Bergbau Verein monitored the developments at Bruchstrasse. The always combative Kirdorf telegraphed Stinnes to remind him that the leadership of the mine owners' association had repeatedly made known its opposition to any negotiations with representatives of striking workers. The more flexible Stinnes was not averse to listening to the miners' grievances, but he refused to submit to arbitration, arguing that the interests not just of his own mine but of the entire industry were at stake.[74]

The strike that grew out of this encounter soon encompassed all of Ruhr mining and became the largest work stoppage in terms of man-days lost in the history of Imperial Germany. The major employers of the region faced their most serious challenge to date. Iron and steel as well as coal industrialists were directly involved since by 1905 no major metallurgical concern was without miners in its employ. In addition, the iron and steel mills were the most important consumers of Ruhr coal and without it would have great difficulty continuing their own production. They successfully strove to keep the confrontation limited to the coal industry by keeping their own workers employed at least part-time at repair work or in production using foreign coal or coal from the Saar. Some supported their idle employees by continuing to pay their wages or by granting advances.[75] At issue in 1905 for all Ruhr employers was their right to undivided and undisputed rule over the terms of labor in the companies under their control.

8
Conflict and Readjustment

The 1905 Coal Strike

Ruhr employers were dismayed by the suddenness with which the local incidents of 1904, discussed at the end of the previous chapter, escalated into a massive regional confrontation, lasting from 14 January to 9 February 1905. Emil Krabler described the strike as coming "like a thief in the night."[1] At its peak, the strike was joined by 73 percent of the workers in Ruhr mines. Words of caution from leaders of the miners' unions failed to check the momentum of this impressive demonstration of miner solidarity and of dissatisfaction with the conditions under which they labored. The mine operators noted the failure of union leaders to control the situation and used this as an argument against negotiating with organized labor. On 14 January, Krabler, speaking on behalf of the leadership of the Bergbau Verein, told officials of the Prussian mining authority that negotiation with the unions would be of dubious utility because there was no guarantee that any agreements could be enforced.[2] This, of course, was not the principal stumbling block to negotiations. The real issue was the mine owners' denial of any role to organized labor, no matter how constituted, in employer-employee relations.

Ruhr coal industrialists refused to recognize any legitimate basis for the strike or for subsequent union demands. Employers claimed that throughout the industry miners were fairly treated. Leaders of the Bergbau Verein indicated they would welcome a government inquiry into conditions in the Ruhr in the confidence that their claims of blamelessness would be verified. They hoped that such an inquiry would shift attention away from the question of whether the basis of labor relations in the mines should be altered to the question of whether existing rules were properly implemented. To demonstrate that the 1905 strike was not based on legitimate grievances, employers pointed out that the miners had struck without giving notice and only later formulated specific demands.[3] According to management, negotiation with workers guilty of breach of contract would sanction lawlessness and encourage irresponsible actions in the future.

Ruhr coal industrialists stood united throughout the 1905 strike in their refusal to negotiate with representatives of striking workers. There was to be no repetition of 1889. According to Emil Kirdorf, who articulated the most extreme opposition to any compromise: "In 1889 Hammacher negotiated in Berlin and imposed obligations upon us. We have learned our lesson as a consequence."[4] There was only one reported instance of an attempt to negotiate a settlement. This occurred at the mine Freie-Vogel und Unverhofft. This medium-sized mine, employing approximately 850 men, was not a member of the coal syndicate. Its management, in an effort to get the men back to work, granted the substance of their demands, recognizing the worker representatives and agreeing to the establishment of a worker committee (*Arbeiterausschuss*). Despite the agreement, however, the mine's employees did not return to work because of pressure from other workers to hold out for a general settlement with the Bergbau Verein.[5]

The uncompromising position of the Bergbau Verein in 1905 met with a general lack of public sympathy. Not only workers but also many influential representatives of bourgeois society and members of what the Ruhr elite liked to call the "state-supporting parties" endorsed the position of the Ruhr miners, at least in part.[6] Contributions for the workers came, for example, from the Archbishop of Cologne, from professors at the University of Bonn, and from city governments such as those of Mainz, Strassburg, and Hanau.[7] Criticism of the mine owners' rigid position came even from certain elements within the entrepreneurial camp itself, notably from spokesmen of the light and finished products industries who believed that refusal of the coal magnates to compromise was giving industrial employers in general a bad name.[8]

To Ruhr employers, the least welcome of all criticisms were those emanating from the government. They greatly resented pressures from Berlin to negotiate with representatives of striking miners. Initially, Minister of Commerce Theodor Adolf von Möller, speaking for the Prussian government, indicated his intention to remain neutral, admonishing the miners to avoid excesses and criticizing employers for their refusal to consider any form of negotiation. As the strike continued, however, pressure for government action mounted. Secretary of the Interior Arthur Graf von Posadowsky-Wehner was in the forefront of those favoring intervention. Posadowsky, a spokesman for cooperation with the Center party, which had an interest in the strike because of the Catholic Gewerkverein's participation, urged Chancellor Bülow to intervene on behalf of the miners. Bülow himself was concerned about the impact of a prolonged coal strike on Germany both internally and externally. Internally, any civil disorder that might result from the strike seemed especially inopportune because of the revolutionary situation in the Russian Empire at the beginning of 1905. Externally, a prolonged coal strike was always cause for concern because adequate coal supplies for Germany's railroads and fleet were crucial for military preparedness.[9]

The argument for government intervention was strengthened by awareness of how unpopular the coal operators had managed to make themselves in this matter. In addition, the 1905 strike came at a time when relations between Ruhr coal industrialists and the Prussian government were already strained. Pricing policies of the coal syndicate since the turn of the century, mine closures in the southern Ruhr, speculation about the possible formation of a trust, and successful entrepreneurial resistance to the state's attempt in 1904 to exercise more influence in the region by purchasing a controlling interest in its third largest mining company, the Hibernia, had all contributed to a growing perception in Berlin of the Ruhr elite as a potentially disruptive force in need of restraint.[10]

On 30 January 1905 Möller reluctantly declared that the Prussian mining law would be revised to accommodate some of the workers' demands. His statement followed Posadowsky's announcement, which had Bülow's backing, that he intended to introduce mining legislation in the Reichstag if the Prussian ministry refused to act. After this public promise of reform legislation, the strike continued only a few more days before being called off by the unions.

As long as the work stoppage lasted, Prussian officials sought to prevent Ruhr employers from using antistrike tactics so harsh that they would provoke violence. Thus, the *Landrat* of the county of Ruhrort refused to provide police support for August Thyssen's plan to evict striking workers from company housing, and the firm subsequently modified its plans, limiting the eviction to about fifty ringleaders.[11] Minister of the Interior Hans Freiherr von Hammerstein refused to sanction the importation of foreign strikebreakers.[12] Government officials encouraged the leaders of the Bergbau Verein in their decision to recommend that mining companies not make use of their right to withhold up to six days' pay from the wages due striking workers as a penalty for breach of contract.[13]

Throughout the strike, most government officials refused to endorse employer demands for military action, demands usually justified in terms of the need to protect strikebreakers.[14] Such requests were viewed with considerable skepticism. The Ruhrort *Landrat*, for example, dismissed pleas for military aid as coming from "an anxious young *Bergassessor*," by which he meant one of Thyssen's deputies at the Deutscher Kaiser, and from a "notoriously hard man," by which he meant Heinrich Kamp, managing di-

Conflict and Readjustment

rector of Phoenix.[15] Those few high-ranking bureaucrats who advocated brandishing the sword remained, in this instance, isolated and ineffective.

On 8 March 1905, the Prussian government placed before the Landtag the promised mining law revision. Through this legislation, the miners gained some of their demands, among them the creation of worker committees, the abolition of the practice of *Wagennullen*, limits on fines, and regulation of the *Seilfahrt* question and of overtime.[16] To be sure, the mandated changes did not impose any severe burden on the employers. For example, *Wagennullen* was replaced by fines that Krabler predicted the workers would find more onerous than the earlier practice.[17] Limits on the duration of the *Seilfahrt* were largely compensated for through reorganization during the following year.[18] Worker committees were given a purely advisory role and could be ignored at will. Nevertheless, the employers, though not greatly inconvenienced, felt betrayed, deprived by state action of a victory over rebellious workers that on the basis of sheer economic power and organizational cohesion should have been theirs.

The most bitter critic of the government's intervention was Emil Kirdorf. He accused the government of shortsightedness, a failure to appreciate that what was at stake was not just industrial profits but the existing order in Germany. No good could come, in his opinion, from even modest concessions to the workers. By showing weakness in the face of the workers' challenge, the government was, Kirdorf contended, siding with its enemies against its most valuable allies. So furious did Gelsenkirchen's managing director become that he could not even maintain a facade of politeness in his dealings with government officials or with anyone else who disagreed with him or even suggested that he moderate the tone, let alone the content, of his statements. In the aftermath of the strike, Kirdorf, disgusted and frustrated, resigned those of his honorary offices, including that of vice-chairman of the Bergbau Verein, that brought him into contact with the government. But as head of the coal syndicate and of the Ruhr's largest coal company, he continued to poison the social atmosphere with his violent statements and dire predictions.[19]

As the strike drew to a close, a minority of Ruhr employers took revenge on those miners they believed had shown themselves to be troublemakers and agitators during the strike by refusing to reemploy them. Most noteworthy was August Thyssen's Deutscher Kaiser, where 131 were not rehired. The strike at Deutscher Kaiser, where an autocratic employer confronted a volatile work force with a high percentage of young migrants, had been particularly bitter.[20] Also among those dismissing substantial numbers of workers were mines under the control of Heinrich Kamp and Emil Krabler.[21] Most unforgivable of the miners' transgressions, in the employers' eyes, appear to have been public statements charging specific wrongdoing on the part of management. Some retribution was taken, despite employer assurances to the contrary, even against workers whose critical comments were made as witnesses in the government inquiry that the coal industrialists themselves had requested.[22]

Most mine operators, however, rehired all who wished to return to work.[23] The Haniel-owned Neumühl mine even took the opportunity to expand its work force by hiring men who had been fired from other mines for strike activities.[24] To assist the reestablishment of industrial peace, a number of employers offered advances and subsidies to returning workers to help them support families until regular wages were once more being paid.[25]

The primary lesson of the mass strike of 1905, for all but the most hard-line of Ruhr employers, was that a posture of total intransigence was ineffective because it alienated all but the most reactionary elements in German society and, most important, in the government. Economic power and rigid resistance to organized labor were no longer sufficient to cope with labor problems in the Ruhr. Some modification of approach was needed if the crippling mass strike and the employers' isolation that had accompanied it were not to be repeated.

Employer Associations

The Ruhr coal strike of 1905 was just one, though the most spectacular, of a series of work stoppages plaguing German employers during the upturn following the 1901–1902 recession. From 1903 on, the number of strikes in Germany increased, especially in the textile, lignite, and metal industries, in addition to over two years of sustained unrest in coal mining, beginning in 1904. From 1.3 million man-days lost due to strikes in the recession year 1902, the rate increased to 2.8 million in 1903 and 3.6 million in 1904 and then soared to 14.5 million in 1905. German strikes resulted in the loss of 8.2 million man-days in 1906 and 6.2 million in 1907. In 1908, a year of renewed recession, the rate sank to 2.3 million.[26]

One of the most noteworthy strikes of these years of labor challenge was the five-month action of more than eight thousand Crimmitschau textile workers in the winter of 1903–1904 for a ten-hour workday. This strike, which was supported by contributions from unions and working-class organizations throughout the country, aroused management fears in many regions and industries of a united and militant labor movement operating on a national scale. Industrialists from all parts of Germany, including Ruhr employers, contributed to the support of the intransigent

Crimmitschau textile mill owners, who resisted government mediation and ultimately, through the use of strikebreakers, defeated the strike.[27] One consequence of the Crimmitschau strike was greater interest among German industrialists in the formation of employer associations, organizations designed specifically to cope with common labor difficulties.

Although there were employer organizations in handicraft and finished products industries prior to the turn of the century, coal, iron, and steel industrialists did not seriously concern themselves with such institutions until 1904–1905.[28] The delayed formation of employer organizations in heavy industry reflected both the later development of labor unions in those industries as compared to other types of production and the great resources of the large corporations, which long sustained the illusion that they could regulate relations with their employees on their own. Events of 1904–1905 ended that illusion by dramatizing the growing number and importance of outside influences on labor-management relations.

The employer associations that Ruhr heavy industrialists formed or participated in after the turn of the century were not new groupings of previously unorganized industrialists. Rather, they were offshoots of existing entrepreneurial coalitions established during the second half of the nineteenth century to meet other needs. Thus, in 1904, after the Crimmitschau textile strike, it was the Centralverband, in which Ruhr industrialists played a dominant role, which took the lead in forming the Hauptstelle deutscher Arbeitgeberverbände. The Hauptstelle was intended to coordinate all existing employer associations and encourage the creation of new ones.[29] This attempt to unite all employers in German industry failed because representatives of light and finished products industries feared the domination of the Centralverband, which advocated labor policies harsher and more rigid than they considered prudent. Therefore, most of them chose to affiliate with the Verein deutscher Arbeitgeberverbände, formed in the same year as the Hauptstelle under the sponsorship of the Gesamtverband deutscher Metallindustrieller, the powerful organization of the finished metal products industry.[30] The two central employer organizations, the Hauptstelle and the Verein, confined their actions primarily to making policy statements and issuing threatening pronouncements against labor unions and the less steadfast employers, the Hauptstelle in particular excelling in extreme formulations of the managerial position. By and large, the task of organizing united entrepreneurial action in specific labor-management confrontations was left to specialized employer associations, some organized by region, others by industry.

Heeding the call of the Hauptstelle, the Northwest Group of the Association of German Iron and Steel Industrialists, whose membership encompassed but was not limited to the leaders of Ruhr metallurgy, formed its own employer association, Arbeitnordwest, in 1904. Given the lack of large-scale union activity and work stoppages in the region's primary iron and steel industry, the creation of Arbeitnordwest did not reflect so much a truly pressing need for collective employer action as it did the close organizational ties between the Northwest Group and the Centralverband. Because the immediate need was minimal, membership in the new employer organization was at first relatively small (thirty-nine companies with 93,227 employees in 1904) and enthusiasm limited, especially among the most powerful Ruhr industrialists.[31]

The idea of employer associations did, however, have its advocates among leading spokesmen of Ruhr metallurgy. Managing Director Heinrich Kamp of Phoenix, for instance, argued that it was important to create such organizations before, rather than after, the need for them became pressing.[32] Two strikes by skilled ironworkers in Dortmund in 1905 aroused increased interest in the new association.[33] Nevertheless, before World War I, Arbeitnordwest was not as strong or active as its counterpart in the Ruhr coal industry.

One of the weaknesses of Arbeitnordwest was its members' diversity of opinion and interests. The most important split was between representatives of the iron-and steel-producing industries on the one hand and the iron- and steel-consuming industries on the other. The primary producers thought the finished products industrialists were too conciliatory toward labor. Conversely, entrepreneurs of the machine-building industry and the manufacturers of finished iron and steel products represented in Arbeitnordwest believed that the leaders of heavy industry were too rigid and that by backing the hard-liners on questions such as hours and refusing to recognize unions they were needlessly inviting the attack of organized labor.[34] In the balancing of interests in Arbeitnordwest between primary production and finished products manufacture, by far the greater weight attached to Ruhr heavy industry because it was the dominant supplier for the Rhenish metal industries and often a major customer.

Slower than Arbeitnordwest to take shape, but much stronger and more cohesive when finally formed, was the Zechenverband, established by the Bergbau Verein. Plans for a powerful employer association in the Ruhr coal industry were long discussed, especially after the strike of 1905. Because of the strength of organized labor in coal mining and government sensitivity to repressive measures in that industry, the coal entrepreneurs chose to wait for a favorable moment to inaugurate their antiunion coalition, especially as it was intended to do more than just issue threats. Thus, the new organization was not formed until 1908, a recession year when economic conditions could be counted on to keep labor protest minimal.[35]

Conflict and Readjustment

The Zechenverband was as different from Arbeitnordwest as labor relations in coal mining were from those in iron and steel production. Unlike its counterpart in the iron and steel industry, the Zechenverband was tightly organized and included almost all important leaders of Ruhr mining. The membership was determined to hold the line against organized labor. The new antiunion league was to play a leading role in labor-management conflict in the last prewar years.

The reason the leaders of Ruhr heavy industry formed and participated in employer associations—the Zechenverband, Arbeitnordwest, and the Hauptstelle—was not because existing entrepreneurial organizations failed to act on labor problems. Indeed, the Bergbau Verein, as already noted, was a dominant force against negotiation in the 1905 coal strike, though all the while maintaining the fiction that it played only an advisory role.[36] True, some reorganization or expansion of resources and powers would have been necessary for existing groupings to have tackled effectively the labor questions of the Wilhelmian era, but the primary reason for separate creations was propagandistic. The formation of employer organizations was intended to advertise to the workers and general public that industrialists meant to put up a united resistance to labor agitation. Employer associations and the sanctions they intended to impose on dissident workers were widely publicized and were intended to serve as deterrents. The idea was to warn workers in advance of the consequences that would befall them in any future disturbances.

Employment Controls

The most immediate consequence of forming employer associations in heavy industry was the refinement of tactics aimed at the control of employment. Among methods of regulating employment, the most important were the lockout, the black list, and employer-sponsored labor exchanges. The lockout was primarily an antiunion measure. The black list and labor exchanges could be used either to punish strikers and labor agitators or to cope with chronic problems associated with the creation of a dependable and disciplined complement of workers.

The lockout is the employer's ultimate weapon. In the years immediately following the 1901–1902 recession, there was a marked increase in the number of lockouts in German industry. From 0.6 million man-days lost due to lockouts in 1902, the rate increased to 1.3 million in 1903, 1.7 million in 1904, and 4.4 million in 1905. In 1906 and 1907, the rates were 3.4 million and 2.8 million, respectively. In the recession year 1908, the number of man-days lost due to lockouts declined to 1.4 million, only to rise again sharply when prosperity returned.[37]

At first glance, it might appear that coal, iron, and steel producers would have been the most likely to make use of lockouts, because they had the financial resources to sustain a prolonged interruption of income and because they represented in many other respects the most determined opposition to the demands of organized labor. But in fact, prior to the First World War, Ruhr heavy industrialists avoided the use of lockouts. In 1907, the Krupp concern did carry out a successful lockout affecting approximately two thousand workers, but this occurred at its Germania shipyards in Kiel, not in the Ruhr.[38]

Lockouts were most prevalent in handicrafts and finished products manufacture, for example in the metal and construction trades, in machine building, and in the new and highly concentrated electrical industry.[39] Those industries making extensive use of lockouts had in common the employment of a high percentage of skilled workers and the existence of highly developed organizations of both labor and management. Where employers were not highly organized, a lockout was usually not effective. The employer had to be certain that other employers in the same or related industries would not hire his workers, and if need be, would even instigate sympathy lockouts so that their employees could not provide financial aid to the other workers. Where workers were not highly organized, as in the primary iron and steel industry, a lockout was not necessary. Less drastic methods sufficed.

Coal, iron, and steel entrepreneurs were reluctant to dismiss, even temporarily, their entire complement of workers. Under the best of conditions, workers were difficult to recruit for the dangerous, arduous, and unpleasant work in mines and steel mills. In industries such as coal mining, where unions were strong but large numbers of workers remained unorganized, industrialists also hesitated to lock out employees for fear of driving unorganized workers into the unions.[40]

Although industrial leaders of the Ruhr usually stopped short of employment controls that threatened to disrupt production, they made extensive use of controls aimed at individual workers. Such tactics were especially prevalent in coal mining, where the need was greater and employers were better organized than those in the iron and steel industries. The latter, however, did make some use of black lists both as a means of attempting to reduce the frequency of job changes and also as a weapon in their infrequent confrontations with striking workers.[41] An example of such a confrontation was a strike at the Hoesch steelworks in the summer of 1909. Striking unions charged the company with firing workers for union membership, though the company denied it. Managing Director Friedrich

Springorum refused to respond to communications from the unions. Strikebreakers were hired to continue production. Hoesch then called upon Arbeitnordwest to black-list the striking workers, depriving them of alternative employment and burdening unions with their support. The number of black-listed Hoesch workers peaked at 675. Springorum claimed this action made a major contribution to the failure of the strike.[42]

In Ruhr mining before the formation of the Zechenverband in 1908, efforts to block the employment of individual workers usually took one of two forms, either permanent local agreements or temporary industry-wide bans during and after strikes. Local agreements were between mines in a single area (*Nachbarzechen*) or mines belonging to a single family or corporation (*Familienzechen*) such as the Haniel or Thyssen mines.[43] The participating companies agreed not to hire workers leaving the employ of any participant unless officials had stipulated in writing (*Überweisungsschein*) that they had no objection to the move.[44] Such local bans had long existed and aimed at discouraging frequent job changes in areas with a heavy concentration of mines where workers might easily shift jobs without changing their place of residence.

Temporary employment bans against strikers, such as those imposed by the Bergbau Verein in 1889 and 1905, were agreements that workers fired for strike participation would not be hired by other employers for a specified period following the strike. Because these bans were secret and unregulated, there were many rumors about their application including allegations of the routine use of secret markings on the papers of all workers. Actually, these bans were not particularly effective because they were very cumbersome and heavy industry's often pressing need for workers meant that hiring officials did not always closely scrutinize the credentials of those applying for work.[45]

In 1908, Ruhr coal industrialists began a determined effort to regulate employment on a permanent, industry-wide basis. Employment control was to be the chief weapon in the arsenal of the newly formed Zechenverband. The original statutes of the Zechenverband contained a provision that no member was to hire a worker who had been dismissed because of strike participation for a period of three months following the dismissal. Moreover, no member was to employ any worker for a period of six months if he had failed to give the required two weeks' notice when quitting his last employment. Employers offending against these provisions were subject to a fine of up to 1,000 marks for each violation.[46] Long lists containing the names of men who were not to be employed circulated secretly, at first weekly, then twice monthly.

The ban was rigorously enforced except in a few small mines outside the Zechenverband. During the recession years 1908 and 1909, the demand for workers was less than normal so employers had less incentive to break the rules. During the first year the number of names on black lists at times exceeded five thousand.[47] Union spokesmen complained that many men were put on the lists for reasons other than those stipulated in the Zechenverband's statutes. Because the lists were secret and names were usually supplied by subordinate officials who might have personal grudges against individual workers, their use could easily be abused. There was no appeal procedure. A vigorous public controversy developed, culminating in extensive Reichstag debates on the subject in late 1908 and early 1909.[48] Criticism of the black lists came not only from representatives of the Social Democrats and the Catholic Center party but even, in qualified form, from National Liberals such as business lobbyist Gustav Stresemann.[49] To the coal industrialists, it seemed like a simple question of their right to employ or not to employ whomever they pleased. But the pressure of public opinion as expressed through the Reichstag was very great, as was the threat of some kind of government intervention. A further problem was that the large number of names involved greatly complicated the hiring procedure. Early in 1909, the Zechenverband advised member companies that blacklisted miners should be informed of the reason they were being denied employment.[50] Later that same year, the Zechenverband dropped its black lists in favor of a more workable system of employer-controlled labor exchanges (*Arbeitsnachweise*).

The formation of employer-controlled labor exchanges in Ruhr coal mining had been discussed by the Bergbau Verein since the strike of 1905 but was not acted upon immediately for fear of intensifying the widespread labor agitation of the years from 1905 to 1907. Prior to 1909, such institutions, first used in the 1890s, had been effective only in highly specialized industries, especially in the metal trades, in urban areas such as Berlin and Hamburg.[51] The placement service of the Zechenverband was exceptional in the prewar period because it encompassed a whole region through the use of sixteen branch offices. The success of this effort was made possible by the concentration and relative homogeneity of Ruhr coal mining and the effectiveness of the coal industrialists' organization.

Statutes of the Zechenverband's employment service reduced the ban for failing to give notice from six months to two weeks. The same two-week ban also applied to workers who accepted a job but did not report on the specified day. The ban for strikers remained at three months. Although the length of the ban for breach of contract was radically reduced, there was much opposition from workers when the plans became known. Miners feared that labor exchanges would limit freedom of movement, their most effective protection against total domination by employers. Employers claimed that the labor exchanges were designed primarily to insure that job changes occurred only after notice had been given. In response to the controvery, Prussian Minister of Commerce Reinhold von Sydow investigated the plans of the coal entrepreneurs and managed to secure one important concession. Management had intended that a miner would have to show proof that he had given notice at his old place of employment before applying for a new job. Under government pressure, the industrialists finally conceded that workers could retain the right of looking around for a new position before giving notice to their current employer. With this concession and management's assurances that the placement service would not be used to limit the mobility of workers but merely to make it more regular, the government gave its blessing.[52]

Despite the initial forebodings of unions and sympathetic liberal public opinion, it soon became apparent even to critical observers that the coal industrialists did intend to keep the substance of their promises.[53] The labor exchanges proved to be less objectionable than the older, less regularized, less open methods of controlling employment. The new institution at least let the workers know when and why they were being punished and provided possibilities for appeal.[54] Thus, the labor exchanges represented an attempt at more regularized and realistic methods of coping with problems of large-scale, impersonal labor-management relations. But at the same time, such employer-controlled employment offices reflected the continued refusal of the entrepreneurial elite to make concessions on questions of authority. Industrialists were willing to modify the means by which they sought to control the labor market but unwilling to consider union demands that job placement be delegated to public labor exchanges in which employers and workers would have equal rights.[55]

Prior to World War I, Ruhr iron and steel industrialists declined to follow the lead of coal industrialists in the creation of labor exchanges. In 1914 such a step was proposed for Arbeitnordwest but rejected by major Ruhr firms. The response of the Phoenix steelworks summarized the reasons for the negative reaction, contrasting the needs and interests of the coal industry with those of iron and steel. It referred to the greater organizational cohesiveness of the coal industry and the greater homogeneity of its work force in terms of required skills, both of which made regional employment control easier to implement. But the most important consideration, according to Phoenix, was that the creation of labor exchanges would destroy the "good relations" between large Ruhr metallurgical concerns and their workers and would give the unions a basis for agitation that would attract previously "peaceful" elements of the work force to their cause.[56] In the iron and steel industry up to 1914, the need to regulate employment opportunities on the regional level was not perceived as sufficiently pressing to warrant potentially disruptive innovation in this area of labor relations.

Employer-Employee Communication

Employer organizations of the prewar Ruhr repeatedly stated their refusal to recognize the labor unions as legitimate representatives of worker interests or as acceptable bargaining partners. This was a central tenet of their creed. Holding to this position, however, left unsolved the problem of establishing procedures within the context of massive industrial concerns to permit effective two-way communication between labor and management. One suggested means of encouraging a dialogue between employer and employed in large-scale industry without resorting to the unions was to create worker committees (*Arbeiterausschüsse*).[57] These were to consist of employees, elected by their fellows, who would present worker suggestions and grievances to management at regular meetings. This proposal came primarily from advocates of moderate social reform, men inside the government as well as out.

Bitter opposition to the creation of worker committees came from spokesmen for heavy industry. They objected that such institutions would conflict with their right to control the internal administration of their firms and would undermine their authority, substituting what Hanns Jencke described as "a caricature of a parliamentary regime."[58] Ruhr employers also claimed the committees would fail to achieve their purpose because the election of worker representatives would fall under the control of unions and the unorganized workers would remain unrepresented. They predicted the unions would use the elections as opportunities for agitation and the committees as a means of embarrassing and harassing management.[59]

Despite employer objections, one of the union demands that the Prussian government enacted into law in 1905 was to make a worker committee obligatory for every mine employing more than one hundred men. The new law, however, limited the committees' powers to such an extent as to make their effectiveness doubtful. The newly established committees were not allowed to discuss any questions reaching beyond the confines of the individual firm. Wages were also outside their province. In other areas, they could discuss and advise only.[60] With such limited powers, it was obvious that the worker committees could be effective only if they secured the good will of individual employers.

Conflict and Readjustment

The response of coal industrialists to the new committees was mixed. Some tried every means of obstructing their operation. In a large number of mines, though not the majority, workers who had been dismissed because of participation in the 1905 coal strike and then subsequently rehired were excluded from the first election because, as the Bergbau Verein reminded its members, such employees failed to meet the requirement of one year's continuous employment.[61] The same organization encouraged employers to limit the worker committees to their prescribed functions and to remind committee members that their mandate did not extend to wage questions or to issues not having to do with their own mine.[62] However, practice was not always as rigid as pronouncement. During the continuing labor unrest in the years immediately following the 1905 strike, wage questions were often unofficially discussed in worker committees and adjustments made in the interests of uninterrupted production.[63]

Despite the hostility and suspicion they encountered from the coal operators, the new worker committees in many instances proved to be useful instruments for regulating potentially disruptive grievances in the mines. Worker committees directed the attention of management to aspects of working conditions, sometimes quite easily and cheaply remedied, that the miners found disagreeable.[64] In addition to improving communication between employer and employed, even if only slightly, worker committees also served to reinforce the trend toward more uniform conditions in Ruhr mines. On the committees, worker representatives, especially those with union ties, bolstered their demands by pointing to improvements at other companies. Similarly, the employers consulted one another to arrive at a common policy toward issues likely to be raised by the worker committees.[65]

One area in which worker committees functioned to meet a need perceived by both workers and the managerial elite was in revealing abuses by lower supervisory personnel. The committees represented a first step toward improving the flow of information from bottom to top in the industrial hierarchy, information that was no longer simply filtered through lower management. Yet, though the leaders of large Ruhr concerns realized that they needed to be better informed about negligence and capriciousness on the part of company officials in the interests of furthering their goal of insuring greater uniformity and predictability in the treatment of workers, they were ambivalent about encouraging worker representatives to criticize supervisors. Much as employers wanted to curb the independence of lower management, they did not want in the process to undermine the authority of supervisory personnel vis-à-vis their subordinates.[66] As a consequence, complaints against company officials emanating from worker committees were investigated but often in halfhearted fashion. The sympathy of the investigator, drawn from middle management, was typically with the supervisor and the burden of proof rested entirely on the workers. Even if the investigation revealed irregularities, upper and middle management were ordinarily willing to excuse or punish mildly all but the most serious abuses against workers because of their conviction that supervisors were often intolerably provoked by a recalcitrant and insubordinate work force.

Similarly grudging investigations were prompted by revelations made by the working-class press or by union officials.[67] The advent of organized labor in the Ruhr gave workers a new forum for protesting and publicizing abuses on the job. Employers, especially after the experience of 1905, complained of a flood of inaccurate reports and irresponsible harassment and slander. Emil Krabler disdainfully noted the zeal with which the working-class press was reporting the slightest incidents such as "the water being at some time a little too cold in the washroom."[68] Officially, upper management took little or no notice of such information, considering its source illegitimate and claiming that adequate opportunities for the redress of individual grievances already existed, so that no worker should hesitate to approach his superiors directly with a legitimate complaint.

However, whatever the employers' distaste for the origins of such reports, they could not be ignored entirely, nor were they. Individual companies as well as the Bergbau Verein and Arbeitnordwest systematically monitored the working-class and bourgeois presses.[69] The primary purpose was to force retractions of unwarranted statements and to inspire greater caution in the future.[70] All this was part of a general heightening of entrepreneurial interest in the press and in the employers' public image in the aftermath of the 1905 coal strike. Yet this monitoring of specific working-class complaints about on-the-job abuses also had the consequence of bringing to the attention of upper management information about such matters that was often otherwise closed to them. For example, in 1905 department heads of the Gutehoffnungshütte were admonished to report accidents more carefully in the future. Recent newspaper accounts had made the firm's directors aware that many serious mishaps went unreported by company officials.[71]

In the last prewar decade, a wide range of developments brought Ruhr employers or their representatives into increasing contact, both official and unofficial, with the spokesmen of organized labor. The result was an opportunity for a greater measure of communication between the two sides, not all of it unrelentingly hostile. Most of these encounters occurred within the context of the single firm or community. However, before 1914 there was one institution in which industrialists and their representatives

Conflict and Readjustment

regularly faced worker representatives on an industry-wide level. This was the miners' *Knappschaft*, the primary function of which was the administration of social insurance. With the growing importance of unions, the miners' delegates in the *Knappschaften* were increasingly selected from union candidates. Employers claimed that the presence of union representatives made cooperation in the *Knappschaften* impossible because the unions were more interested in agitation than in improved relations between labor and management. Spokesmen for the coal industry painted the picture of formerly idyllic agreement and cooperation in the *Knappschaften* being turned into a complete deadlock by the unions.[72] But the dire predictions of industrialists did not prove to be completely accurate. Management and union delegates found they could work together within the *Knappschaften*, as demonstrated by the successful reform of the statutes of the Bochum *Knappschaft* after a debate lasting from 1906 to 1908. For the first time, a negotiated settlement on a question of mutual concern was reached between industrialists and union representatives on an industry-wide level, though only with great reluctance on the part of the employers.[73]

9
Containment

Resistance to Government Regulation

During the years of prosperity from 1905 to 1907, Ruhr industrialists had been on the defensive in their confrontations with labor. Their need for workers was pressing. They could ill afford long disruptions of production in view of the strong demand for coal, iron, and steel. The recession years of 1908 and 1909 gave the entrepreneurial elite a chance to regroup and to strengthen its position. The creation of the Zechenverband in 1908 and the labor exchanges in 1909 was part of this attempt. After 1907, labor agitation decreased sharply, so management had less to worry about on that front. But government attempts to regulate working conditions continued. Ruhr industrialists were already bitter about state interference, especially after the strike of 1905. Now that they were momentarily free of significant union pressure, they concentrated on opposing government intervention.

In 1908 the government made its first feeble attempt to regulate working conditions in primary iron and steel production. The proposed regulation was mild, but the leaders of the iron and steel industry feared that if it were successful, more extensive controls would follow. Iron and steel industrialists were unaccustomed to outside interference in labor questions. They objected more to the principle of state intervention than to the actual proposal. Government involvement seemed to them both malicious and mischievous.

The new regulation was issued by the Bundersrat under its power to protect the health of laborers. Its main purpose was to limit the excessive hours of iron- and steelworkers. This was an issue on which the industry was particularly vulnerable to attack because much of its work force put in hours significantly longer than the norm in other kinds of production. The debate on hours of labor in metallurgy stimulated by the Bundesrat order of 1908 was to find no satisfactory resolution prior to 1914.

The characteristic work day in the iron and steel industry lasted from 6 A.M. to 6 P.M., with quarter-hour pauses in the morning and afternoon and an hour-and-a-half pause for lunch at midday. However, in those departments in which production was continuous, as in blast furnaces, hammerworks, and rolling mills, regular pauses were not provided. Molten metal would not wait, and those who tended it typically had to take their breaks at such times as the production process permitted. Some were not even allowed to leave the work site long enough to eat lunch elsewhere.[1]

The biggest labor problem peculiar to continuous production was the regulation of Sunday work. Prior to the war, Sundays were used to change shifts, the day shift changing to night and the night shift changing to day. Workers on one shift would have a free Sunday, but workers on the other shift would have to be on the job for twenty-four hours to keep production going while their comrades had a day of rest. The regular use of twenty-four hour shifts invited criticism. Industrial spokesmen attempted to argue that the situation was not as bad as it seemed because there were natural lulls in production during which the workers could rest. They claimed that the workers were not really working a continuous twenty-four hours.

Ruhr iron and steel industrialists were actually unhappy with a practice that put them in such a bad light. But they justified it, both to themselves and others, as the only economically viable option. Whereas in noncontinuous production, labor and government managed over a period of years to secure reductions of the workday an hour at a time, the solution was not as easy in continuous production industries where the only logical alternative was the radical readjustment from two twelve-hour to three eight-hour shifts, with attendant increases in labor costs and serious shortages of certain kinds of workers.[2]

In addition, the primary iron and steel industry was largely impervious to the frequently heard argument of social reformers that shorter hours need not necessarily result in decreased labor productivity because workers could be motivated to a compensatory increase in the pace and regularity of their efforts. What was being suggested was conversion from an extensive to an intensive use of labor. But in metallurgy, the pace was largely set, not by workers, but by the production process itself.[3] Thus, employers in the primary iron and steel industry had even less incentive than most other kinds of manufacturers to consent to a reduction in hours. At the end of 1907, the leadership of the Northwest Group of the Association of German Iron and Steel Industrialists enjoined members engaged in the primary production of ferrous metals not to make any changes in hours without first securing approval from their fellows.[4]

Since employers would not act to improve the situation, the government took it upon itself to intervene, but cautiously at first. As a beginning, the Bundesrat order of 1908 stipulated that in each shift of eight hours or longer, workers were to be given two hours of pauses, including a one-hour lunch break. The worst abuses, namely, the twenty-four hour shift changes and excessive overtime, were not regulated, but there was a provision that the hours of overtime were to be recorded as the government was hoping to collect information to support future legislation.[5]

On 6 February and 23 September 1908 representatives of the iron and steel industry held closed meetings at the Stahlhof in Düsseldorf to discuss the problems posed by government intervention. They agreed "to concede as little as possible."[6] Each employer was to send a letter to the *Regierungspräsident* of the district in which his firm was located asking that he be given the privilege of limiting lunch pauses to a half hour instead of the legally stipulated hour because of the insurmountable technical difficulties involved. These protest letters were sent regardless of whether the sender was seriously inconvenienced by the implementation of the new pauses or not. For instance, Managing Director Paul Reusch of the Gutehoffnungshütte sent such a letter asking for permission to restrict the lunch period to a half hour even though the lunch break of his workers had been set at an hour even before the Bundesrat decree of 1908. When a factory inspector asked him the reason behind his protest, Reusch replied that though he had no intention of reducing the lunch pause even if permission were granted, he was objecting as a matter of principle and professional solidarity. Reusch stated that he wished to retain freedom of movement in regulating hours and did not wish to be subject to denunciation by his employees for every minor infraction of the law.[7] To Reusch, as to other powerful industrial managers in the prewar Ruhr, the question was not one of economics but of authority.

Observance of the new regulations was uneven and the number of infractions large. As before, pauses for workers in the primary iron and steel industry, especially in the less modern plants, were usually brief, irregular, and determined by the rhythm of production.[8] Where longer rest periods were actually granted, this was sometimes an excuse for lowering wages. For instance, in 1909 the Rheinische Stahlwerke made known to its employees that when the two-hour pauses came into effect, wages would be reduced by 10 percent.[9] A circular of the Association of German Iron and Steel industrialists in 1911 cynically suggested that reductions of wages accompanying the introduction of longer pauses be carefully documented and utilized in governmental circles as an argument in favor of repealing the regulation.[10]

The position taken by iron and steel industrialists in response to the Bundesrat decree of 1908 was closely paralleled by that of the coal entrepreneurs in response to the proposed introduction of worker safety inspectors (*Sicherheitsmänner*) in 1909. Following the explosion at the mine Radbod in November 1908 that resulted in the loss of 348 lives, there was widespread public demand for new safety legislation.[11] The government's proposal was to introduce worker safety inspectors, elected employee representatives who would have the privilege of making inspections on a regular basis. In January 1909, Prussian Minister of Commerce Clemens Delbrück called spokesmen of both labor and management to Berlin to discuss the proposed legislation. On the day before the meeting, representatives of the entrepreneurial associations of the Prussian coal industry met to devise a common strategy. They decided they would attend the meeting but would refuse to discuss the proposed legislation in any detail with labor representatives or even in their presence. It was further decided that they would voice their objections but would make no suggestions for amending the legislation until it reached the Landtag, lest any proposals be interpreted as meaning that the legislation was acceptable to the industrialists with certain modifications. The representatives of Ruhr mining, Eduard Kleine and Paul Randelbrock, took the lead in reaching these decisions. Kleine summarized his position as being "completely negative."[12] Yet it should be noted that in the discussion of specific points, Kleine and his colleague from the Ruhr proved more reasonable than their counterparts from the coal industry in the less urbanized areas of Prussia, particularly Silesia. The latter did not want to meet at all in the presence of union representatives.

Employers' fears of the disruptive potential of the new legislation proved to be grossly exaggerated. The safety inspectors were ineffective and unsatisfactory to all concerned—management, unions, and state officials. The behavior of management was at best formally correct, offering no encouragement or aid, and at worst actively hostile, making use of the numerous possibilities for intimidating and harassing independent-minded employees.[13] However, the experiment was probably sabotaged as much or more by the workers, who resented being cited for unsafe practices by one of their own number; by the unions, which competed among themselves for control; and by the officials of the *Oberbergamt*, who identified closely with the employers on this issue because of the large number of safety inspectors elected from the ranks of the Social Democratic miners' union.[14]

At the same time that the iron and steel industrialists were contesting the Bundersrat decree on pauses and the coal industrialists were contesting the introduction of safety inspectors, they joined in a collective campaign against the proposed introduction of chambers of labor (*Arbeitskammern*) that were intended, as an alternative to the unions, to give workers a forum for their interests. Unlike the worker committees already mandated for mining, the *Arbeitskammern* would transcend the individual company. The government presented such a proposal to the Reichstag in

1908. Ruhr industrialists responded to this initiative, as they had responded to earlier reformist proposals, with the argument that the result would be not greater social harmony but rather one more opportunity for disruptive agitation.[15] Because the government proved unwilling to alter its proposal to meet the demand of the Reichstag majority that union secretaries be eligible for election to the *Arbeitskammern*, the law failed to pass.[16]

Political Initiatives

Government attempts to increase regulation of working conditions in private industry diminished during the last prewar years. This shift was the product of a widely held feeling of present or impending crisis, part of a European-wide malaise. In Germany, a number of events fed this uneasiness. After 1908, there was increased internal ferment in the empire, partly triggered by a struggle over tax reform. There was at the same time increased popular demand for democratic reforms, especially relating to Landtag franchises. Internal tensions were reinforced by the series of foreign crises leading up to World War I. The combined effect heightened concern for national unity and power, which appeared to beneficiaries of the established system to be endangered by the activities of working-class organizations, and convinced them of the need for a more united and forceful antisocialist, antidemocratic front. Proposals to build national unity through conciliation rather than coercion were largely rejected by defenders of the status quo because of the reallocation of power and resources this would entail.

Ruhr coal, iron, and steel entrepreneurs attempted to capitalize on this social and political atmosphere. They expanded their efforts to influence national policy making relative to labor questions, demanding increased government intervention on their behalf and stiffer resistance to the "danger of revolution."[17] Their political offensive in the years just prior to World War I differed from that of the 1890s in that it focused to a greater degree on influencing public opinion and the Reichstag.[18]

One technique used in attempting to influence the Reichstag was that of election contributions. Major contributions were first supplied for the 1907 election, with substantial sums being collected by the Northwest Group of the Association of German Iron and Steel Industrialists and by the Bergbau Verein. The share of the Haniel mines alone for that campaign came to 15,000 marks.[19] The candidates to be supported were chosen more on the basis of their willingness to commit themselves to industrial interests than on the basis of party affiliation.

Paralleling efforts to use Ruhr money more generously and systematically to further the election of congenial candidates were efforts to use Ruhr money to influence the press. To be sure, there had been earlier efforts to influence the press, usually through purchase, but results had not been encouraging. Newspapers known to be controlled by industrialists had limited readership.[20] The entrepreneurial elite needed ways of influencing the press that were less obvious and more pervasive than investment in a few right-wing publications.[21] One option was the planned and centralized disbursement of industrial advertising funds. An agreement to this end was reached by leading Ruhr magnates in 1912 and implemented at the beginning of 1914 with the establishment of an organization known, not very revealingly, as the Ausland GmbH.[22] Heavy industrialists, given the nature of their customers, actually had comparatively little interest in newspaper advertising for its own sake. But in order to support the Ausland GmbH, which, according to Paul Reusch, existed "to give industry a mighty weapon to be used against the entire domestic and foreign press," major concerns substantially increased their advertising budgets and entrusted them to the new association. Kirdorf's Gelsenkirchener Bergwerks-AG, for instance, increased its annual allocation for this purpose from 20,000 to 60,860 marks.[23]

The central figure in the campaign to modernize the political tactics of the Ruhr elite was Krupp director Alfred Hugenberg.[24] New to the Ruhr and to industry, politically and ideologically committed—to a degree alien to most of the rest of the region's managerial elite—to causes that transcended the immediate interests of industry, the former civil servant and future press lord and party leader took upon himself the task of reorganizing and redirecting the use of political funds provided by Ruhr companies. Appalled by the lack of coordination and accountability he had initially encountered in this area, Hugenberg, upon becoming chairman of the Bergbau Verein in 1912, insisted that all political contributions emanating from the industry should pass through his office. He wanted to make certain that those individuals and groups receiving financial aid would secure tangible benefits for the donors.[25]

In national politics, the collapse of the liberal-conservative Bülow bloc in 1909 because of an inability to reach agreement on the issue of tax reform confronted the leaders of Ruhr industry with the question of whether to reach an understanding with conservative agrarian forces as in times past or to align themselves with a newly forming liberal coalition, represented by the Hansabund, which supported tax reform, especially an inheritance tax, and opposed the excessive power of the landed elite. Included in the Hansabund were representatives of commerce, finance, and handicrafts as well as all types of industry. The leaders of Ruhr heavy industry reluctantly endorsed the Hansabund in 1909 in order to avoid being labeled allies of the extreme agrarians; to avoid alienating the more liberal elements within the Centralverband; to exercise such control as they could over the new organization; and to warn the agrarians to be more reasonable in the future.[26] But for most coal, iron, and steel magnates, it was from the beginning an uncomfortable alliance, so uncomfortable, indeed, that the supervisory board of the Krupp concern insisted that Max Roetger not assume a leadership role in the antiagrarian Hansabund until after he had left the company's executive committee. It was feared that, otherwise, Conservatives influential in the government, upon which the firm depended for important orders, might take offense.[27]

Ruhr industrialists were at odds with other members of the Hansabund on questions of tariffs, social legislation, and the gravity of the socialist threat. At the first meeting, Emil Kirdorf stated his opposition to the inheritance tax and to "excessive" social legislation, thereby provoking hisses and jeers.[28] In fact, there were few issues on which the heavy industrialists and most of the other groups represented in the Hansabund could agree. The history of that organization in its first two years provides an excellent illustration of the degree of alienation of the Ruhr entrepreneurial elite from much of the rest of the German business community.

From the very beginning, the leaders of Ruhr heavy industry looked for an excuse to withdraw. In 1911, the Centralverband, the Bergbau Verein, and the Rhenish-Westphalian branch of the Hansabund withdrew under the leadership of Roetger and Kirdorf.[29] The reason given by Roetger for withdrawal was that the Hansabund had moved too far to the left since its formation. Its attacks against the landed interests were too severe and its attacks against the socialists were not severe enough to suit most coal, iron, and steel producers.[30] The entrepreneurial elite of the Ruhr then formed a separate organization called the Regional Group of Lower Rhineland-Westphalia for Trade, Commerce, and Industry (Niederrheinisch-Westfälische Bezirksgruppe für Gewerbe, Handel und Industrie) with Emil Kirdorf as chairman. The stated goals of the new association were "the insurance of adequate protection for the national economy in all its sectors and a persistent battle against Social Democracy as the most dangerous enemy of the sound continued development of our industry."[31]

Secession by the Ruhr industrial magnates from the Hansabund made possible a renewed rapprochement between the interest groups of heavy industry and agriculture. In 1912 Paul Reusch noted his impression that the representatives of agriculture were showing more understanding than in the past of the needs of industry.[32] One expression of this rapprochement was the formation in 1913 of the Cartel of the Productive Estates (Kartell der schaffenden Stände), a loose coalition of antiparliamentary forces including the Bund der Landwirte and the Centralverband.[33] The stated goals of the Kartell were identical to those of the association formed by the Ruhr entrepreneurial elite in 1911: preservation of authority in all economic enterprises, protection of the national economy, and opposition to social democracy.[34]

Ruhr business leaders were not, however, exclusively committed to the Kartell.[35] They liked, as always, to keep their options open. Besides, alliance with the extreme agrarians in the Bund der Landwirte was uncomfortable. All too often, it was believed, the agrarians were unwilling to make reasonable compromises with other economic interest groups when the interests of the estate owners were at stake. Still looking for congenial allies, the leaders of Ruhr heavy industry sought to patch up some of the divisions between themselves and other industrialists, especially those in the Bund der Industriellen.[36] They had not given up completely on achieving a measure of unity among industrial employers. In 1909, the Hauptstelle deutscher Arbeitgeberverbände, which had been dominated by heavy industry since its creation in 1904, managed to form a cartel with the other central employer association, the Verein deutscher Arbeitgeberverbände. In 1913, the two organizations merged to form the Vereinigung deutscher Arbeitgeberverbände. Perfect harmony was not thereby attained, but the heavy industrialists had achieved at least outwardly the unity of German employers that they had sought for almost a decade.[37] The harsh nature of the policies advocated by the new association is indicated by its campaign for the legal prohibition of picketing.[38]

Response to Renewed Labor Agitation

Stepped-up interest politics in the last prewar years, even under the determined direction of men like Hugenberg and Kirdorf, held out little prospect of any immediate resolution of the most pressing problems posed by the confrontation of labor and management in the Ruhr, problems that flared into renewed prominence with the upsurge of union activity, nationally and regionally, during the years of economic recovery following the 1908–1909 recession. Nationally, the number of man-days lost due to strikes rose from 2.8 million in 1909 to 4.6 million in 1910, 7.7 million in both 1911 and 1912, and 8.8 million in 1913. Strikes were particularly prevalent in construction, in machine building, in metal working, and in mining.[39] Employers in the above-mentioned industries, with the exception of mining, responded with an increased use of lockouts. Most notable was a massive lockout in the building trades in 1910, affecting between 175,000 and 200,000 workers. The most militant building contractors received the support of the leaders of heavy industry, who refused to supply materials to employers who failed to join the lockout. This confrontation, expensive to both labor and management, ended in the acceptance of government mediation.[40]

In the Ruhr, strike activity in iron and steel production remained limited to isolated groups of specialized, strategically placed workers. In March 1911, for example, 379 machinists and stokers struck the Dortmunder Union (total work force: ca. 7,000), recently acquired by Stinnes's Deutsch-Luxemburg concern. Confronted with reduced wages and an increased pace of work under the Stinnes regime, the strikers demanded higher pay, shorter hours, and premiums for overtime. This unsuccessful two-week strike attracted considerable attention because it was accompanied by what was for the Ruhr a rare instance of alleged worker sabotage.[41] Such partial walkouts in the primary iron and steel industry along with campaigns for higher wages and shorter hours in the closely allied machine-building and finished metal products industries in the Rhineland motivated Reusch of the Gutehoffnungshütte to advocate in November 1911 the collection of higher contributions from members of Arbeitnordwest in preparation for "the battles with organized labor that will doubtless soon materialize."[42]

In Ruhr mining, concern with union activity was more immediately pressing than it was in metallurgy. The region's coal operators were most anxious that there be no repetition of 1905. If another mass strike could not be avoided, they hoped to cope with it in such a manner as to forestall the kind of isolation and general opprobrium they had experienced that year. A step in that direction was to begin a cautious policy of conciliating the Catholic Gewerkverein so as to deepen the divisions plaguing the labor movement in the Ruhr. Rapproachement with Catholic workers had the additional advantage of pleasing the government, since the Center party, following the collapse of the Bülow bloc in 1909, was now a government party. Also, as the first socialist representatives were managing to get themselves elected to communal councils in the Ruhr, the region's entrepreneurial elite was coming to see the Catholic Center party as potential ally rather than as arch rival in local politics. It did not escape the employers' notice that in Ruhr cities there was an inverse relationship between the percentage of Catholics in the population and the percentage of socialist voters.⁴³ Collaboration with the Center party in local politics was fostered in particular by the employer-supported Deutsche Vereinigung and was eased by political Catholicism's increasing abandonment of its earlier critique of the German state and of industrial capitalism.

However, despite the strong arguments in favor of a more conciliatory treatment of the Catholic union, this was not a policy the entrepreneurial elite could easily bring itself to adopt. Ruhr coal industrialists had long insisted that competition for the allegiance of the miners forced Catholic labor leaders to be just as "radical" as the socialists.⁴⁴ Just as in the political sphere it was democracy, not just social democracy, that Ruhr industrialists opposed with such determination, so in the industrial sphere it was unionism, not just socialist unionism, that the employers struggled to contain. Thus the change in the relations between the leaders of the coal industry and the Catholic labor movement hesitantly inaugurated in 1910 represented for the employers a triumph of expediency over ideology.

The wooing of the Catholic miners could not, under the circumstances, proceed smoothly. The Zechenverband attempted to be conciliatory toward the union, though stopping short of actual recognition. It was argued that requests from the Catholic Gewerkverein were to receive, "for tactical reasons," responses that were "friendlier and fuller" than those given to the socialist union.⁴⁵ But these replies were kept vague, holding out the promise of future concessions while at the same time avoiding specific commitments.

The campaign to win over the Catholic workers placed the Zechenverband in the position of having to deny that it had, in effect, recognized their union. On 8 December 1910, the liberal *Kölnische Zeitung* printed an overly optimistic article in which a reply by the Zechenverband to the Christian union was interpreted as being an example of "negotiation" between labor and management in the coal industry.⁴⁶ The business manager of the Zechenverband, Hans von und zu Löwenstein, immediately drafted a reply to the newspaper that denied that any "negotiation" had taken place or that the association's response was in any essential way different from several given in the past. But objections to Löwenstein's draft came from two quarters within the Zechenverband. On the one hand, Eduard Kleine, intransigent as ever, argued that the interpretation of the *Kölnische Zeitung* could not be successfully refuted, because its claim was actually not far from the truth. He had thought at the time the Zechenverband's response to the union was drafted that it represented a dangerous departure from precedent and had therefore opposed it. On the other hand, Hugo Stinnes argued in an opportunistic vein that though he did not agree with the interpretation of the *Kolnische Zeitung*, it made no sense to deny it. After all, the intention had been to win the good will of the Catholic workers.

Therefore, let them continue to believe that they had been given especially favorable treatment.[47] For its part, the Catholic union subsequently complained that the promise of higher wages it believed it had received from the Zechenverband had not been honored. The leadership of the Zechenverband replied irritably that no promise had been made. The association's chairman, Paul Randebrock, concluded that the episode constituted a lesson not to consider future petitions from the Christian union.[48]

The 1912 Coal Strike

The wave of labor agitation in Ruhr mining that had begun in 1910 culminated in the mass strike of 7–20 March 1912, a strike in which the Catholic union did not participate. The confrontation of 1912 had long been expected and prepared for on both sides. The employers had accumulated large stores of coal, enough to ensure uninterrupted steel production for the probable duration of the strike.[49] More important, they had won a larger measure of support for their position from outside their own camp than they had been able to muster in 1905. In part this was because this strike, unlike those of 1889 and 1905, was widely perceived as being the result of union initiative. In part, it was because Ruhr employers had been paying more attention to cultivating their public image.

In 1912, the Zechenverband, under Randebrock's leadership, initially pursued a policy of relative restraint in responding to the demands of the three contentious unions—Social Democratic, Polish, and Hirsch-Duncker. The purpose of this restraint was to ensure that the onus for initiating the strike would rest entirely on the unions and that the Zechenverband would not undermine the more favorable position it had achieved since 1910 relative to the government, bourgeois public opinion, and the Catholics. Randebrock recommended to the members of the Zechenverband that though they should refuse to discuss demands with the three striking unions, they should indicate a willingness to hear grievances raised by the worker committees, the only bodies legally empowered to speak for the workers in the mines. Stinnes supported this proposal but wanted it made clear that the committees would not be allowed to discuss the question of wages, a matter legally outside their competency.[50]

The recommendation of the Zechenverband and the Bergbau Verein to individual employers to summon their worker committees met with a variety of responses. Some refused to meet with the committees.[51] Paul Reusch of the Gutehoffnungshütte believed that the calling of such meetings and the discussion of issues with worker representatives in the midst of a strike would only cause greater dissension.⁵² Other employers called meetings only to announce that the workers' demands were unacceptable. At some meetings, the wage question, in line with Stinnes's admonition, was not even mentioned. At others, the employers agreed to discuss the wage issue informally after the official meeting had been closed.⁵³ Finally, there were meetings at which some effort was made to come to terms with worker grievances, most notably at the Amalie mine under the direction of Otto Krawehl. There the promised concessions included not only a number of physical improvements in the mine but also the granting of paid vacations for workers who had been employed for a minimum of five years.⁵⁴

Facing a divided labor movement, the coal industrialists were confident of their prospects, provided the government refrained from intervention on the side of the workers. At the beginning of the strike, Gustav Krupp von Bohlen und Halbach turned directly to the emperor with a fervent plea for such restraint. He advised his sovereign that "the employers expect and demand only one thing: namely, that in this conflict the state should not again hamper their freedom of action, that ministers should not come into the strike area in order to arbitrate, which at all times works only to the advantage of the workers, and that the government should make no statements in the Reichstag or Landtag that would affect the employers unfavorably."⁵⁵ He promised that if the employers were not betrayed by the government, they would be able to achieve a victory over social democracy that would be beneficial for "the entire bourgeois world." The role of the government, he continued, should be strictly limited to the maintenance of public order and the protection of life and property. Employers would take care of everything else. William II covered Krupp's statement with marginalia indicating his complete and enthusiastic agreement and directed government authorities to consult with him before departing from any of its prescriptions.

Because the work force was divided and there were many more strikebreakers in 1912 than there had been in 1905, the maintenance of public order loomed as a more serious problem than it had been in the past. Even before the strike began, Ruhr coal industrialists were pressing hard for a maximum show of force by the state. And the state obliged.⁵⁶ In anticipation of the strike, extra police began to pour in from cities outside the Ruhr. During the strike, Arnsberg *Regierungspräsident* Alfred Georg von Bake felt compelled to call in the military, a step that had been avoided in 1905.⁵⁷ After the strike, employers showed their appreciation of the efforts of the police and their hopes for similar service in the future by providing gratuities to those who had helped protect their mines and harass the strikers.⁵⁸ Prussian Minister of the Interior Johannes von Dallwitz, however, was displeased by this action and forbade employers to make similar gifts to individual policemen in the future.[59]

For their part, police officials in the Ruhr, beginning at least as early as 1893, had encouraged employers to establish auxiliary police forces consisting of armed supervisory personnel to aid in protecting mines during periods of labor unrest. Encouragement to establish such forces had intensified in the wake of the Moabit disturbances in Berlin.[60] The Moabit riots of September 1910, much commented upon at the time, had left two dead and over two hundred injured. The riots grew from a strike of 141 workers at a Berlin coal-handling firm. The company refused to consider their demand for higher wages, turning to strikebreakers instead. The company's owner pressed hard for stronger government action to protect his interests. The owner in question was Hugo Stinnes.[61]

Auxiliary police forces were widely used in the 1912 Ruhr coal strike. At the beginning of the strike, August Thyssen received permission from the Hamborn city council to arm his mine officials with revolvers and night sticks.[62] At the Gutehoffnungshütte, company officials were also armed with revolvers, but Managing Director Reusch stressed the importance of making certain that these weapons were never actually used because of the public furor that would result.[63] An important function of company officials posted as extra guards during strikes was to identify for the police and for the firm those workers who picketed or otherwise demonstrated against their employers. The presence of supervisors robbed the striking workers of the shield of anonymity.[64]

As a result of the insurmountable forces employers were able to array against the miners in 1912, the strike had to be called off after only nine days with nothing gained. The government did not step in afterwards as it had in 1889 and 1905 with legislation to secure for the workers at least part of what they had failed to obtain directly by striking. In view of their unqualified triumph in 1912, Ruhr employers felt free to punish striking miners with greater severity and in larger numbers than in 1889 or 1905. In 1912 the industrialists carried out their threat, as they had not done in the two previous mass strikes, to withhold the legally permitted fine of up to six days' wages for unexcused absences lasting more than three days.[65] They were prompted to implement their threat by the belief that if it were not carried out this time, it would have little force in the future.[66] Any employer who did not impose the fine was required to pay the Zechenverband 1,000 marks for every such failure.[67] Strikers who were rehired were regarded as newly employed and lost accumulated pension and other claims on the company and the *Knappschaft*.[68] Whereas strikers were punished, those who had continued to work throughout the strike were rewarded with premiums added to their wages for that period.[69] How much the defeated miners resented their treatment in 1912 is reflected in demands made during postwar strikes for payment of wages withheld in the earlier confrontation.

Subordination of Salaried Employees

Harsh as they were, the measures taken against striking miners in 1912 were not as harsh as those used against the small number of salaried employees in Ruhr heavy industry who dared to question, through word or deed, whether there was complete identity between their interests and those of their employers. The entrepreneurial elite considered the issue especially crucial in regard to supervisory personnel, those indispensable bearers of delegated authority from whom unconditional loyalty was demanded. Few in number compared to ordinary laborers, their actions and associations off-the-job could be and often were monitored with a care that was not possible with respect to the masses of nonsalaried employees.

Efforts to establish an independent organization to represent the interests of Ruhr *Steiger* yielded meager dividends before World War I, as a result of unyielding employer opposition. The Steigerverband, formed in 1907 partly in response to stepped-up measures taken by the managerial elite to discipline mine supervisors more rigorously, had by 1911 achieved a membership reported to be about sixteen hundred. But at that point, almost all Ruhr mining companies informed their officials in writing that membership in the organization was grounds for immediate dismissal. By the following year, membership in the Steigerverband had declined to a little over two hundred.[70]

In the iron and steel industry, leadership in the battle against the independent organization of lower management was taken by Paul Reusch of the Gutehoffnungshütte. By 1911, forty-five out of about five hundred officials of that company belonged to organizations—the Deutscher Techniker-Verband and the Bund der technisch-industriellen Beamten—which by sympathizing with strike actions had made themselves anathema to Ruhr employers. These forty-five men were told to give up their memberships and submit written statements to that effect or face immediate dismissal. If they did give up their memberships, they would be compensated for the dues they had paid to date. Seven refused to comply and were not only fired but were also black-listed through Arbeitnordwest. In future hirings, the company further stipulated, only those applicants who would guarantee in writing that they were not members of suspect associations would be considered.[71]

Management and Labor in Imperial Germany

In explaining why the Gutehoffnungshütte had to take the harshest possible measures against any trade unionist activity among company officials, management stressed both the obligation of salaried employees to provide models for their subordinates of faithful and obedient service and the willingness of employers to meet the legitimate expectations of their lieutenants without the need for outside intervention. The company claimed that it presented its salaried employees not with a choice between organization and the Gutehoffnungshütte but, rather, between "Social Democracy, terrorism, and loathsome agitation on the one hand and culture, inner freedom, and trust in senior colleagues on the other hand." It was assumed that salaried employees would be better able to appreciate the reasonableness of the company's position in such matters than would the masses of workers who "lacked the capacity for independent judgment."[72]

Reusch wanted other members of the Union of German Metal Industrialists (Gesamtverband deutscher Metallindustrieller) to join in the good fight. Max Roetger, however, argued that though he agreed in principle, the association as a whole would have to take a more moderate stance than that of the Gutehoffnungshütte because members outside the Ruhr did not have the same massive resources. Both Reusch and Roetger stressed the importance of counteracting the proletarianization of lower management not only by resisting union activity but also by granting increased pay and other benefits to justify the loyalty demanded.[73] Only two weeks after these statements were made, officials of the Gutehoffnungshütte earning less than 3,600 marks a year were granted a bonus of one month's extra salary to help meet the increased cost of living.[74]

In addition to providing better pay, Ruhr employers attempted to prevent the proletarianization of lower management by filling their need for association by encouraging membership in safe, closely monitored organizations both within the company itself and within the industry as a whole. Thus, at the same time that the Gutehoffnungshütte forced withdrawal from suspect associations, it promised the creation of a separate organization for its salaried employees. At Krupp in 1914 a separate organization was established for salaried employees, partly in response to their desire for an alternative to membership in the worker-oriented company union.[75] Collectively, Ruhr employers subsidized organizations such as the Werkmeisterverband, subjecting the associations in question to continuous and careful scrutiny to detect any hint of unwelcome independence.[76]

There were close parallels between the ways in which Ruhr employers sought to come to terms with salaried employees and with workers: the same combination of repression and appeal to loyalty, the same stress on the organic unity of the company from top to bottom, the same insistence on unquestioning obedience, the same frustrated desire for standardized

Containment

response, the same puzzlement that their good will and superior wisdom should be questioned. What was different was the greater intensity and emotion of employer reaction to any resistance to their will from lower management, such resistance being viewed as even less justified, less reasonable, and more dangerous than that coming from laborers. And because supervisors were fewer in number than workers, the counterblows against them could be much more devastating.

10
Unsolved Problems

By 1912, the leaders of Ruhr heavy industry had cause to be reasonably satisfied with the results of their campaign to contain the union challenge in their region. Unions had failed to make any appreciable inroads into the primary iron and steel industry. Employers in metallurgy stressed their continuing "good" relations with their work force. Coal industrialists could take encouragement from their victory in the 1912 strike and from the government support their efforts had received in that confrontation. The striking unions had not been destroyed, but they had suffered a substantial setback.[1]

Nonetheless, none of this was, from the employers' point of view, grounds for complacency. Rather it was an invitation to use their currently strengthened position vis-à-vis the labor movement to consolidate existing industrial authority and to tackle some of the long-term problems of managing labor. They perceived the most pressing of these problems to be winning or preserving the loyalty and willing cooperation of at least a core of the work force and forestalling any renewed surge of governmental regulation and public censure by finding alternatives to those employment practices, most notably the long hours in the iron and steel industry, that departed dramatically from the norm in the rest of German manufacturing.

Company Unions

Ruhr employers had long faced a growing problem of finding a convincing sanction for their authority, both on the job and in the wider community. Since the 1870s, their self-justification had often taken the form of an appeal to nationalism. The spokesmen of industry emphasized the supposed antinational character of the German working-class movement. The entrepreneurial elite attempted to supplement the theory of the identity of employer and worker interests within the individual factory community with the theory of the identity of management and labor interests within the national community.

Unsolved Problems

The most effective expression of this national, integrative appeal in the last prewar years was the formation of company unions. The first such organization in Germany was formed at a large machine-building factory, the Maschinenfabrik Augsburg-Nürnberg, in 1905 and the first in the Ruhr in 1908 at the Krupp steelworks.[2] The Krupp initiative was at least in part a response to National Liberal losses in the 1908 Prussian Landtag election. Among company unions in prewar Germany, the Krupp organization, which claimed 10,003 members by the end of 1913, was noted for its political engagement. One of its stated goals was to support the election of "nationally committed" individuals.[3]

Initially, directors of other large Ruhr corporations hesitated to follow the Krupp lead, despite the efforts of Krupp spokesmen Max Roetger and Alfred Hugenberg.[4] Even within the Krupp hierarchy there was resistance to the new creation.[5] In Ruhr mining, as late as the fall of 1911, there were only seven company unions with a total membership of 131. It was not until the beginning of 1912, which brought the dual stimulus of socialist gains in the Reichstag election and the coal strike in the Ruhr, that there was a rush to create such unions throughout the region's coal industry. By the spring of 1914, the number of mine-sponsored unions in the Ruhr had reached ninety-three with a combined membership of 21,241.[6]

Ruhr company unions of the immediate prewar years were intended by their sponsors to be loyal to the firm and to a prescribed conception of the national interest. In practice this meant that the company unions were, on the one hand, supposed to renounce the use of strikes and instead rely on cooperation with management to improve working conditions and, on the other, to renounce any collaboration with the independent working-class organizations as being "antinational."[7]

In return for the company unions' renunciation of the strike and of cooperation with independent labor organizations, the industrialists supplied them with financial subsidies to provide benefits competing with those of the free unions.[8] The employers promised to give serious consideration to complaints and suggestions of their company unions. At the same time, new Krupp employees were reminded that membership in one of the independent unions could bring only financial loss. Workers were told that the strike unions "never had and never would secure any concessions from the firm."[9]

In view of their dependent character, it is easy to dismiss the creation of company unions in the Ruhr as a compound of entrepreneurial cynicism and old paternalistic ideas dressed up in the language of modern nationalism, a snare for the naive or timid worker. Although such a view contains a large measure of truth, it overlooks the significant change in attitude required on the part of the entrepreneurial elite before company unions could be seriously considered. Such creations would have been unthinkable in the Ruhr even ten years earlier, as they continued to be in Silesia. Forming company unions was not undertaken by the employers without hesitation.[10] For the most conservative industrialists, *any* worker organization, even one sponsored by the firm, was potentially dangerous. That Ruhr heavy industrialists sponsored unions, whatever their nature and limitations, indicated a reorientation in their view as to the inevitability of labor organization.[11] They realized that if they did not organize and indoctrinate their employees, others would.[12]

Prewar Paternalism

The considerations that stimulated the formation of company unions in the last prewar years also reinforced changes taking place in corporate welfare programs. The earliest industrial social services such as housing, insurance, and company stores, which made workers dependent upon their employers for more than just employment, were best suited to industry in isolated areas. The increased urbanization of the Ruhr and the increased activity of the state and of working-class organizations in providing services to workers reduced the effectiveness of employer efforts to bind the laborer and his family in this manner.

Employer-financed social services introduced during the last prewar years were characterized by a growing emphasis on providing benefits designed to increase the worker's loyalty to his place of employment rather than to bind him with threats of economic loss.[13] The most ambitious efforts were informed as well by the desire to win worker loyalty for the existing social, political, and economic order of Imperial Germany. Some of these new services were a direct response to those offered by labor organizations. For instance, in 1909 the Gutehoffnungshütte established an office providing free legal counsel for its employees so they would not turn to the union secretaries for legal advice.[14] Many of the welfare endowments of the last prewar years made provisions that would have been considered luxuries by earlier generations of Ruhr entrepreneurs: libraries, club houses, vacations for children, Christmas gifts, new clothes for confirmations, and housekeepers to help employees' wives who had just given birth.[15]

The proliferation of new services did not mean abandonment of older forms of company welfare. Most of these, too, continued to flourish. Between December 1912 and March 1914, the number of mine-owned dwellings in the Ruhr increased from 81,780 to 94,027, and the number of miners housed in them from 129,372 to 148,583. Between 1900 and 1914 the percentage of Ruhr miners living in company housing increased from 18.5 percent to 34.3 percent.[16] By 1913 there were only three Ruhr mines that did not provide any housing to their work forces.[17]

Before the war there was, however, at least one member of the Ruhr managerial elite, Krupp director Alfred Hugenberg, who perceived possibly negative consequences of concentrating and isolating the workers of heavy industry in company-owned colonies, namely, facilitating the development of working-class solidarity and the dissemination of disapproved ideas. He favored, instead, employer subsidies to help workers buy their own homes. Such subsidies were included among the bequests made in honor of the Krupp centenary in 1912. Drawing in part on the American experience, Hugenberg believed that home ownership would give the workers a stake in the system.[18]

Among developments influencing the changing emphasis in types of social services offered to employees were growing restrictions on the employers' freedom of action where the provision of basic necessities was concerned. Where the opportunities for abuse were greatest, there also was the greatest likelihood of government intervention or public outcry. Even Paul Reusch had to admit, in the context of a scandal involving the actions of officials responsible for the administration of one of the company's boardinghouses, that a degree of public concern in such matters was justified. He conceded that though the boardinghouse was private property, the institution was so large and had such significance for the community that the public had a legitimate interest in its orderly functioning.[19]

Before the war, Ruhr industrialists were being forced, by legislation or the threat of legislation, by unfavorable press reports, and by employee dissatisfaction, to alter some of the more restrictive or repressive clauses governing so-called welfare benefits. A notable instance was the reform of the Krupp pension fund undertaken in 1912. The complaint against the fund that had caused the most frequent comment in the press and in the Reichstag was its failure to make any repayment to workers who left the employ of Krupp before becoming eligible for a pension. The continuing bad publicity, particularly damaging for a firm doing so much business with the government, and the threat of legislation, finally forced the Krupp directors to agree to return most of an employee's pension contributions when he left the company.[20]

Vacations for Workers?

Within the Ruhr entrepreneurial elite, the most hotly contested of possible new fringe benefits was the provision of paid vacations for workers. The chief advocates of this idea were not in the ranks of organized labor, where more central issues such as better pay and shorter hours were the focus of attention, but among bourgeois social reformers. At the very end of the nineteenth century and the beginning of the twentieth, some German employers, including, in 1909, the giant Siemens electrical concern, introduced paid vacations, usually making the enjoyment thereof dependent upon long years of faithful service. In this form, vacations served an obvious disciplinary function.[21]

Among prewar employers experimenting with vacations for workers was the Prussian state. Of particular concern to Ruhr employers was the state's decision in 1907 to grant vacations to selected workers in its coal mines. Eligibility was limited to those aged thirty-five years or older who had worked in the state mines for at least five years. Ruhr coal industrialists noted that though state mining officials in Recklinghausen approved of the initiative, hoping it would reduce absenteeism, those in Saarbrücken viewed it as potentially disruptive. Ruhr employers also noted that the decision had been made by the ministerial rather than the technical bureaucracy. This initiative therefore represented in their view one more instance in which inadequately informed officials in Berlin dictated economically questionable practices for government mines with an eye to bringing pressure on the private mines to follow suit.[22]

Despite the model provided by state mining, most Ruhr industrial leaders remained strongly opposed to granting paid leave for workers. After all, for decades one of their prime concerns had been to reduce the number of days their employees stayed away from work. They had fought long and hard to eradicate unauthorized absences on Mondays and for church festivals and pre-Lenten Carnival celebrations. As recently as 1906 a rare strike had broken out among the blast-furnace workers of Thyssen's Deutscher Kaiser when those employees who had stayed away from their jobs to celebrate Carnival were punished with the loss of their monthly premiums.[23]

The Ruhr elite denied any need for vacations on the part of healthy manual laborers, though paid leaves were granted to salaried employees as part of the effort to differentiate further their status from that of workers. Ruhr employers argued that since workers failed to show up for so many assigned shifts, they did not need additional time off.[24] The Harpener Bergbau-AG argued that vacations were not needed in the coal industry because of the "short" eight-hour workday, failing to mention the frequent imposition of overtime shifts.[25] Worker representatives at the König Ludwig mine were told that as long as huge sums were wasted by strikes, the industry could not afford to provide vacations.[26]

When in January 1911 the Zechenverband inquired about the granting of vacations, the Bergbau Verein replied that it knew of no member company doing so and encouraged the collection of information substantiating the burden such an innovation would entail.[27] According to Ruhr employers, the burden consisted not only of additional wage costs but also the difficulty in procuring replacements and the litigation that might arise from worker claims. They generally ignored the testimony of employers in other industries who had tried vacations and found they paid for themselves through increased productivity on the job and fewer unauthorized absences.[28]

Under the circumstances, it caused a great stir in the ranks of Ruhr coal industrialists when the Helene & Amalie mining company, under the direction of Otto Krawehl, agreed, at the time of the 1912 coal strike, to a request from the worker committee of the Amalie mine to grant five-day paid summer vacations to miners after five years' employment.[29] Krawehl subsequently maintained that the decision to award vacations had already been made before the worker committee raised the issue. Zechenverband members complained indignantly that before taking such a precedent-setting step, Krawehl should have checked first with other Ruhr coal industrialists.[30]

The Zechenverband launched an inquiry into the matter, calling upon Krawehl to explain his action. Krawehl argued that in the long run, the general introduction of vacations for workers was inevitable. By making early voluntary provision, according to Krawehl, employers would not only gain considerable public approval but would be able to control the new practice to suit themselves. What he had in mind became clear as he outlined the terms under which vacations would be granted by his company. The firm set aside only two marks a year per worker for vacations. This meant that not all eligible employees could be awarded leave. The company would decide who would be the recipients. Only loyal employees who had never been guilty of unexcused absences from work would be considered.

The Zechenverband reluctantly accepted Krawehl's plan but warned other industrialists, for the time being, not to follow suit. However, as this warning was being issued, Alfred Hugenberg announced that Krupp had decided to include provision for vacations for selected workers among the grants being made in honor of the firm's centenary. Although the exact terms had not yet been decided, Hugenberg stressed that the workers would have no legal claim to the vacations, which were to function as a "disciplinary measure to strengthen the position of the employer."[31] In line with this purpose, it was understood at Krupp that requests for vacations from members of the company union would be given first priority.[32] Four-day vacations would be granted to loyal workers after a minimum of ten years' service, six days after fifteen years. Recipients had to be at least forty years old. A further provision, inspired by the conception of vacations as a welfare measure rather than as an earned right of the worker, was that the time was to be used for rest only. Anyone found trying to make extra money by working during his vacation would never be granted another.[33]

Just before the outbreak of war, Krawehl reported that his experiment with worker vacations had yielded favorable results at minimal cost and would therefore be extended to the company's other mines.[34] Most Ruhr heavy industrialists, however, remained unconvinced, and actively resisted the spread of the practice.[35] Even among those who claimed to recognize the desirability of vacations for workers, there was unwillingness to assume the extra costs.

Work Hours in Metallurgy

More immediately pressing than the question of whether or not to grant paid vacations was the problem of what to do about excessive hours in metallurgy. This became, both inside and outside the Ruhr entrepreneurial elite, the single most debated issue affecting labor relations on the eve of war.

Iron and steel industrialists had been on notice, since the Bundesrat decree of 1908 regulating pauses, that they should do something on their own to reduce the burden of excessive hours or face further government intervention. Relative to the possible future regulation of overtime, the decree had provided for the collection of statistics to indicate the dimensions of the problem and the changes needed. The resulting statistics did not, to be sure, show the full extent of the problem because management took care that not all overtime was recorded.[36] But despite this, the statistics still indicated a significant increase during the last prewar years in already unreasonable hours. It was not unusual for individual workers to put in sixty or ninety hours of overtime in a month, in addition to their regular twelve-hour shifts.[37] And it should be noted that generally there was no extra pay beyond the regular hourly rate for overtime, especially on weekdays.[38]

Spokesmen for the iron and steel industry attempted to rationalize these abuses with some curious arguments. They maintained, for instance, that Sunday work, whether included in the normal twenty-four-hour shift changes or not, could be considered overtime only if there were no break between it and regular weekday shifts. They also claimed that the amount of overtime recorded was deceptive, as it was largely offset by absenteeism.[39]

However, despite their public disclaimers, the industrialists admitted in private that serious abuses existed. In May 1913 the problem of excessive overtime was discussed at a meeting of the executive committee of the Association of German Iron and Steel Industrialists. It was decided to recommend to the members that excessive hours be reduced voluntarily to avoid continued criticism and the possibility of government intervention at some later date. In June a secret memorandum was sent to all members, outlining the extent of existing abuses and recommending self-regulation.[40]

How this was to be done was left up to the individual companies. In May 1914, for example, Reusch queried a lieutenant as to whether it would be possible to limit overtime by offering premiums to supervisors who were successful in avoiding its use. He also wanted absolutely unavoidable overtime spread among as many workers as possible so that the burden on individual employees could be lessened.[41] However, just a few months earlier, when the government was considering a proposal to limit the number of continuous hours a single individual could work, even if his replacement failed to show up, Reusch had proposed unconditional opposition. He suggested that under those circumstances, the entire production unit should be shut down and all workers sent home. After this had happened a few times, he was sure, the workers themselves would bring pressure to bear on the government to change the ruling.[42]

The problem of the twenty-four-hour shift change was even more difficult than that of overtime. But the need for a solution was becoming pressing. In 1912, the Düsseldorf *Regierungspräsident* Francis Kruse suggested to leaders of the Association of German Iron and Steel Industrialists that they should voluntarily regulate shift changes so that the government would not have to intervene.[43] In response, it was decided to form a commission of blast furnace directors to discuss possible solutions. The commission reported at a closed meeting of the association in November 1913 that they had failed to agree on a proposal. But they stressed that change was inevitable.[44]

There were some members of the association who still opposed any change. That position was most common among industrialists from the smallest, least modern, least diversified, and least profitable firms, which would have the greatest difficulty implementing changes. But leading entrepreneurs in the primary iron and steel industry of the Ruhr agreed that some reform of existing conditions was necessary.[45]

However, before World War I, Ruhr iron and steel industrialists were not yet ready to consider seriously the most obvious solution to the problem of shift regulation in continuous production, namely, substitution of three eight-hour shifts for the two twelve-hour shifts. This alternative was rejected because it would have entailed increased labor costs and the additional workers required would have been difficult to obtain. According to Director Arnold Woltmann of the Gutehoffnungshütte, spokesman and frequent stand-in for Paul Reusch, the problem of obtaining enough additional workers was an even greater obstacle than the added costs. He estimated that the German iron and steel industry would need sixty to ninety thousand additional employees if the eight-hour day were introduced. Given the existing labor shortage, he saw an unwanted influx of foreign workers as the inevitable consequence.[46]

The eight-hour shift or anything pointing in that direction remained anathema to the elite of Ruhr metallurgy. For this reason, in late 1913, at a time when a downturn in the economy was forcing cutbacks in production, members of Arbeitnordwest were instructed to idle workers a half or whole shift at a time, if necessary, but under no circumstances to shorten the workday by four hours or less. Workers were not to be given, even temporarily, anything approaching an eight-hour day.[47]

Still without a viable solution to the problem of shift changes, the executive committee of the Association of German Iron and Steel Industrialists recommended to the government in January 1914 the establishment of a committee to consider the alternatives.[48] The proposed group was to be composed of representatives of labor and management. The war prevented anything coming of this suggestion. After the war, the length of a workday in Ruhr heavy industry reemerged as a central, bitterly contested issue.

Conclusions and Comparisons

Ruhr Employers on the Eve of War

In the final years before the outbreak of war in 1914, Ruhr employers saw little reason, barring some great catastrophe of the kind that actually did finally overtake them, not to continue with their prevailing policies. This meant continued efforts to combat and contain unions as much as possible, to resist further government intervention, to create integrated and cohesive communities of loyal workers and company officials, and to achieve stricter and more uniform work discipline. The intent was to regularize and stabilize labor-management relations as much as possible and to hold the line against new concessions.

Useful to this end were two developments that were otherwise far from welcome to the Ruhr elite. The first of these was the electoral success of the Social Democrats in the 1912 Reichstag election, making them the largest party in that body. The gains socialists made in that year were used by Ruhr employers to bolster their argument that Germany's nonsocialist majority should join with them in a common defense of established authority, especially theirs. The second of these developments was the recession that began to affect Ruhr heavy industry in the second half of 1913. The resulting reduction in the demand for labor, coming in the wake of the defeat of the 1912 coal strike, served to strengthen the employers' hand vis-à-vis the "agitators." With declining membership, Ruhr labor unions faced a bleak prospect on the eve of war. They seemed farther than ever from recognition by the entrepreneurial elite as legitimate bargaining agents.

Looking back from the perspective of the early months of 1914, Ruhr coal, iron, and steel industrialists were generally proud of their performance as employers during the Wilhelmian era. They were proud of the standard of living of their employees, compared, for example, to that of workers in Silesian heavy industry where wages were lower, hours longer, amenities fewer, discipline at least as harsh, and women and children were employed in substantial numbers. They welcomed domestic and foreign visitors to view their highly publicized welfare institutions, the fame of which had spread not only to other European countries but to the United States and Japan as well. They stressed their successes in providing employment for hundreds of thousands of men. As always, they warned against additional restrictions on their freedom of action that might make it difficult or impossible for them to continue to fulfill this vital function for the nation.[1]

When critics of the Ruhr elite pointed out that real wages had failed to keep pace with profits and that the region's workers still labored under unnecessarily dangerous, unhealthy, and demeaning conditions, the employers responded that they did the best they could in such matters, within the limits of what seemed to be technologically and economically feasible. They, of course, were to be the only judges of feasibility. When their critics objected that they unreasonably and unfairly refused to recognize organized labor as a bargaining agent, their response continued to be that they could not tolerate the disruptive presence of troublemakers and outside agitators. Some day it might be necessary to come to terms with organized labor, but not yet. It troubled Ruhr employers not at all that many of their labor policies were condemned by working-class spokesmen and bourgeois social reformers as outmoded, lagging behind more "progressive" and flexible responses in other industries and other countries, thereby creating a dangerous backlog of frustrated demands for change. They believed that Germany should define its own future, not slavishly imitate models of development provided by other industrial societies, especially Britain.

Ruhr employers liked to think of themselves as tough and determined defenders of an orderly and productive society. They continued to react harshly whenever they perceived a threat to established authority, both inside and outside the Ruhr. They made a major contribution to the language of irreconcilability that dominated the political discourse of Imperial Germany. But Ruhr employers were not all-powerful, and they knew it. The entrepreneurial elite could not rely solely upon repression. Despite the employers' frequently unwarranted rigidity in their relations with their workers, particularly in the political arena, some adaptation to the changing character of the working class and of German society as a whole was unavoidable.

In the massive corporations that had come to dominate Ruhr heavy industry before the First World War, it was becoming increasingly apparent to many members of the managerial elite that the often capricious and uncoordinated labor policies of earlier decades needed modification in the name of greater efficiency, predictability, and governmental approval. In addition, Ruhr employers were aware that flagrant abuses in such sensitive areas as safety regulation and hours of labor provided ammunition for embarrassing attacks in the press and in legislative bodies. The great size that made Ruhr corporations so powerful also made them conspicuous. At the same time, there was concern not to drive aggrieved workers into the arms of union organizers. Steady and productive workers remained in short supply in the prewar Ruhr. A generally high demand for labor kept Ruhr industrialists from purging their work forces as ruthlessly as they would have liked. And the prospect of readily finding alternative employment helped cushion many of the region's workers against the full impact of entrepreneurial domination.

Comparisons with English and American Employers

Although this book is specifically a study in German social history, it was conceived in a comparative frame of reference. So it would be appropriate at this point to suggest briefly some differences and similarities between labor-management relations in heavy industry in the Ruhr, on the one hand, and in England and the United States, on the other, and indicate the extent to which such differences and similarities might be accounted for by the characters and experiences of their respective entrepreneurial elites. This approach in no way implies that other factors were less important in determining variations in industrial relations among these societies but merely reflects the specific orientation of this study.

England and the United States are appropriate for such a comparison not only because they shared with Imperial Germany the distinction of being the industrial leaders of the pre-1914 world but also because Ruhr industrialists themselves were aware of what was happening in those countries and repeatedly made such comparisons. Foreign study and travel, either their own or that of their lieutenants, along with the reading of technical journals, kept Ruhr employers abreast of developments in the two English-speaking countries.[2] Technological and organizational innovations introduced by major foreign competitors, especially those with either labor-saving or labor-controlling potential, were carefully noted. American heavy industry was especially admired as a model for such innovations.

Often the same labor-related issue was debated simultaneously on both sides of the English Channel or on both sides of the Atlantic. For example, the debate among Ruhr iron and steel industrialists about regulation of twenty-four hour shifts was paralleled by a similar debate in American metallurgy during the same years. There too, the entrepreneurial elite was under pressure to bring its own house in order or face government intervention. In 1910, the American Iron and Steel Institute devised a plan calling for rotating days off during the week. This plan was accepted by the huge United States Steel Corporation, representing about half the American steel industry.[3] Similar plans were considered in the Ruhr as well but were rejected. Employers argued that workers themselves preferred the existing system, which gave them every other Sunday off, to a system that spread days off throughout the week. It was also argued that the churches would oppose such a change, a recognition that cultural and political differences could hamper the adoption of foreign solutions to labor problems.[4]

The international wave of industrial unrest during the last prewar years provides another example of shared employer difficulties. In 1912 the Ruhr coal strike was paralleled by a five-week work stoppage in the English coalfields. But the consequences were very different. Whereas Ruhr employers, enjoying government support, neither negotiated nor compromised in 1912, in England the strike was settled through government-sponsored negotiations and was followed by the passage of a minimum wage bill, a concept still anathema in the Ruhr.[5] Ruhr industrialists bitterly opposed a minimum wage or anything approaching it because they believed that their unrestricted freedom to manipulate the relationship between pay and performance was the only way to maintain or raise productivity.[6]

Increasing labor militance in British industry in the last prewar years, especially the 1912 coal strike, occasioned a shift in the arguments Ruhr employers used to justify their refusal to recognize unions or to bargain collectively. Previously they had argued, rather defensively, that though negotiations might be helpful in preventing major work stoppages in Britain, such negotiations were possible only because English unions were more unified, more responsible, and less ideological than those in the Ruhr. However, as British labor became more militant, Ruhr employers argued more confidently that industrialists on the other side of the channel obviously had little to teach them about the maintenance of peaceful labor relations and, indeed, would ultimately find themselves forced to adopt the tougher antiunion stance of their German counterparts.[7]

In its timing and swiftness of development, the growth of heavy industry in the Ruhr more closely paralleled that of the United States than it did the earlier industrialization of Britain. Coal, iron, and steel industrialists in the Ruhr and in the United States simultaneously faced many of the same problems of quickly organizing a new and disparate work force for large-scale primary production. Indeed, workers in American heavy industry were even more diverse than those in the Ruhr.[8] Even more than Ruhr employers, the leaders of American heavy industry faced the challenge of introducing great masses of immigrant labor to industrial work discipline.[9]

Conclusions and Comparisons

Leaders of American big business were generally no more willing than their German counterparts to accept labor organizations or to recognize labor demands as legitimate.[10] Operating within a democratic political system did not make the elite of American heavy industry any less authoritarian in its treatment of workers and their organizations than were Ruhr industrialists. American advocates of an industrial democracy to parallel the national form of government received little encouragement from those who presided over the giant corporations of the prewar era. This was especially true of those who came from the side of production rather than finance. American corporate leaders of the period were more likely to endorse the open shop campaign than they were collective bargaining.[11]

Indeed, in prewar America management's struggle against organized labor was accompanied by greater turbulence and violence, though by less long-term and pervasive bitterness, than in the Ruhr. Heavy industrialists in the United States made freer use of such provocative measures as importing large numbers of armed guards and strikebreakers during labor disputes.[12] The Imperial German government, fearful that labor unrest might escalate into political revolution, was less willing than the United States government to tolerate violent clashes of private interest.

Although Ruhr entrepreneurs shared a common timing of industrial development with their American counterparts, they shared with English industrialists the problem of coming to terms with an entrenched agrarian aristocracy—and in their own case, with a powerful state bureaucracy as well—that dominated the top of the social and political hierarchies before the onset of industrialization. They had to establish a position for themselves within a ruling elite that held values different from, and sometimes opposed to, their own. In both England and Germany prior to World War I, but particularly in Germany, the aristocracy retained much of its social and political, though not economic, preeminence. Marked divergence in the social and political development of the two states in the course of industrialization resulted less from differences in the nature and degree of accommodation between agrarian and business elites than from differences in the character of the aristocracy in each case. Entrepreneurial interaction with an aristocracy having strong parliamentary traditions produced very different results than did interaction with an aristocracy possessing strong military and bureaucratic associations. In England, with its tradition of parliamentary government, political leaders ultimately came to compete for the support of working-class voters and made political concessions to them in the process, whereas in Germany the propertied elites, supported by and supporting an authoritarian state, combined to exclude the workers as much as possible from social and political participation.[13]

In this study, three characteristic features of labor-management relations in Ruhr coal, iron, and steel production have been noted. First and most readily discernible was the extensive provision for welfare benefits, such as pensions, health services, housing, education, and recreational facilities, by Ruhr employers. When English workers were sent to imperial Germany to study working conditions, this was the most obvious difference to attract their attention.[14] In England and the United States, especially the latter, laissez-faire principles and a distaste for bureaucracy were long used to justify failure to develop extensive welfare institutions, either by the state or by private industry. Management and government in those two countries propagated the ideal of "self-help" for adult male workers. Management in particular stressed its virtues, though more for workers than for themselves.[15] In line with this self-help bias, the wealthiest American businessmen of the prewar era were more likely to make philanthropic contributions for the support of education than for welfare benefits.[16] In American heavy industry, the ready availability of immigrant labor discouraged the early implementation of industrial welfare programs and the building of a sense of industrial community.[17] At the end of the nineteenth century, the general disinclination of American industrialists to make a major commitment to comprehensive company welfare programs may have been strengthened by the failure of George Pullman's much publicized model community to deter workers of his railway sleeping car company from launching a bitter strike in 1894.[18] It should be noted, however, that in both Britain and the United States, experiments with welfare capitalism, such as those of Judge Elbert Gary of United States Steel, were becoming more numerous on the eve of World War I.[19] And in Britain, there was a burst of social legislation in the last prewar years.

In Imperial Germany, both state and industry used welfare gestures, with great fanfare, in an attempt to overcome bitterness between labor and management or, in a broader context, between labor and the existing social and political order. T. H. Marshall's model of the extension of citizenship rights to workers, which fits the experience of England and the United States, must be reversed in the case of Germany. In Britain and the United States political rights for industrial workers preceded social welfare. A common commitment to political liberalism in the two English-speaking countries favored the extension of political rights, whereas in Germany social benefits were used in both the public and private spheres to attempt to compensate for refusal to admit the workers as partners in either the industrial or the national community.[20] As some of their British and American counterparts appeared to be moving in the direction of welfare capitalism during the last years of peace, Ruhr employers felt reassured that paternalism, properly bureaucratized, was not outmoded as their liberal critics charged but, rather, represented the wave of the future.

Conclusions and Comparisons

A second characteristic of industrial relations in the Ruhr was the ideological schism dividing management and organized labor. Prior to World War I, more workers voted socialist in Germany than in any other country. In England and the United States, there was more agreement between employers and employed as to the fundamental nature of the social and political system. As a consequence, labor-management conflict in the two English-speaking countries was more likely to emphasize specific economic issues. In Germany there was disagreement between the two parties not only on economic issues but also on fundamental questions of social and political organization, a disagreement that Ruhr employers chose to exaggerate for their own ends. Given the industrialists' commitment to an authoritarian social and political order, they were as alienated by the workers' desire for democracy as by the socialism that some workers proclaimed.

A third characteristic of Ruhr labor-management relations prior to World War I was the growing importance of disciplined organizations in both camps. The elaborate and comprehensive nature of big business associations in Germany reflected a disposition to solve common problems, including labor issues, collectively. In contrast, American big business, sheltered by massive trusts, remained generally aloof from such associations. British entrepreneurs proved difficult to organize.[21] The proliferation and expansion of entrepreneurial associations in Germany, among them employer organizations, in part reflected the extent to which industrial leaders felt defensive about their position in Wilhelmian society. Ruhr heavy industrialists had created for themselves a place in the national ruling elite that was more ambivalent than that enjoyed by American and British entrepreneurs in their respective countries. The ambiguity in the position of the Ruhr entrepreneurial elite gave rise to a defensiveness that encouraged them to turn inward and organize themselves. Their propensity to organize for mutual defense was reinforced by a lack of a strong tradition of economic individualism, with its condemnation of restrictive association, and by the government's encouragement of such defensive efforts. The employers' defensiveness was also responsible for their sensitivity to censure and their feelings of being often misunderstood and betrayed by their social allies. Many peculiar aspects of their behavior in confrontations with labor may be explained by their search for security and recognition in an authoritarian society that they defended politically but that was being transformed by the social and economic changes their own entrepreneurial activities fostered.

Ruhr employers believed that in any international comparison they deserved a favorable rating, though this was strongly contested by bourgeois reformers and labor spokesmen throughout Germany who viewed them as highly repressive and as socially and politically shortsighted. Ruhr industrialists perceived themselves as tougher and more dynamic than their British counterparts, and more socially responsible than the leaders of American big business. They prided themselves on being as up-to-date as any group of businessmen in the world. The ability to anticipate and prepare for the future was taken to be absolutely essential to the exercise of leadership in massive companies engaged in fierce international competition. This, rather than day-to-day administration, Ruhr industrial leaders perceived as their essential task. They believed that British and American employers had at least as much to learn from them as vice versa.

Ruhr employers were most willing to learn from foreign experience as it related to technology and to the organization and direction of production. They found foreign experience least relevant in addressing societal problems that transcended the corporation. Yet it was in precisely this sphere that they were unable to devise constructive proposals of their own. They had little to propose beyond defense of the social and political status quo. They could only hope that through a combination of authoritarian firmness, perpetual vigilance, and full employment, German industrial society, at least for the foreseeable future, would be able to maintain its unique character and avoid the democratization of western Europe and the instability of the east and south. War and military defeat destroyed that hope.

World War I and Beyond

The war years, 1914 to 1918, brought marked changes in the composition and expectations of the Ruhr work force but not of the region's entrepreneurial elite. For miners and steelworkers, the war meant an influx of new, inexperienced workers, including prisoners of war, as well as longer hours, increased accident rates, lower real wages, and serious food shortages. For Ruhr employers, the war meant an urgent demand for their products and handsome profits. But it also meant mounting concern for the survival of the existing order, which had served them so well. Their ardent advocacy of annexationist war aims was linked in part to their hope that German conquests would help bolster authoritarian institutions.[22]

Only at the very end of the war, when no amount of wishful thinking could obscure the imminence of military defeat, did Ruhr industrial leaders, most notably Hugo Stinnes, begin to cast about for alternatives to collaboration with the traditional elites of Prussian-German society. The result was an agreement with organized labor, signed on 15 November 1918. In return for union cooperation in efforts to maintain orderly production

Conclusions and Comparisons

during demobilization, industrial leaders conceded recognition of the unions as bargaining agents. In addition, they agreed, for the time being, to sacrifice their sponsorship of company unions and to accept the eight-hour day.[23] Thus, as the empire collapsed, those whom the Ruhr entrepreneurial elite had repeatedly stigmatized as subverters of order were grudgingly, and ironically, enlisted as partners in maintaining order.

At the end of the war, worker unrest swept the Ruhr, with widespread strikes and calls for socialization of the mines in 1919 and a major armed insurrection in 1920.[24] Social Democratic and union leaders, already discredited in the eyes of many workers by their support for the war effort and by their commitment to collaboration with the entrepreneurial elite, attempted to control rather than intensify dissent, ultimately sanctioning the use of armed force against the protesters. Ruhr industrialists, however, showed scant gratitude, especially after the immediate crisis had passed, and subsequently dedicated themselves to revoking the concessions wrested from them in 1918. Facing an economic and political order much less to their liking than that which had existed before the war, coal, iron, and steel producers intensified their commitment to interest politics and to industrial concentration, while forging ahead with the rationalization of production. Their bitter determination to reassert control over labor was dramatized during the 1920s by their willingness to make use of economically costly and politically risky lockouts, a tactic they had been able to avoid before 1914. Although the economic importance of heavy industry was declining relative to such comparative newcomers as the chemical and electrical industries, Ruhr industrialists continued to be a major force in German society, powerful enough to contribute to the ultimate destabilization of the Weimar Republic, a regime whose legitimacy they did not accept and for whose survival they were unwilling to make sacrifices.[25]

Appendix A
Ruhr Coal, Iron, and Steel Corporations

Employment figures are for 1912 or for the date closest to that year for which information is available.

Arenberg: Arenberg'sche AG für Bergbau und Hüttenbetrieb (est. 1856); 9,266 employees in 1912.

Bochumer Verein: Bochumer Verein für Bergbau und Gusstahlfabrikation (est. 1854; successor to Mayer & Kühne, est. 1842); 14,529 employees in 1912–1913.

Concordia: Concordia Bergbau AG (est. 1850); 5,458 employees in 1912.

Consolidation: Bergwerks-AG Consolidation (est. 1862; organized as *Aktiengesellschaft* in 1889); 6,701 employees in 1912.

Constantin der Grosse: Gewerkschaft Vereinigte Constantin der Grosse (est. 1849); 8,816 employees in 1912.

Deutsch-Luxemburg: Deutsch-Luxemburgische Bergwerks- und Hütten-AG (est. 1901; successor to AG für Eisenindustrie und Kohleindustrie Differdingen-Dannebaum, est. 1899); 49,427 employees in 1912–1913.

Deutscher Kaiser: Gewerkschaft Deutscher Kaiser (est. 1871); 25,714 employees in 1913.

Dortmunder Union: Union, AG für Bergbau, Eisen- und Stahlindustrie (est. 1872; merged with Deutsch-Luxemburg in 1910); 12,583 employees in 1909–1910.

Essener Steinkohlenbergwerke AG (est. 1906); 7,420 employees in 1912.

Ewald: Gewerkschaft des Steinkohlenbergwerks Ewald (est. 1871); 7,098 employees in 1912.

Gelsenkirchener Bergwerks-AG (est. 1873); 44,589 employees in 1909–1910.

Graf Bismarck: Gewerkschaft Graf Bismarck (est. 1868); 6,870 employees in 1912.

Gutehoffnungshütte: Gutehoffnungshütte Aktienverein für Bergbau- und Hüttenbetrieb (est. 1872; successor to Jacobi, Haniel & Huyssen, est. 1810); 27,720 employees in 1912–1913.

Harpener Bergbau-AG (est. 1856); 28,879 employees in 1912.

Hibernia: Bergwerksgesellschaft Hibernia (est. 1873 through the fusion of the Gewerkschaft Hibernia, est. 1854, and the Gewerkschaft Shamrock, est. 1857); 18,438 employees in 1912.

Hoesch: Eisen- und Stahlwerk Hoesch (est. 1871); 11,166 employees in 1912–1913.

Hoerder Verein: Hoerder Bergwerks- und Hüttenverein (est. 1852; successor to the Hermannshütte, est. 1841; merged with Phoenix in 1906); 7,963 employees in 1905–1906.

Appendix A: Corporations

Köln-Neuessener Bergwerksverein (est. 1912 through the fusion of the Kölner Bergwerksverein, est. 1847, and the Bergwerksgesellschaft Neu-Essen, est. 1855); 5,152 employees in 1912.

König Ludwig: Gewerkschaft König Ludwig (est. 1872); 5,244 employees in 1912.

Krupp: Friedrich Krupp AG (est. 1812; organized as *Aktiengesellschaft* in 1903); 66,454 employees in 1912–1913.

Lothringer Hüttenverein: Lothringer Hüttenverein Aumetz Friede (est. 1897); 8,505 employees in 1909–1910.

Neumühl: Gewerkschaft Neumühl (est. 1867); 5,163 employees in 1912.

Nordstern: AG Steinkohlenbergwerk Nordstern (est. 1873; merged with Phoenix in 1907); 9,387 employees in 1904.

Phoenix: Phoenix, AG für Bergbau und Hüttenbetrieb (est. 1852); 39,735 employees in 1912–1913.

Rheinische Stahlwerke (est. 1870); 11,697 employees in 1912–1913.

Rheinpreussen: Gewerkschaft Rheinpreussen (est. 1856); 9,221 employees in 1912.

Schalker Verein: Schalker Gruben- und Hüttenverein (est. 1872; merged with the Gelsenkirchener Bergwerks-AG in 1907); 7,091 employees in 1906.

Thyssen & Co. (est. 1871); 5,880 employees in 1909–1910.

Zollverein: Gewerkschaft Zollverein (est. 1848); 6,045 employees in 1912.

Appendix B
Members of the Ruhr Entrepreneurial Elite

Baare, Fritz (1855–1917), managing director (*Generaldirektor*) of the Bochumer Verein, 1895–1914 (successor to his father in that position)
Birthplace: Bochum (Ruhr)
Father: Louis Baare, managing director of the Bochumer Verein, 1854–1895
Education and Training: Studied at technical universities in Berlin and Karlsruhe
Employment outside Ruhr Industry: Two years' work in the English iron industry
Religion: Protestant

Behrens, Karl (1854–1906), managing director of the Bergwerksgesellschaft Hibernia, 1889–1906
Brithplace: Triebsees (Pomerania)
Father: ?
Education and Training: Educated as state mining official (*Bergassessor*)
Employment outside Ruhr Industry: Served as state mining official in Silesia
Religion: Protestant

Beukenberg, Wilhelm (1858–1923), managing director of the Hoerder Verein, 1903–1906, and after the Hoerder Verein's merger with Phoenix, managing director of that company until 1922
Birthplace: Werne (Ruhr)
Father: Heinrich Wilhelm Beukenberg, mine supervisor (*Steiger*)
Education and Training: Studied mechanical engineering at the technical university in Berlin (*Regierungsbaumeister*)
Employment outside Ruhr Industry: Director of railroads in the Ruhr and in Venezuela
Religion: Protestant

Brauns, Hermann (1838–1911), managing director of the Dortmunder Union, 1885–1902
Birthplace: Uslar (Hanover)
Father: Wilhelm Brauns, forestry official
Education and Training: Studied engineering at the mining academy in Clausthal (*Diplomexamen für Hütten- und Bergingenieure*)
Employment outside Ruhr Industry: Technical director of the Georgs-Marien Hütte in Osnabrück
Religion: Protestant

Burgers, Franz (1845–1911), managing director of the Schalker Verein, 1878–1911 (selected by shareholder August Thyssen)
Birthplace: Geldern (Rhine province)
Father: Customs official
Education and Training: Attended trade school in Cologne; apprenticed as mechanic in a Cologne workshop; traveled in England
Employment outside Ruhr Industry: Worked in Rhenish iron industry
Religion: Old Catholic (one of those who rejected papal infallibility)

Appendix B: Members of the Elite

Dehnke, Reinhold (1864–1941), managing director of the Gewerkschaft Graf Bismarck, 1908–1926
Birthplace: Strelno (Posen)
Father: Estate owner
Education and Training: Educated as state mining official at the mining academies in Berlin and Clausthal
Employment outside Ruhr Industry: Served as state official in the Ruhr and in the Saar
Religion: Protestant

Funke, Carl (1855–1912), chairman of the board (*Vorsitzender des Aufsichtsrates*) of the Essener Steinkohlenbergwerke AG and chairman of the executive committee (*Vorsitzender des Grubenvorstandes*) of the Gewerkschaft König Ludwig (inherited father's mining interests)
Birthplace: Essen (Ruhr)
Father: Friedrich Funke, building contractor and mine promoter
Education and Training: Attended a Realgymnasium in Essen, followed by a stay in Geneva to learn French and a commercial apprenticeship with chemical companies in Cologne and Schalke
Employment outside the Ruhr: None
Religion: Protestant

Goecke, Emil (1842–1910), managing director of the Rheinische Stahlwerke, 1878–1910 (appointed by his lawyer brother, Feodor Goecke, who was the company's bank-selected chairman of the board)
Birthplace: Duisburg (Ruhr)
Father: Heinrich Wilhelm Goecke, lawyer
Education and Training: Gymnasium; commercial apprenticeship
Employment outside Ruhr Industry: Worked for a bank
Religion: Protestant

Haniel, Franz (1842–1916), chairman of the executive committees of the *Gewerkschaften* Rheinpreussen, Neumühl, and Zollverein, and chairman of the board of the Gutehoffnungshütte, 1894–1916 (successor to his father and grandfather as head of the Haniel industrial empire)
Birthplace: Ruhrort (Ruhr)
Father: Hugo Haniel, founder of the Gewerkschaft Rheinpreussen and son of Franz Haniel, one of the pioneers of Ruhr mining
Education and Training: Commercial apprenticeship
Employment outside Ruhr Industry: None
Religion: Protestant

Hasslacher, Johann (1869–1940), managing director of the Rheinische Stahlwerke, 1910–1936
Birthplace: Saarbrücken (Saar)
Father: Franz Anton Hasslacher, state mining official
Education and Training: Studied law at the Universities of Bonn and Berlin
Employment outside Ruhr Industry: Member of the Prussian judiciary
Religion: Catholic

Hoesch, Albert (1847–1898), chief executive (sole *Vorstandsmitglied*) of the Eisen- und Stahlwerk Hoesch, 1873–1898
Birthplace: Düren (Eifel)
Father: Leopold Hoesch, Eifel iron manufacturer who moved his base of operations to Dortmund
Education and Training: Studied at technical universities in Zurich and Berlin; traveled for two years in England
Employment outside Ruhr Industry: Briefly managed family firm in Eifel
Religion: Protestant

Hugenberg, Alfred (1865–1951), chairman of the executive committee (*Vorsitzender des Direktoriums*) of the Krupp steelworks, 1909–1919 (recommended for the position by Freiherr von Rheinbaben, *Oberpräsident* of the Rhine province and formerly Hugenberg's superior at the Prussian ministry of finance)
Birthplace: Hanover

Appendix B: Members of the Elite

Father: Karl Hugenberg, city official in Hanover
Education and Training: Studied law at the Universities of Göttingen, Heidelberg, and Berlin; studied economics at the University of Strassburg
Employment outside Ruhr Industry: Served in the Prussian high civil service; director of a bank in Frankfurt
Religion: Protestant

Jencke, Hanns (1843–1910), chairman of the executive committee of the Krupp steelworks, 1879–1902 (recommended for the position by Albert Maybach, Prussian minister of commerce)
Birthplace: Dresden
Father: Johann Friedrich Jencke, founder and director of an institute for the deaf and dumb
Education and Training: Studied law at the Universities of Leipzig and Heidelberg
Employment outside Ruhr Industry: Worked in a lawyer's office; director of the Saxon state railroads
Religion: Protestant

Kamp, Heinrich (1841–1927), managing director of Phoenix, 1898–1908
Birthplace: Wetter (Ruhr)
Father: Hermann Kamp, foundry owner and son of Heinrich Kamp, who together with Friedrich Harkort established one of Germany's first machine-building firms in Wetter in 1819
Education and Training: Studied at the technical institute in Berlin; traveled in England
Employment outside Ruhr Industry: Managed foundry in the Rhineland
Religion: Protestant

Kirdorf, Emil (1847–1938), managing director of the Gelsenkirchener Bergwerks-AG, 1893–1926
Birthplace: Mettmann (Rhine province)
Father: Martin Kirdorf, owner of a handloom weaving company
Education and Training: Commercial apprenticeship
Employment outside Ruhr Industry: None
Religion: Catholic (repudiated Christianity by 1913)

Kleine, Eduard (1837–1914), director of several medium-sized mines in the Dortmund-Hoerde area in which his wife's family had an interest (included in this list because he served from 1905–1909 as chairman of the Bergbau Verein)
Birthplace: Herford (Westphalia)
Father: Johann Ludwig Kleine, clergyman
Education and Training: Studied at mining academies in Halle and Berlin (*Bergreferendar*)
Employment outside Ruhr Industry: None
Religion: Protestant

Kleine, Eugen (1867–1928), managing director of the Harpener Bergbau-AG, 1914–?
Birthplace: Dortmund (Ruhr)
Father: Eduard Kleine (see above)
Education and Training: Educated as a state mining official at the mining academy in Berlin
Employment outside Ruhr Industry: None
Religion: Protestant

Kloeckner, Peter (1863–1940), chairman of the board of the Lothringer Hüttenverein (appointed in 1903 by banking interests with a mandate to reorganize the tottering firm)
Birthplace: Koblenz (Rhine province)
Father: Peter Kloeckner, dockyard owner
Education and Training: Commercial apprenticeship
Employment outside Ruhr Industry: None
Religion: Catholic

Kost, Heinrich (1855–?), managing director of the AG Steinkohlenbergwerk Nordstern, 1896–1907

Appendix B: Members of the Elite

Birthplace: Witten (Ruhr)
Father: ?
Education and Training: Educated as state mining official; studied at Universities of Bonn and Berlin
Employment outside Ruhr Industry: Served as state mining official in the Saar, Silesia, and the Ruhr
Religion: Protestant

Krabler, Emil (1839–1909), managing director of the Kölner Bergwerksverein, 1886–1907
Birthplace: Crossen a. d. Oder
Father: Johann Eduard Krabler, merchant, later mine director
Education and Training: Educated as state mining official at the mining academy in Berlin
Employment outside Ruhr Industry: None
Religion: Protestant

Krawehl, Otto (1875–1936), chairman of the board of the Arenberg'sche AG, 1906–? (successor to his uncle, Oskar von Waldthausen, in that position)
Birthplace: Aachen (Rhine province)
Father: Georg Krawehl, wool merchant
Education and Training: Educated as state mining official; studied at the technical universities in Freiburg and Berlin
Employment outside Ruhr Industry: None
Religion: Protestant

Krupp, Friedrich Alfred (1854–1902) owner of the Krupp steelworks, 1887–1902
Birthplace: Essen (Ruhr)
Father: Alfred Krupp, owner of the Krupp steelworks until his death in 1887
Education and Training: Brief study at the technical university in Braunschweig; trained primarily at the Krupp works under his father's supervision
Employment outside Ruhr Industry: None
Religion: Protestant

Krupp von Bohlen und Halbach, Gustav (1870–1950), chairman of the board of the Krupp steelworks, 1910–1945 (married to Bertha Krupp, eldest daughter of F. A. Krupp)
Birthplace: The Hague
Father: Court official, Baden, ennobled 1871
Education and Training: Studied law at the Universities of Lausanne, Strassburg, and Heidelberg
Employment outside Ruhr Industry: Diplomatic service in Washington, D.C., Peking, and Rome
Religion: Protestant

Lueg, Carl (1833–1905), chairman of the executive committee (*Vorstandsvorsitzender*) of the Gutehoffnungshütte, 1872–1903 (successor to his father in that position)
Birthplace: Sterkrade (Ruhr)
Father: Wilhelm Lueg, chief executive of the Gewerkschaft Jacobi, Haniel & Huyssen, forerunner of the Gutehoffnungshütte
Education and Training: Studied at the technical university in Karlsruhe
Employment outside Ruhr Industry: None
Religion: Protestant

Müser, Robert (1849–1927), managing director of the Harpener Bergbau-AG, 1893–1914 (successor to his father in that position)
Birthplace: Dortmund (Ruhr)
Father: Friedrich Wilhelm Müser, M.D., one of the founders of the Harpener Bergbau-AG
Education and Training: Gymnasium; commercial apprenticeship
Employment outside Ruhr Industry: Eight years with a New York bank
Religion: ?

Pieper, Hermann, Sr. (1839–1904), managing director of the Gewerkschaft

Appendix B: Members of the Elite

Vereinigte Constantin der Grosse, 1875–1904
Birthplace: Sprockhövel (Ruhr)
Father: ?
Education and Training: Educated as state mining official; studied in Bonn, Breslau, and Berlin
Employment outside Ruhr Industry: None
Religion: ?

Pieper, Hermann, Jr. (1872–1913), managing director of the Gewerkschaft Vereinigte Constantin der Grosse, 1904–1913 (successor to his father in that position)
Birthplace: Bochum (Ruhr)
Father: Hermann Pieper, Sr. (see above)
Education and Training: Educated as state mining official; studied at Universities of Göttingen, Berlin, and Aachen
Employment outside Ruhr Industry: Served as state official in the Ruhr
Religion: ?

Randebrock, Paul (1856–1912), mining director of the Gelsenkirchener Bergwerks-AG, 1908–1912 (included in this list because he served from 1909–1912 as chairman of the Bergbau Verein)
Birthplace: Recklinghausen (Ruhr)
Father: Landowner
Education and Training: Educated as state mining official; studied at the mining academy in Berlin and at the Universities of Berlin and Bonn
Employment outside Ruhr Industry: Served as state official in the Ruhr
Religion: Catholic

Reusch, Paul (1868–1956), chairman of the executive committee of the Gutehoffnungshütte, 1908–1942
Birthplace: Königsbronn (Württemberg)
Father: Hermann Reusch, director of a state-owned foundry in Württemberg

Education and Training: Studied at the technical university in Stuttgart
Employment outside Ruhr Industry: Worked as engineer in the Habsburg Empire
Religion: Protestant

Roetger, Max (1860–1923), chairman of the executive committee of the Krupp steelworks, 1902–1909
Birthplace: East Prussia
Father: ?
Education and Training: Studied law
Employment outside Ruhr Industry: Served as *Landrat* (highest county civil official) in Essen
Religion: Protestant

Servaes, August (1832–1923), managing director of Phoenix, 1859–1902
Birthplace: Düsseldorf (Rhine province)
Father: ?
Education and Training: Studied law at the Universities of Heidelberg, Bonn, and Greifswald
Employment outside Ruhr Industry: None
Religion: ?

Springorum, Friedrich (1858–1938), managing director of the Eisen- und Stahlwerk Hoesch, 1905–1920
Birthplace: Schwelm (Westphalia)
Father: Friedrich Springorum, owner of a small steel mill in Schwelm
Education and Training: Studied metallurgy at the technical university in Aachen
Employment outside Ruhr Industry: Managed steel mill in Aachen
Religion: ?

Stinnes, Hugo (1870–1924), chairman of the board of the Deutsch-Luxemburgische Bergwerks- und Hütten-AG, 1906–1924
Birthplace: Mülheim (Ruhr)
Father: Hermann Hugo Stinnes, chief executive of the Stinnes mines, 1864–1887, and son of Mathias Stinnes, one of the pioneers of Ruhr mining

Appendix B: Members of the Elite

Education and Training: Commercial apprenticeship; one semester at the mining academy in Berlin
Employment outside Ruhr Industry: None
Religion: Protestant

Tengelmann, Ernst (1870–1954), managing director of the Essener Steinkohlenbergwerke AG, 1913–?
Birthplace: Samborn (Ruhr)
Father: Wilhelm Tengelmann, mine director
Education and Training: Attended the Bochum *Bergschule*
Employment outside Ruhr Industry: None
Religion: Protestant

Thyssen, August (1842–1926), owner of Thyssen & Co., 1871–1926, and of Deutscher Kaiser, 1885–1926
Birthplace: Eschweiler (Rhine province)
Father: Friedrich Thyssen, owner of a small rolling mill, later became banker
Education and Training: Attended a business school in Antwerp and the technical university in Karlsruhe
Employment outside Ruhr Industry: None
Religion: Catholic

Tull, Matthias (1835–1913), managing director of the Hoerder Verein, 1892–1903 (selected by banking interests to reorganize the tottering firm)
Birthplace: Trier (Rhine province)
Father: ?
Education and Training: ?
Employment outside Ruhr Industry: Director of Rhenish railroads
Religion: Catholic

Waldthausen, Oskar von (1854–1906), chairman of the board of the Arenberg'sche AG für Bergbau und Hüttenbetrieb, 1883–1906 (successor to his father in that position)
Birthplace: Essen (Ruhr)
Father: Ernst Waldthausen, one of the founders of the Arenberg'sche AG
Education and Training: Trained in the family enterprise
Employment outside Ruhr Industry: None
Religion: Protestant

Winkhaus, Friedrich (1865–1932), managing director of the Kölner Bergwerksverein, 1907–1932 (successor to his father-in-law Emil Krabler in that position)
Birthplace: Oeckinghausen (Sauerland)
Father: Iron implement merchant
Education and Training: Studied chemistry at the University of Marburg; studied at the mining academy in Berlin; traveled in the United States
Employment outside Ruhr Industry: Served as state official in the Ruhr
Religion: Protestant

Notes

Abbreviations Used in Notes

AG	*Aktiengesellschaft*	Reg.	*Regierung*
BA	Bundesarchiv Koblenz	RPr	*Regierungspräsident*
HA/GHH	Historisches Archiv der Gutehoffnungshütte	StAD	Staatsarchiv Düsseldorf
		StAK	Staatsarchiv Koblenz
OBA Dort.	*Oberbergamt* Dortmund	StAM	Staatsarchiv Münster
OP	*Oberpräsidium*	VdESI	Verein deutscher Eisen-und Stahlindustrieller
OPr	*Oberpräsident*		

The general order of archival citations is: item cited; name of archive; designation of general series or collection; volume used; and finally, page numbers for volumes that have them. Variations reflect usage at individual archives.

Introduction

1. Alfred Hugenberg, *Streiflichter aus Vergangenheit und Gegenwart*, p. 210. All translations are the author's unless otherwise indicated.
2. See, for example, Klaus Saul, *Staat, Industrie, Arbeiterbewegung im Kaiserreich*.
3. A book that does fruitfully link an industrial case study with broader social and political themes in the history of Imperial Germany is Jürgen Kocka's *Unternehmensverwaltung und Angestelltenschaft am Beispiel Siemens 1847–1914*.
4. For economic trends and business cycles in Imperial Germany, see Gerhard Bry, *Wages in Germany, 1871–1945*, pp. 474–480; Volker Hentschel, *Wirtschaft und Wirtschaftspolitik im wilhelminischen Deutschland*, pp. 205–259;

Notes

Joseph Schumpeter, *Business Cycles*, 1:446–448; Arthur Spiethoff, *Die wirtschaftlichen Wechsellagen*, 1:45, 83–84, 130–139; and Reinhard Spree, *Wachstumstrends und Konjunkturzyklen in der deutschen Wirtschaft von 1820 bis 1913*, pp. 32–97. See also David Landes, *The Unbound Prometheus*, pp. 231–237; and W. W. Rostow, "Kondratieff, Schumpeter, and Kuznets." Hans Rosenberg, *Grosse Depression und Bismarckzeit*, pp. 1–25, and Hans-Ulrich Wehler, *Bismarck und der Imperialismus*, pp. 15–111, discuss the use of economic trend periods like the one from 1896 to 1914 as a basis for periodization in social history. Cf. Jürgen Kocka's reservations in "Theoretical Approaches to Social and Economic History in Modern Germany," pp. 110–111. Spree and Hentschel, cited above, also express reservations, but these apply primarily to industries other than those being investigated in this book. The same is true of S. B. Saul, *The Myth of the Great Depression 1873–1896*. Saul, whose critique of the theory of long waves focuses on the British economy, denies any unity to the years 1873–1896, but he does concede coherence to 1896–1914 as a period of price recovery. See pp. 13 and 27.

5. *Glückauf* 49 (30 August 1913):1472–1473.

6. On the problem of the identification of industrial leaders, see Alfred D. Chandler, Jr., and Fritz Redlich, "Recent Developments in American Business Administration and Their Conceptualization"; and Redlich, *Der Unternehmer*, pp. 42, 67, 96, 132. See also Heinz Hartmann, "Manager and Entrepreneur."

7. Toni Pierenkemper stresses the impossibility of using such an approach when large numbers of entrepreneurs are to be investigated. See his *Die westfälischen Schwerindustriellen 1852–1913*, p. 19.

8. These individuals, or at least the most vocal and politically active among them, are no strangers to anyone familiar with the recent historiography of the German Empire. For examples of recent studies of Imperial Germany in which the political role of Ruhr industrialists is discussed, see Helmut Böhme, *Deutschlands Weg zur Grossmacht*; Fritz Fischer, *Krieg der Illusionen*; Hartmut Kaelble, *Industrielle Interessenpolitik in der Wilhelminischen Gesellschaft*; Saul, *Staat, Industrie, Arbeiterbewegung*; Dirk Stegmann, *Die Erben Bismarcks*; and Wehler, *Bismarck und der Imperialismus*. Apart from current historical interest in the political activities of Ruhr business leaders, there is an older tradition of study of this group deriving its impulse in part from entrepreneurial history and in part from local and regional history. In such studies, the Ruhr elite is frequently treated as part of the economic leadership of the provinces of Rhineland and Westphalia. See Gerhard Adelmann, "Führende Unternehmer im Rheinland und Westfalen, 1850–1914"; Horst Beau, *Das Leistungswissen des frühindustriellen Unternehmertums in Rheinland und Westfalen*; Helmuth Croon, "Die wirtschaftlichen Führungsschichten des Ruhrgebietes in der Zeit von 1890 bis 1933"; Hansjoachim Henning, "Soziale Verflechtungen der Unternehmer in Westfalen 1860–1914"; Pierenkemper, *Die westfälischen Schwerindustriellen*; Ludwig Puppke, *Sozialpolitik und soziale Anschauungen frühindustrieller Unternehmer in Rheinland-Westfalen*; and Friedrich Zunkel, *Der Rheinisch-Westfälische Unternehmer, 1834–1879*.

Chapter 1: Coal, Iron, and Steel

1. Norman J. G. Pounds, *The Ruhr*, pp. 19–25.

2. Carl-Ludwig Holtfrerich, *Quantitative Wirtschaftsgeschichte des Ruhrkohlenbergbaus im 19. Jahrhundert*, p. 15.

Notes

3. *Jahresbericht des Vereins für die bergbaulichen Interessen im Oberbergamtsbezirk Dortmund für 1913*, p. 8.

4. Hans Marchand, *Säkularstatistik der deutschen Eisenindustrie*, pp. 118–119.

5. Hans Spethmann, *Das Ruhrgebiet im Wechselspiel von Land und Leuten, Wirtschaft, Technik und Politik*, 2:465–466.

6. For a list of corporate links between Ruhr mining and the iron industry of Lorraine and Luxemburg, see Paul Wiel, *Wirtschaftsgeschichte des Ruhrgebiets*, p. 212.

7. Ibid., p. 238.

8. See Appendix A.

9. Holtfrerich, *Quantitative Wirtschaftsgeschichte*, pp. 95–98.

10. See Appendix A.

11. Holtfrerich, *Quantitative Wirtschaftsgeschichte*, p. 16.

12. Ibid., p. 145.

13. Ibid., p. 146.

14. Ibid., p. 23.

15. Ibid., p. 146.

16. Walther Daebritz, *Bochumer Verein für Bergbau und Gusstahlfabrikation in Bochum*, pp. 189, 244; and Wilfried Feldenkirchen, *Die Eisen- und Stahlindustrie des Ruhrgebiets 1879–1914*, p. 55.

17. See, for example, Klaus Tenfelde, *Sozialgeschichte der Bergarbeiterschaft an der Ruhr im 19. Jahrhundert*, pp. 192–193.

18. Holtfrerich, *Quantitative Wirtschaftsgeschichte*, pp. 17–18.

19. Ibid., p. 145.

20. Ibid., p. 55.

21. Gerhard Bry, *Wages in Germany, 1871–1945*, p. 346.

22. Walter Bacmeister, *Louis Baare*, pp. 209–210. See also Feldenkirchen, *Die Eisen- und Stahlindustrie des Ruhrgebiets*, p. 56; Wolfram Fischer, *Herz des Reviers*, pp. 261–264; and Donald Paul Panzera, "Organization, Authority, and Conflict in the Ruhr Coal Mining Industry," pp. 215–216.

23. Helmut Böhme, "Bankenkonzentration und Schwerindustrie, 1873–1896"; and Wilfried Feldenkirchen, "Kapitalbeschaffung in der Eisen- und Stahlindustrie des Ruhrgebiets 1879–1914."

24. Oskar Martens, "Kommerzienrat Robert Müser," pp. v–vi.

25. Erich Maschke, *Grundzüge der deutschen Kartellgeschichte bis 1914*, p. 43.

26. Helmut Böhme, "Emil Kirdorf," p. 22.

27. Maschke, *Grundzüge der deutschen Kartellgeschichte*, p. 20.

28. Steven B. Webb, "Tariffs, Cartels, Technology, and Growth in the German Iron and Steel Industry, 1879 to 1914."

29. Friedrich Schunder, *Tradition und Fortschritt*, pp. 33–38.

30. Helmut Böhme, *Deutschlands Weg zur Grossmacht*, pp. 359–365.

31. On the history of the Centralverband, see H. A. Bueck, *Der Centralverband deutscher Industrieller, 1876–1901*; and Hartmut Kaelble, *Industrielle Interessenpolitik in der Wilhelminischen Gesellschaft*. On the challenge from the Bund der Industriellen, see Helga Nussbaum, *Unternehmer gegen Monopole*, and Dirk Stegmann, "Hugenberg contra Stresemann." See also Hans-Peter Ullmann, *Der Bund der Industriellen*.

32. On the protectionist campaign, see Böhme, *Deutschlands Weg zur*

Grossmacht; Karl W. Hardach, *Die Bedeutung wirtschaftlicher Faktoren bei der Wiedereinführung der Eisen- und Getreidezölle in Deutschland 1879*; Ivo N. Lambi, *Free Trade and Protection in Germany, 1868–1879*; Hans Rosenberg, *Grosse Depression und Bismarckzeit*; and Friedrich Zunkel, *Der Rheinisch-Westfälische Unternehmer, 1834–1879*.
33. Bacmeister, *Louis Baare*, p. 198.
34. Hans Ehrenberg, *Die Eisenhüttentechnik und der deutsche Hüttenarbeiter*, p. 136.
35. See the works listed in note 4 to the introduction. Specifically on the Ruhr, see Feldenkirchen, *Die Eisen-und Stahlindustrie des Ruhrgebiets*, pp. 98–109, and Wolfram Fischer, "Konjunkturen und Krisen im Ruhrgebiet seit 1840 und die wirtschaftspolitische Willensbildung der Unternehmer." The economic fortunes of the Ruhr coal industry can be followed in the *Jahresberichte des Vereins für die bergbaulichen Interessen* and those of the iron and steel industry in *Stahl und Eisen*.
36. Cf. James E. Cronin, "Theories of Strikes"; Hartmut Kaelble and Heinrich Volkmann, "Konjunktur und Streik während des Übergangs zum Organisierten Kapitalismus in Deutschland"; and Eduard Shorter and Charles Tilly, *Strikes in France, 1830–1968*, pp. 82–97.
37. Holtfrerich, *Quantitative Wirtschaftsgeschichte*, pp. 20–24.
38. Feldenkirchen, *Die Eisen- und Stahlindustrie des Ruhrgebiets*, pp. 277–282.
39. *Glückauf* 50 (17 January 1914):101.
40. Daebritz, *Bochumer Verein*, p. 309.
41. Böhme, "Bankenkonzentration und Schwerindustrie," p. 438; and Richard Tilly, "The Growth of Large-scale Enterprise in Germany," pp. 159, 165. See also Emil Kirdorf, "Das Verhältnis der Kartelle zum Staat," p. 285.
42. *Stenographischer Bericht der 39. Generalversammlung des Vereins für die bergbaulichen Interessen im Oberbergamtsbezirk Dortmund, 28 Juni 1897*, pp. 4–5.
43. Wilhelm Beukenberg, "Die Entwicklung der Schwerindustrie in der Regiergungszeit Wilhelms II."
44. See, for example, *Bergassessor* Hilgenstock, "Über Lohntarife im britischen und rheinisch-westfälischen Steinkohlenbergbau," p. 1680. See also a 30 January 1911 speech by Alfred Hugenberg in *Der Nationale Arbeiter-Verein Werk Krupp*, pp. 26–28.
45. Kenneth D. Barkin, *The Controversy over German Industrialization, 1890–1902*, pp. 184–185; and Hermann Lebovics, "'Agrarians' versus 'Industrializers.'"
46. Holtfrerich, *Quantitative Wirtschaftsgeschichte*, p. 18.
47. Wiel, *Wirtschaftsgeschichte des Ruhrgebiets*, p. 227.
48. Gerhard Adelmann, *Quellensammlung zur Geschichte der sozialen Betriebsverfassung Ruhrindustrie unter besonderer Berücksichtigung des Industrie- und Handelskammerbezirks Essen*, 1:144.
49. Stenogramme der Kommissionsverhandlungen in Dortmund betreffend Stillegen von Ruhrzechen, 28 April 1904, StAM, OBA Dort. B, group 119, no. 280, pp. 408–435; and Eingabe der vereinigten Zechenbetriebsgemeinden des südlichen Ruhrkohlengebiets um Herbeiführung von Massnahmen zur Erhaltung der in ihrem Bezirke gelegenen von der Stillegung bedrohten Zechen, 3 February 1913, StAK, OP Koblenz 403/13123.

Notes

50. Gerhard Gebhardt, *Ruhrbergbau*, p. 494.
51. Adelmann, *Quellensammlung*, 1:144.
52. Spethmann, *Das Ruhrgebiet*, 2:469–473. See also Feldenkirchen, *Die Eisen- und Stahlindustrie des Ruhrgebiets*, table 39, pp. 418–419, and table 42, pp. 422–423; and Wiel, *Wirtschaftsgeschichte des Ruhrgebiets*, p. 211.
53. Volkmar Muthesius, *Ruhrkohle, 1893–1943*, p. 32.
54. Fritz Siebrecht, *Der Köln-Neuessener Bergwerksverein*, p. 51.
55. Fritz Siebrecht, *Fritz Winkhaus*, p. 17.
56. Muthesius, *Ruhrkohle, 1893–1943*, p. 93.
57. Feldenkirchen, *Die Eisen- und Stahlindustrie des Ruhrgebiets*, pp. 112–117, 129–136.
58. Pounds, *The Ruhr*, p. 103.
59. *Glückauf* 49 (30 August 1913):1472.
60. Gebhardt, *Ruhrbergbau*, pp. 212–214.
61. Erich Maschke, *Es entsteht ein Konzern*, p. 89.
62. *Glückauf* 50 (17 January 1914):110.
63. Wiel, *Wirtschaftsgeschichte des Ruhrgebiets*, p. 120.
64. See, for example, Wilhelm Treue, *Die Feuer verlöschen nie*, pp. 156–157, for a listing of the far-flung holdings of the Thyssen concern in 1913.
65. Feldenkirchen, *Die Eisen- und Stahlindustrie des Ruhrgebiets*, table 104, pp. 510–511.
66. Fischer, *Herz des Reviers*, p. 14.
67. Maschke, *Grundzüge der deutschen Kartellgeschichte*, p. 32, and Treue, *Die Feuer verlöschen nie*, p. 163.
68. Böhme, "Emil Kirdorf," p. 294.
69. Treue, *Die Feuer verlöschen nie*, p. 74.
70. Charles Medalen, "State Monopoly Capitalism in Germany."
71. Cf. David Landes, *The Unbound Prometheus*, p. 302.

Chapter 2: The Entrepreneurial Elite

1. On Thyssen's career, see Wilhelm Treue, *Die Feuer verlöschen nie*.
2. Rudolf Martin, *Jahrbuch des Vermögens und Einkommens der Millionäre in der Rheinprovinz*, pp. 132–140; and Walter Serlo, *Bergmannsfamilien in Rheinland und Westfalen*, p. 125.
3. *Rheinisch-Westfälische Wirtschaftsbiographien*, 5:129.
4. *Deutsche Bergwerks-Zeitung*, 15 August 1912.
5. See, for example, Wolfgang Benz, "Die Entstehung des Kruppschen Nachrichtendienstes," p. 211.
6. Dankwart Guratzsch, *Macht durch Organisation*, pp. 66–68.
7. *Glückauf* 50 (3 January 1914):14; Carl-Ludwig Holtfrerich, *Quantitative Wirtschaftsgeschichte des Ruhrkohlenbergbaus im 19. Jahrhundert*, pp. 42–48; and Paul Wiel, *Wirtschaftsgeschichte des Ruhrgebiets*, pp. 164, 339.
8. Martin, *Millionäre in der Rheinprovinz*, pp. 169–175; and *Zur Feier der 25-jährigen Tätigkeit des Herrn Kommerzienrats Oscar von Waldthausen im Dienste der Arenbergschen Aktien-Gesellschaft für Bergbau und Hüttenbetrieb*.
9. On Funke's holdings, see *Carl Funke und seine Werke*.
10. Werner Schiefel, *Bernhard Dernberg, 1865–1937*, p. 26; and Peter Wulf, *Hugo Stinnes*, pp. 22–29.

Notes

11. Gert von Klass, *Hugo Stinnes*, p. 54.
12. On Kloeckner's career, see Volkmar Muthesius, *Peter Klöckner und sein Werk*.
13. The earliness of corporate development in Ruhr coal, iron, and steel production compared to that in German industry in general is discussed in Jürgen Kocka, *Unternehmer in der deutschen Industrialisierung*, pp. 69–73.
14. Walter Bacmeister, *Louis Baare*, pp. 76–77, 96. Cf. Alfred D. Chandler, Jr., and Herman Daems, eds. *Managerial Hierarchies*, esp. pp. 13–14.
15. Wilfried Feldenkirchen, *Die Eisen- und Stahlindustrie des Ruhrgebiets 1879–1914*, pp. 308, 317.
16. Helmut Böhme, "Emil Kirdorf," p. 285.
17. Cf. Ralf Dahrendorf, *Class and Class Conflict in Industrial Society*, pp. 42–46; Heinz Hartmann, *Authority and Organization in German Management*, p. 97; and Lawrence Schofer, *The Formation of a Modern Labor Force*, p. 139.
18. *Nekrologe aus dem rheinisch-westfälischen Industriegebiet, Jahrgang 1939–1951*, pp. 195–197.
19. Justus Hashagen, *Geschichte der Familie Hoesch*, 2:571; Klass, *Hugo Stinnes*, p. 58; Georg Tischert, "Carl Funke," p. 605; and Treue, *Die Feuer verlöschen nie*, p. 23.
20. Klass, *Hugo Stinnes*, p. 55; *Deutsche Bergwerks-Zeitung*, 13 August 1912.
21. Hashagen, *Geschichte der Familie Hoesch*, 2:571; Karl Mews, "Otto Krawehl," p. 175; and Treue, *Die Feuer verlöschen nie*, p. 22.
22. Serlo, *Bergmannsfamilien in Rheinland und Westfalen*, pp. 52, 168, 175, 190; and Serlo, *Westdeutsche Berg- und Hüttenleute und ihre Familien*, p. 110.
23. Volkmar Muthesius, *Ruhrkohle, 1893–1943*, p. 47, and *Stahl und Eisen* 27 (1907):684 and 30 (1910):273.
24. Serlo, *Bergmannsfamilien in Rheinland und Westfalen*, pp. 85–88.
25. Cf. Hartmut Kaelble, "Long-Term Changes in the Recruitment of the Business Elite."
26. Muthesius, *Ruhrkohle, 1893–1943*, p. 47.
27. *Rheinisch-Westfälische Wirtschaftsbiographien*, 10:197.
28. *Nekrologe, Jahrgang 1939–1951*, pp. 195–197.
29. For information on where members of the Ruhr elite studied, worked, and traveled, see Appendix B.
30. Fritz Siebrecht, *Fritz Winkhaus*, p. 8.
31. In addition to the former Saxon railroad director (Hanns Jencke of Krupp), two other members of the Ruhr elite (Wilhelm Beukenberg of the Hoerder Verein and later of the Phoenix steelworks and Matthias Tull of the Hoerder Verein) had directed railroads before coming to metallurgy. In their cases, however, the railways were private. Alfred D. Chandler, Jr., *The Visible Hand*, pp. 81–121, stresses the importance of railways as early models for the management of big business in the United States.
32. Martin, *Millionäre in der Rheinprovinz*.
33. Cf. the financial difficulties of the Bochumer Verein's first managing director. Bacmeister, *Louis Baare*, pp. 73–74.
34. Martin, *Millionäre in der Rheinprovinz*; and Martin, *Jahrbuch des Vermögens und Einkommens der Millionäre in Preussen*. Government documents relating to the award of titles contain information about the financial situation of the recipients. See *Die Verleihung des Titels Kommerzienrat beziehungsweise*

Notes

Geheimer Kommerzienrat, StAM, OP Münster 1514, vols. 2–4; and Akten betreffend der Verleihung von Titeln, StAK, OP Koblenz 403/9881-90.

35. F. A. Krupp to v. Studt, 15 July 1902, in Willi Boelcke, ed., *Krupp und die Hohenzollern*, p. 94; and Paul Brandi, *Essener Arbeitsjahre*, pp. 20–21.

36. Brandi, *Essener Arbeitsjahre*, p. 10; Helmut Croon, "Die Einwirkungen der Industrialisierung auf die gesellschaftliche Schichtung der Bevölkerung im rheinisch-westfälischen Industriegebiet," p. 313; *Deutsche Bergwerks-Zeitung*, 18 May and 13 August 1912; and Serlo, *Bergmannsfamilien in Rheinland und Westfalen*, pp. 168–169.

37. Heinrich Class, *Wider den Strom*, p. 219; and Hans Fürstenberg, *Carl Fürstenberg*, p. 371.

38. Wilhelm Schulte, *Westfälische Köpfe*, pp. 12–13; and Serlo, *Bergmannsfamilien in Rheinland und Westfalen*, pp. 168–169.

39. OPr Münster to Minister für Handel und Gewerbe, 20 July 1899, StAM, OP Münster 1514, vol. 2, pp. 87–88.

40. See listings of supervisory board members for Ruhr concerns and German investment banks in *Handbuch der deutschen Aktien-Gesellschaften*.

41. On interaction between bank representatives and Ruhr industrialists, see, for example, Willibald Gutsche, "Die Deutsche Bank und die Entstehung der Stahlwerks-Verband AG."

42. Maura Kealey, "Kampfstrategien der Unternehmerschaft im Ruhrbergbau seit dem Bergarbeiterstreik von 1889."

43. On differences within the entrepreneurial camp, see Siegfried Mielke, *Der Hansa-Bund für Gewerbe, Handel und Industrie 1909–1914*, and Helga Nussbaum, *Unternehmer gegen Monopole*.

44. Schofer, *The Formation of a Modern Labor Force*, pp. 29–31. See also Toni Pierenkemper, "Entrepreneurs in Heavy Industry."

45. On the extensive interrelationships among prominent Prussian mining families, see Serlo, *Die preussischen Bergassessoren*.

46. Fritz Hellwig, *Carl Ferdinand Freiherr von Stumm-Halberg*, pp. 565–567.

47. On the relationship of the Catholic church and organized labor in Imperial Germany, see Klaus Michael Mallmann, *Die Anfänge der Bergarbeiterbewegung an der Saar 1848–1904*; and Mary Nolan, *Social Democracy and Society*.

48. Schofer, *The Formation of a Modern Labor Force*, pp. 22–28.

49. O. Taeglichsbeck, ed., *Die Belegschaft der Bergwerke und Salinen im Oberbergamtsbezirk Dortmund nach der Zählung vom 16. Dezember 1893*, 1:viii.

50. On the religious affiliation of Ruhr employers, see Appendix B.

51. *Carl Funke und seine Werke*, p. 13; and *Deutsche Bergwerks-Zeitung*, 19 April 1912.

52. Dora Freifrau von Bodenhausen-Degener, *Eberhard von Bodenhausen*, pp. 216–217.

53. Ibid., p. 31.

54. Treue, *Die Feuer verlöschen nie*, pp. 121, 164.

55. Friedrich Zunkel, *Der Rheinisch-Westfälische Unternehmer, 1834–1879*, p. 126.

56. *Deutsche Bergwerks-Zeitung*, 13 August 1912.

57. Walter Bacmeister, *Emil Kirdorf*, p. 152; *Deutsche Bergwerks-Zeitung*, 18 May 1912; and Conrad Matschoss, *Männer der Technik*, p. 147.

58. See, for example, OPr Münster to Minister für Handel und Gewerbe,

20 July 1899, StAM, OP Münster 1514, vol. 2, pp. 87–88. The *Oberpräsident* cited the granting of *Kommerzienrat* titles to managing directors Hermann Brauns of the Dortmunder Union and Emil Kirdorf of the Gelsenkirchener Bergwerks-AG as precedents for offering such a title to Fritz Baare of the Bochumer Verein.
59. Richard Lewinsohn, *Das Geld in der Politik*, p. 27. See also Lamar Cecil, "The Creation of Nobles in Prussia, 1871–1918."
60. Boelcke, *Krupp und die Hohenzollern*; Lamar Cecil, *Albert Ballin*; and Hellwig, *Carl Ferdinand Freiherr von Stumm-Halberg*.
61. *Amtsblätter*, 26 November 1902, in StAD, Reg. Düsseldorf, Präs. Büro, no. 1063.
62. Bacmeister, *Emil Kirdorf*, p. 137; and Hans Jaeger, *Unternehmer in der deutschen Politik, 1890–1918*, p. 259.
63. Dirk Stegmann, *Die Erben Bismarcks*, p. 426.

Chapter 3: Ruhr Workers

1. Carl-Ludwig Holtfrerich, *Quantitative Wirtschaftsgeschichte des Ruhrkohlenbergbaus*, p. 68.
2. Ibid., p. 52.
3. Such complaints were especially frequent during 1906. See, for example, *Deutsche Bergwerks-Zeitung*, 11 October 1906; and *Jahresbericht des Vereins für die bergbaulichen Interessen im Oberbergamtsbezirk Dortmund für 1906*, p. 14.
4. Friedrich Syrup, "Die Arbeitszeit in der Grosseisenindustrie," p. 195.
5. *Rhein- und Ruhrzeitung*, 5 September 1896, clipping in StAK, OP Koblenz 403/8326.
6. Gert von Klass, *Stahl vom Rhein*, p. 42; and Wilhelm Treue, *Die Feuer verlöschen nie*, p. 130.
7. See, for example, Adolf Günther and René Prevôt, *Die Wohlfahrtseinrichtungen der Arbeitgeber in Deutschland und Frankreich*, pp. 47–48, 105–106; *Nekrologe aus dem rheinisch-westfälischen Industriegebiet, Jahrgang 1939–1951*, pp. 67–68; and Fritz Quint, "50 Jahre Bergbau vom Kumpel gesehen," p. 67.
8. See Wilhelm Brepohl, *Der Aufbau des Ruhrvolkes im Zuge der Ost-West-Wanderung*; and Wolfgang Köllmann, *Bevölkerung in der industriellen Revolution*, pp. 106–124, 171–185.
9. Helmuth Croon, "Die Einwirkungen der Industrialisierung auf die gesellschaftliche Schichtung der Bevölkerung im rheinisch-westfälischen Industriegebiet," p. 306.
10. Paul Wiel, *Wirtschaftsgeschichte des Ruhrgebiets*, pp. 8, 12.
11. Wilhelm Brepohl, *Industrievolk im Wandel von der agraren zur industriellen Daseinsform dargestellt am Ruhrgebiet*, p. 387; and E. A. Wrigley, *Industrial Growth and Population Change*, p. 61.
12. Norman J. G. Pounds, *The Ruhr*, pp. 97–101.
13. On Ruhr zones, see Brepohl, *Industrievolk im Wandel*, pp. 1–28.
14. Max König, "Über den wirtschaftlichen und politischen Einfluss der Grossindustrie auf die Gemeinde-Vertretung und -Verwaltung im Ruhrgebiet," col. 901.
15. Hans Spethmann, *Das Ruhrgebiet im Wechselspiel von Land und Leuten, Wirtschaft, Technik und Politik*, 2:559.

Notes

16. Gerhard Adelmann, *Quellensammlung zur Geschichte der sozialen Betriebsverfassung Ruhrindustrie unter besonderer Berücksichtigung des Industrie- und Handelskammerbezirks Essen*, 2:328; Richard Ehrenberg and Hugo Racine, *Krupp'sche Arbeiterfamilien*, pp. 350–352; Wolfram Fischer, *Herz des Reviers*, p. 252; and Wiel, *Wirtschaftsgeschichte des Ruhrgebiets*, pp. 70–71.
17. Recruitment at one such mine is described in H. Th. Schmidt, "Belegschaftsbildung im Ruhrgebiet im Zeichen der Industrialisierung."
18. Gutehoffnungshütte to Arnold Ottawa, 13 August 1912, and Gilfert to Ludwig Frisch, 10 September 1912, HA/GHH 30 100/9 Anwerbung von Arbeitern. See also Christoph Klessmann, *Polnische Bergarbeiter im Ruhrgebiet 1870–1945*, p. 39.
19. Cf. Schofer, *The Formation of a Modern Labor Force*, pp. 37, 61.
20. Wolfgang Köllmann, "The Process of Urbanization in Germany at the Height of the Industrialization Period," p. 65.
21. Pounds, *The Ruhr*, p. 128. For the social consequences of Hamborn's rapid growth, see Erhard Lucas, *Zwei Formen von Radikalismus in der deutschen Arbeiterbewegung*, pp. 21–136.
22. Spethmann, *Das Ruhrgebiet*, 2:563.
23. Croon, "Die Einwirkungen der Industrialisierung," p. 306. See also Brepohl, *Industrievolk im Wandel*, p. 374; and Franz J. Brüggemeier and Lutz Niethammer, "Schlafgänger, Schnapskasinos und schwerindustrielle Kolonie," pp. 139, 148.
24. On development in this part of the Ruhr coalfield, see Helmuth Croon and Kurt Utermann, *Zeche und Gemeinde*.
25. Klessmann, *Polnische Bergarbeiter*, pp. 262, 267; and Klaus Tenfelde, *Sozialgeschichte der Bergarbeiterschaft an der Ruhr im 19. Jahrhundert*, p. 242.
26. Klessmann, *Polnische Bergarbeiter*, pp. 262, 267; Spethmann, *Das Ruhrgebeir*, 2:562; and Wiel, *Wirtschaftsgeschichte des Ruhrgebiets*, pp. 69–70.
27. Klessmann, *Polnische Bergarbeiter*, pp. 40–41; and Spethmann, *Das Ruhrgebiet*, 2:562; See Max Jürgen Koch, *Die Bergarbeiterbewegung im Ruhrgebiet zur Zeit Wilhelms II, 1889–1914*, pp. 21–22, for a list of Ruhr mines employing especially large numbers of Polish workers.
28. Treue, *Die Feuer verlöschen nie*, p. 130.
29. Wiel, *Wirtschaftsgeschichte des Ruhrgebiets*, pp. 69–71.
30. Richard C. Murphy, "Polnische Bergarbeiter im Ruhrgebiet," pp. 97–99; Tenfelde, "Die 'Krawalle von Herne' im Jahre 1899," pp. 86, 100–104; and Spethmann, *Das Ruhrgebiet*, 2:564.
31. Klessmann, *Polnische Bergarbeiter*, p. 63.
32. See, for example, Otto Neuloh, *Die deutsche Betriebsverfassung*, p. 185.
33. Geoff Eley, *Reshaping the German Right*, p. 141; Karl Wilke, *50 Jahre im Dienste des Ruhrbergbaus*, p. 44; and Beukenberg to Reusch, 20 January 1914, HA/GHH 300 193 26/25 Deutsche Vereinigung, vol. 1, 1909–1914.
34. See Tenfelde, *Sozialgeschichte der Bergarbeiterschaft*, p. 239, for the initial reluctance of Ruhr industrialists to hire workers from the eastern provinces until forced to do so by the labor shortages of the last quarter of the nineteenth century.
35. Gutehoffnungshütte to Bergwerksdirektor Kocks, 27 February 1902, HA/GHH 30103/0 Bergwerksverwaltung: Rundschreiben und Verfügungen 1901–1908.
36. Gutehoffnungshütte to Bergwerksverwaltung, 1 December 1905,

Notes

HA/GHH 30103/0 Bergwerksverwaltung: Rundschreiben und Verfügungen 1901–1908; and Verwaltungsberichte des OBA Dort. 1907, 1908, 1909, StAK, OP Koblenz 403/8176.

37. Schofer, *The Formation of a Modern Labor Force*, pp. 26–27; and O. Taeglichsbeck, ed., *Die Belegschaft der Bergwerke und Salinen im Oberbergamtsbezirk Dortmund nach der Zählung vom 16. Dezember 1893*, 1:vii.

38. Pounds, *The Ruhr*, p. 130.

39. David Crew, *Town in the Ruhr*, pp. 62–64; and Lutz Niethammer, "Wie wohnten Arbeiter im Kaiserreich?" p. 75.

40. Spethmann, *Das Ruhrgebiet*, 2:526.

41. Verwaltungsbericht des OBA Dort. für das Jahr 1909, StAK, OP Koblenz 403/8176, p. 84.

42. Adelmann, *Quellensammlung*, 1:145. See also Lorenz Pieper, *Die Lage der Bergarbeiter im Ruhrrevier*, pp. 99–100, 102.

43. Cf. David Montgomery, *Workers' Control in America*, p. 140; Schofer, *The Formation of a Modern Labor Force*, pp. 121–136; and Peter Stearns, *Lives of Labor*, pp. 242–247.

44. Klaus Mattheier, *Die Gelben*, p. 148.

45. Niethammer, "Wie wohnten Arbeiter im Kaiserreich?" p. 85.

46. Tenfelde, *Sozialgeschichte der Bergarbeiterschaft*, pp. 630–633.

47. Wolfgang Köllmann, *Der Bergarbeiterstreik von 1889 und die Gründung des "Alten Verbandes" in ausgewählten Dokumenten der Zeit*, p. 110.

48. Albin Gladen, "Die Streiks der Bergarbeiter im Ruhrgebiet in den Jahren 1889, 1905 und 1912"; and Stephen Hickey, "The Shaping of the German Labour Movement."

49. On the formation of the Alter Verband, see Köllmann, *Der Bergarbeiterstreik von 1889*, pp. 240–291.

50. Adelmann, *Quellensammlung*, 1:257.

51. Klessmann, "Klassensolidarität und nationales Bewusstsein," p. 154.

52. Klaus Tenfelde, "Linksradikale Strömungen in der Ruhrbergarbeiterschaft 1905 bis 1919," p. 208.

53. Schofer, *The Formation of a Modern Labor Force*, p. 156.

54. Klessmann, "Klassensolidarität und nationales Bewusstsein," describes some of the union infighting of the prewar era. See also Murphy, "The Polish Trade Union in the Ruhr Coal Field."

55. Jencke, 17 November 1899, in *Verhandlungen, Mitteilungen und Berichte des Centralverbandes deutscher Industrieller*, 84:58.

56. Emil Kirdorf, "Das Verhältnis der Kartelle zum Staat," p. 289.

57. Elisabeth Domansky-Davidsohn, "Der Grossbetrieb als Organisationsproblem des Deutschen Metallarbeiter-Verbandes vor dem Ersten Weltkrieg."

58. Quoted in *Stahl und Eisen* 30 (1910):483.

59. Crew, *Town in the Ruhr*, pp. 186–190. Cf. Alvin Gouldner, *Patterns of Industrial Bureaucracy*, p. 113.

60. Klessmann, *Polnische Bergarbeiter*, p. 272.

61. David Crew, "Definitions of Modernity"; Hans Ehrenberg, *Die Eisenhüttentechnik und der deutsche Hüttenarbeiter*, p. 160; and W. Viebig, "Die technischen Grubenbeamten beim Steinkohlenbergbau im Oberbergamtsbezirk Dortmund," p. 1138.

62. See the variety of positions and wage rates for metallurgical workers at Deutscher Kaiser listed in Klessmann, *Polnische Bergarbeiter*, pp. 277–279.

Notes

63. Great Britain, Board of Trade, *Cost of Living in German Towns*, pp. 85, 181.
64. Adolf Zimmermann, *Von Haspe bis Duisburg*, p. 67. Cf. Gouldner, *Patterns of Industrial Bureaucracy*, p. 147. For examples of intra- and intergenerational mobility at Krupp, see Ehrenberg and Racine, *Krupp'sche Arbeiterfamilien*.
65. Crew, *Town in the Ruhr*, pp. 81–84. At the Gutehoffnungshütte, positions as office boys were reserved for the sons of company employees. Verfügung an sämtliche Abteilungen, 24 May 1911, HA/GHH 30103/1 Rundschreiben und Verfügungen, 1908–1911. However, only the sons of better paid employees would typically be eligible because boys with middle school training were preferred for such positions over those with only an elementary education. See Otto Heinemann, *Kronenorden Vierter Klasse*, p. 100. In addition, the poorly dressed sons of the poorest workers were made to feel out of place in the white collar environment. See Georg Werner, *Ein Kumpel*, p. 27.

Chapter 4: Industry and Government

1. Ruhr employers frequently complained that the interventionist theories of the Verein für Sozialpolitik did great harm by providing justification for ill-advised bureaucratic regulations that made their task more difficult than need be. According to Krupp spokesman Max Roetger, such theories were "the root of all evil." Quoted in Siegfried Mielke, *Der Hansa-Bund für Gewerbe, Handel und Industrie 1909–1914*, p. 96. See also Emil Kirdorf, "Das Verhältnis der Kartelle zum Staat." On the association itself, see Dieter Lindenlaub, *Richtungskämpfe im Verein für Sozialpolitik*.
2. Karl Erich Born, *Staat und Sozialpolitik seit Bismarcks Sturz*, pp. 33, 138, 248; and Hartmut Kaelble, *Industrielle Interessenpolitik in der Wilhelminischen Gesellschaft*, p. 79. For a sampling of bureaucratic opinion on social issues, see the documents collected in Peter Rassow and Karl Erich Born, *Akten zur staatlichen Sozialpolitik in Deutschland, 1890–1914*.
3. *Stenographischer Bericht über die Versammlung vom 12. 6. 1909 im Zirkus Schumann zu Berlin betreffend Reichsfinanzreform und Gründung des Hansabundes*, p. 31.
4. Alfred Hugenberg, 25 April 1914, in *Stenographischer Bericht der 56. Generalversammlung des Vereins für die bergbaulichen Interessen im Oberbergamtsbezirk Dortmund*, p. 22; Wilhelm Beukenberg, 12 April 1910, in *Verhandlungen, Mitteilungen und Berichte des Centralverbandes deutscher Industrieller*, 118:102–103; and Adolf Zimmermann, *Von Haspe bis Duisburg*, pp. 57–58.
5. Besprechung der Bergbau Vereine über Änderung des Allgemeinen Berggesetzes, 6 January 1909, StAD, Reg. Düsseldorf, no. 15934, p. 34.
6. Helmut Böhme, "Emil Kirdorf," pp. 34–35; and Emil Kirdorf, "Das Verhältnis der Kartelle zum Staat," p. 277.
7. Meeting, 15 December 1908, in *Berichte der Hauptstelle deutscher Arbeitgeberverbände*, 6:38.
8. Alfred Hugenberg, *Streiflichter aus Vergangenheit und Gegenwart*, p. 217.

Notes

9. Quoted in Kaelble, *Industrielle Interessenpolitik*, p. 119.
10. Dirk Stegmann, *Die Erben Bismarcks*, pp. 222, 227–230, 357–358; and Stegmann, "Hugenberg contra Stresemann," p. 337.
11. RPr Arnsberg, 21 June 1898, StAM, OP Münster 1514, vol. 2, pp. 58–59.
12. On the formation of the Navy League, see Geoff Eley, *Reshaping the German Right*, pp. 79–81.
13. Heinrich Class, *Wider den Strom*, pp. 46–47, 216–219; Eley, *Reshaping the German Right*, pp. 249–250; Dankwart Guratzsch, *Macht durch Organisation*, pp. 23–25; and Stegmann, *Die Erben Bismarcks*, pp. 139, 298.
14. Klaus Saul, *Staat, Industrie, Arbeiterbewegung im Kaiserreich*, pp. 115–132; Reusch to Woltmann, 27 July 1910, HA/GHH 300 193 003/11 Schriftwechsel Reusch-Woltmann; and Abt. G, Hauptverwaltung Gutehoffnungshütte to company officials, 17 October 1910, HA/GHH 300 127/0 Reichsverband gegen die Sozialdemokratie 1907–1916.
15. HA/GHH 300 193 26/25 Deutsche Vereinigung, vol. 1, 1909–1915; and Reusch to Woltmann, 27 October 1913, HA/GHH 300 193 003/11 Schriftwechsel Reusch-Woltmann.
16. Klaus J. Mattheier, "Drei Führungsorganisationen der wirtschaftsfriedlich-nationalen Arbeiterbewegung."
17. Efforts to disguise the degree of industrial sponsorship led to secret subsidies like that paid in cash-filled envelopes by Krupp officials to General August Keim, founder and chairman of the Defence League (Wehrverein). See Wolfgang Benz, "Die Entstehung des Kruppschen Nachrichtendienstes," p. 203.
18. See, for example, Reusch to the Hauptgeschäftsstelle der Deutsche Vereinigung, 3 October 1910, HA/GHH 300 193 26/25 Deutsche Vereinigung, vol. 1, 1909–1915.
19. Zimmermann, *Von Haspe bis Duisburg*, p. 19. See also Eley, *Reshaping the German Right*, p. 144.
20. Speech, 8 August 1912, in Hugenberg, *Streiflichter aus Vergangenheit und Gegenwart*, p. 210.
21. Hans Jaeger, *Unternehmer in der deutschen Politik, 1890–1918*, p. 102; and Emil Kirdorf, "Das Verhältnis der Kartelle zum Staat," p. 277.
22. *Deutsche Bergwerks-Zeitung*, 26 April 1908.
23. Gerhard A. Ritter, *Die Arbeiterbewegung im Wilhelminischen Reich*, p. 70.
24. Joseph Risse, "Eduard Kleine," pp. 15–16.
25. Wilhelm Henning, *Geschichte der Stadtverordnetenversammlung von Essen, 1890–1914*, pp. 78–82; and Jaeger, *Unternehmer in der deutschen Politik*, pp. 63, 205.
26. The fate of this legislation can be followed in Saul, *Staat, Industrie, Arbeiterbewegung*.
27. See, for example, Stegmann, *Die Erben Bismarcks*, p. 200.
28. Jaeger, *Unternehmer in der deutschen Politik*, pp. 326–332, lists representatives of industrial interests in the Prussian Landtag. See also Stegmann, *Die Erben Bismarcks*, p. 359.
29. Gisbert Knopp, *Die preussische Verwaltung des Regierungsbezirks Düsseldorf in den Jahren 1899–1919*, pp. 157–159; and Stegmann, *Die Erben Bismarcks*, p. 273.

Notes

30. Erich Hoffmann, *Dr. Francis Kruse*, p. 87; Lysbeth W. Muncy, "The Prussian Landräte in the Last Years of the Monarchy," p. 317; and Alfred Wilke, *Probleme der Verwaltung im Industriebezirk mit besonderer Berücksichtigung der rheinisch-westfälischen Kohlendistrikts*, pp. 10–11. See also my discussion of the relationship between Ruhr industrialists and local and provincial officials in "Businessmen, Bureaucrats, and Social Control in the Ruhr, 1896–1914."

31. Willi Boelcke, ed., *Krupp und die Hohenzollern*, pp. 84–86; and Stegmann, *Die Erben Bismarcks*, pp. 49, 84, 406. On the career patterns of Prussian officials with jurisdiction over the Ruhr, see Knopp, *Die preussische Verwaltung des Regierungsbezirks Düsseldorf*; and Dietrich Wegmann, *Die leitenden staatlichen Verwaltungsbeamten der Provinz Westfalen 1815–1918*.

32. Roetger, 8 December 1909, in *Berichte der Hauptstelle deutscher Arbeitgeberverbände*, 7:40–41; and Reusch to Bürgermeister Dr. zur Nieden, 29 June 1911 and 6 August 1912, HA/GHH 300 193 7/17 Bürgermeister zur Nieden, Sterkrade, 1906–1913.

33. Helmuth Croon, "Die Einwirkungen der Industrialisierung auf die gesellschaftliche Schichtung der Bevölkerung im rheinisch-westfälischen Industriegebiet," p. 315; and Wolfgang Hofmann, "Preussische Stadtverordnetenversammlungen als Repräsentativ-Organe," pp. 43–48.

34. Max König, "Über den wirtschaftlichen und politischen Einfluss der Grossindustrie auf die Gemeinde-Vertretung und -Verwaltung im Ruhrgebiet," col. 921.

35. Henning, *Geschichte der Stadtverordnetenversammlung von Essen*, p. 38; König, "Über den wirtschaftlichen und politischen Einfluss der Grossindustrie," col. 924; and Fritz Mogs, "Die sozialgeschichtliche Entwicklung der Stadt Oberhausen (Rhld.) zwischen 1850 und 1933," p. 145. HA/GHH 300 10 12/71 Gemeinderatswahl Osterfeld 1908–1919 contains instructions for department heads to make certain workers have time off to vote in communal elections and that they cast their ballots for the proper candidates. In contrast, for Reichstag elections, in which secret ballots were used, company officials were directed to give time off for voting only to "safe" workers. Reusch to directors, 24 January 1912, HA/GHH 300 10 12/26 Reichstagswahl 1911–1912.

36. Helmuth Croon, *Die gesellschaftlichen Auswirkungen des Gemeindewahlrechtes in den Gemeinden und Kreisen des Rheinlandes und Westfalens im 19. Jahrhundert*, p. 74; and Henning, *Geschichte der Stadtverordnetenversammlung von Essen*, p. 46.

37. Henning, *Geschichte der Stadtverordnetenversammlung von Essen*, p. 37.

38. Ibid., p. 150.

39. Wilhelm Treue, *Die Feuer verlöschen nie*, p. 74.

40. Helmuth Croon, "Das Vordringen der politischen Parteien im Bereich der kommunalen Selbstverwaltung," pp. 41, 52.

41. Henning, *Geschichte der Stadtverordnetenversammlung von Essen*, pp. 88, 150.

42. König, "Über den wirtschaftlichen und politischen Einfluss der Grossindustrie," col. 921.

43. Henning, *Geschichte der Stadtverordnetenversammlung von Essen*, pp. 31, 81.

44. Ibid., pp. 39–41.

Notes

Chapter 5: Initial Challenges

1. David F. Crew, *Town in the Ruhr*, pp. 25–26; and Klaus Tenfelde, *Sozialgeschichte der Bergarbeiterschaft an der Ruhr im 19. Jahrhundert*, pp. 276–277.
2. Wolfgang Köllmann, *Der Bergarbeiterstreik von 1889 und die Gründung des "Alten Verbandes" in ausgewählten Dokumenten der Zeit*, p. 110.
3. Alex Bein and Hans Goldschmidt, *Friedrich Hammacher*, p. 104; Köllmann, *Der Bergarbeiterstreik von 1889*, pp. 26–78; *Aufsätze über den Streik der Bergarbeiter im Ruhrgebiet*, pp. 5–8; and Tenfelde, *Sozialgeschichte der Bergarbeiterschaft*, pp. 580–581.
4. Albin Gladen, "Die Streiks der Bergarbeiter im Ruhrgebiet in den Jahren 1889, 1905 und 1912," p. 128; Köllmann, *Der Bergarbeiterstreik von 1889*, pp. 43–69; and Tenfelde, *Sozialgeschichte der Bergarbeiterschaft*, pp. 584, 588–589.
5. Paul Grebe, "Bismarcks Sturz and der Bergarbeiterstreik vom Mai 1889," p. 91.
6. Bein and Goldschmidt, *Friedrich Hammacher*, p. 105; Gladen, "Die Streiks der Bergarbeiter," p. 130; and Köllmann, *Der Bergarbeiterstreik von 1889*, p. 95.
7. Grebe, "Bismarcks Sturz;" and Walter Wittwer, "Zur Taktik der herrschenden Klassen gegenüber dem Bergarbeiterstreik von 1889."
8. Bein and Goldschmidt, *Friedrich Hammacher*, pp. 108–113; and Gustav Seeber and Walter Wittwer, "Friedrich Hammachers Aufzeichnungen über den Bergarbeiterstreik von 1889."
9. Bein and Goldschmidt, *Friedrich Hammacher*, pp. 117–118; Köllmann, *Der Bergarbeiterstreik von 1889*, pp. 118–119; and Tenfelde, *Sozialgeschichte der Bergarbeiterschaft*, p. 586.
10. Bein and Goldschmidt, *Friedrich Hammacher*, pp. 127–129; and Maura Kealey, "Kampfstrategien der Unternehmerschaft im Ruhrbergbau seit dem Bergarbeiterstreik von 1889," pp. 183–191.
11. Köllmann, *Der Bergarbeiterstreik von 1889*, p. 190.
12. Dietrich Wegmann, *Die leitenden staatlichen Verwaltungsbeamten der Provinz Westfalen 1815–1918*, pp. 100–101.
13. Tenfelde, *Sozialgeschichte der Bergarbeiterstreik*, p. 594.
14. *Jahresbericht des Vereins für die bergbaulichen Interessen im Oberbergamtsbezirk Dortmund für das Jahr 1896*, p. 67. It is interesting to note that there was a direct business link between Bismarck and Ruhr mining. The Hibernia mining company, cofounded by the chancellor's personal banker Gerson Bleichröder, was the chief buyer of the timber produced on Bismarck's estate. See Fritz Stern, *Gold and Iron*, p. 297.
15. Manfred Hank, *Kanzler ohne Amt*, p. 408.
16. See, for example, Eduard Kleine's comments in Stenogramme der Kommissionsverhandlungen in Dortmund betreffend Stillegen von Ruhrzechen, 28 April 1904, StAM, OBA Dort. B, group 119, no. 280, p. 416; and Helmut Böhme, "Emil Kirdorf," p. 30.
17. Hans Jürgen Teuteberg, *Geschichte der industriellen Mitbestimmung in Deutschland*, pp. 376–390, 410–421.
18. Karl Erich Born, *Staat und Sozialpolitik seit Bismarcks Sturz*, p. 110; and Teuteberg, *Geschichte der industriellen Mitbestimmung*, p. 420.

Notes

19. Bein and Goldschmidt, *Friedrich Hammacher*, p. 152; and Tenfelde, *Sozialgeschichte der Bergarbeiterschaft*, p. 587.
20. Wolfram Fischer, *Herz des Reviers*, pp. 285–286.
21. Jencke to Krupp, 17 January 1893, in Willi Boelcke, ed., *Krupp und die Hohenzollern*, p. 73.
22. *Jahresbericht des Vereins für die bergbaulichen Interessen im Oberbergamtsbezirk Dortmund für das Jahr 1893*, pp. 56–60.
23. Fritz Hellwig, *Carl Ferdinand Freiherr von Stumm-Halberg*, pp. 491–565.
24. Klaus Michael Mallmann, *Die Anfänge der Bergarbeiterbewegung an der Saar, 1848–1904*, pp. 288–305; and Horst Steffens, "Arbeiterwohnverhältnisse und Arbeitskampf."
25. Christoph Klessmann, *Polnische Bergarbeiter im Ruhrgebiet 1870–1945*, pp. 75–79; and Tenfelde, "Die 'Krawalle von Herne' im Jahre 1899." See the documents on the Herne strike to StAM, Reg. Arnsberg 1, nos. 41–42.
26. Born, *Staat und Sozialpolitik*, p. 113; and H. A. Bueck, *Der Centralverband deutscher Industrieller, 1876–1901*, 2:565.
27. J. C. G. Röhl, *Germany without Bismarck*, p. 151; and Teuteberg, *Geschichte der industriellen Mitbestimmung*, p. 399.
28. *Stenographischer Bericht der 40. Generalversammlung des Vereins für die bergbaulichen Interessen im Oberbergamtsbezirk Dortmund, 23 Juli 1898*, pp. 11–12.
29. See Hanns Jencke's arguments in defense of such a program, 29 April 1898, in *Verhandlungen, Mitteilungen und Berichte des Centralverbandes deutscher Industrieller*, 79:52–53.
30. Bueck, *Der Centralverband*, 3:423.
31. Röhl, *Germany without Bismarck*, p. 262.
32. Bueck, *Der Centralverband*, 3:463–464, 487.
33. Jencke, 17 November 1899, in *Verhandlungen, Mitteilungen und Berichte des Centralverbandes deutscher Industrieller*, 84:53–58.
34. Born, *Staat und Sozialpolitik*, p. 152; Bueck, *Der Centralverband*, 3:487; and Jencke, 17 November 1899, in *Verhandlungen, Mitteilungen und Berichte des Centralverbandes deutscher Industrieller*, 84:52–53.

Chapter 6: Company Welfare Programs

1. On the development of welfare institutions by employers in Rhineland-Westphalia in the early and mid-nineteenth century, see Ludwig Puppke, *Sozialpolitik und soziale Anschauungen frühindustriellen Unternehmer in Rheinland-Westfalen*.
2. *Deutsche Bergwerks-Zeitung*, 20 October 1912.
3. Walter Bacmeister, *Louis Baare*, pp. 219–228; and W. J. Mommsen, ed., *The Emergence of the Welfare State in Britain and Germany 1850–1950*, pp. 71–83, 133–149.
4. Jencke, 1897, quoted in H. A. Bueck, *Der Centralverband deutscher Industrieller, 1876–1901*, 2:506; and Ausfuhrungen Herrn Bergassessor Kleine in Generalversammlung des Allgemeinen Knappschafts-Verein zu Bochum, 11 December 1911, StAM, OP Münster 2838 VI, pp. 183–184.

Notes

5. Cf. Adolf Günther and René Prevôt, *Die Wohlfahrtseinrichtungen der Arbeitgeber in Deutschland und Frankreich*, p. 96.

6. Gerhard Adelmann, *Quellensammlung zur Geschichte der sozialen Betriebsverfassung Ruhrindustrie unter besonderer Berücksichtigung des Industrie- und Handelskammerbezirks Essen*, 2:57.

7. *Glückauf* 39 (1903):4; Lutz Niethammer, "Wie wohnten Arbeiter im Kaiserreich?" p. 77; Christoph Klessmann, *Polnische Bergarbeiter im Ruhrgebiet 1870–1945*, p. 270; and O. Taeglichsbeck, ed., *Die Belegschaft der Bergwerke und Salinen im Oberbergamtsbezirk Dortmund nach der Zählung vom 16. Dezember 1893*, 2:xi.

8. See, for example, Verhandlung der Arbeiterausschüsse, Consolidation 3/4, 13 March 1912, StAM, OBA Dort. B, group 119, no. 299.

9. Otto Jeidels, *Die Methoden der Arbeiterentlohnung in der rheinisch-westfälischen Eisenindustrie*, p. 233.

10. Great Britain, Board of Trade, *Cost of Living in German Towns*, p. 242.

11. Adelmann, *Quellensammlung*, 2:66; Niethammer, "Wie wohnten Arbeiter im Kaiserreich?" p. 77; and Wolfram Fischer, *Herz des Reviers*, p. 268. Richard Ehrenberg and Hugo Racine, *Krupp'sche Arbeiterfamilien*, p. 377, calculated that in 1906 living in company housing represented a saving for Krupp workers equivalent to an average 5.4 percent of their annual wage.

12. Verwaltungsbericht des OBA Dort. für das Jahr 1907, StAK, OP Koblenz 403/8176, p. 90.

13. Norman J. G. Pounds, *The Ruhr*, p. 238.

14. Paul Mieck, *Die Arbeiter-Wohlfahrts-Einrichtungen der industriellen Unternehmer in den preussischen Provinzen Rheinland und Westfalen und ihre volkswirtschaftliche und soziale Bedeutung*, pp. 151, 212.

15. Günther and Prevôt, *Die Wohlfahrtseinrichtungen der Arbeitgeber*, pp. 36–38, 45–46.

16. Bergreferendar Tegeler, "Liegt es im Interesse der Besitzer und der Arbeiter der Steinkohlenbergwerke des Bergreviers Ost-Recklinghausen, wenn die Besitzer Arbeiterwohnungen auf eigene Kosten einrichten?" p. 16.

17. Mieck, *Die Arbeiter-Wohlfahrts-Einrichtungen*, p. 157; and Tegeler, "Liegt es im Interesse?" p. 21.

18. Arbeitsordnung der Zeche Shamrock, 12 December 1892, StAM, Reg. Arnsberg 1, no. 41; and Justizminister to Oberlandesgerichtspräsident in Hamm, 28 January 1905, StAD, Reg. Düsseldorf 15925.

19. Great Britain, Board of Trade, *Cost of Living in German Towns*, p. 242.

20. Tegeler, "Liegt es im Interesse?" p. 35.

21. Günther and Prevôt, *Die Wohlfahrtseinrichtungen der Arbeitgeber*, pp. 47–48, 105.

22. Tegeler, "Liegt es im Interesse?" p. 17.

23. Niethammer, "Wie wohnten Arbeiter im Kaiserreich?" p. 109.

24. Günther and Prevôt, *Die Wohlfahrtseinrichtungen der Arbeitgeber*, pp. 79–80.

25. Adelmann, *Quellensammlung*, 2:553–558.

26. Günther and Prevôt, *Die Wohlfahrtseinrichtungen der Arbeitgeber*, p. 87.

27. VdESI, Generalversammlung, 5 November 1913, BA, R 13 I/141, p. 32.

28. Lorenz Pieper, *Die Lage der Bergarbeiter im Ruhrrevier*, p. 63.

29. See, for example, Vortrag Dr. Woltmann zur Frage der Arbeitsverhält-

nisse in der Grosseisenindustrie, 1913, HA/GHH 300 140/16. Cf. David Montgomery, *Workers' Control in America*, pp. 139–152; and Peter Stearns, *Lives of Labor*, pp. 85–108.

30. Oberbürgermeister der Stadt Essen to RPr Düsseldorf, 20 October 1912, and Handelskammer für die Kreise Essen, Mülheim/Ruhr, und Oberhausen to RPr Düsseldorf, 20 October 1913, StAD, Reg. Düsseldorf, Präs. Büro, no. 1062; and Walter Bacmeister, *Emil Kirdorf*, p. 123.

31. Minister für Handel und Gewerbe to RPr Düsseldorf, 26 September 1913, StAD, Reg. Düsseldorf, Präs. Büro, no. 1062.

32. Günther and Prevôt, *Die Wohlfahrtseinrichtungen der Arbeitgeber*, p. 69.

33. Ibid., p. 61.

34. Heinrich Herkner, *Die Arbeiterfrage*, 1:424.

35. Adelmann, Quellensammlung, 2:37, 73.

36. Sitzung des Vorstandes des Bergbau Vereins, 20 July 1906, HA/GHH 301054/3 Arbeiterausschuss 1905–1919.

37. *Deutsche Bergwerks-Zeitung*, 26 June 1912.

38. Adelmann, *Quellensammlung*, 2:206.

39. *Deutsche Bergwerks-Zeitung*, 3 August 1912.

40. Fritz Mogs, "Die sozialgeschichtliche Entwicklung der Stadt Oberhausen (Rhld.) zwischen 1850 und 1933," p. 72; and Otto Neuloh, *Die deutsche Betriebsverfassung*, p. 161.

41. Adelmann, *Quellensammlung*, 2:428; and Günther and Prevôt, *Die Wohlfahrtseinrichtungen der Arbeitgeber*, pp. 130, 146.

Chapter 7: The Terms of Labor

1. Gerhard Bry, *Wages in Germany, 1871–1945*, pp. 342, 354, 358–359. The stagnation of real wages, or at least a decline in their growth rate, was not limited to Ruhr heavy industry, but characterized industry elsewhere in Germany and in other European countries. See Ashok V. Desai, *Real Wages in Germany, 1871–1913*, pp. 1–3.

2. Bry, *Wages in Germany*, pp. 111, 391, 434.

3. Ibid., p. 342.

4. Great Britain, Board of Trade, *Cost of Living in German Towns*, p. iv.

5. *Reichsarbeitsblatt* 5 (1906):246 and 12 (1913):227. The administrative subdivisions of the *Oberbergamtsbezirk* Dortmund included in the wage statistics of the northern Ruhr were Recklinghausen, Dortmund 2 and 3, North Bochum, Herne, Gelsenkirchen, Wattenscheid, East and West Essen, Oberhausen, and Duisburg. Included in the statistics of the southern Ruhr were Dortmund 1, Witten, Hattingen, South Bochum, South Essen, and Werden.

6. Gerhard Adelmann, *Quellensammlung zur Geschichte der sozialen Betriebsverfassung Ruhrindustrie unter besonderer Berücksichtigung des Industrie- und Handelskammerbezirks Essen*, 2:328.

7. Richard Ehrenberg and Hugo Racine, *Krupp'sche Arbeiterfamilien*, p. 392; and Wolfram Fischer, *Herz des Reviers*, p. 264.

8. Bry, *Wages in Germany*, pp. 363, 390.

9. See, for example, Bergbau Verein to Central-Vorstand des Gewerk-

Notes

vereins christlicher Bergarbeiter, 2 March 1897, in *Glückauf* 33 (6 March 1897):192–193. Cf. E. H. Phelps Brown, *The Growth of British Industrial Relations*, p. 125; and J. H. Porter, "Wage Bargaining under Conciliation Agreements, 1860–1914."

10. Otto Jeidels, *Die Methoden der Arbeiterentlohnung in der rheinisch-westfälischen Eisenindustrie*, p. 148.

11. Otto Heinemann, *Kronenorden Vierter Klasse*, p. 98.

12. See, for example, Adolf Levenstein, *Die Arbeiterfrage*, pp. 17–25.

13. *Glückauf* 43 (14 December 1907):1677.

14. *Glückauf* 43 (14 December 1907):1681; and *Schriften der Gesellschaft für Soziale Reform*, December 1908, pp. 113–118, 187.

15. Georg Werner, *Ein Kumpel*, pp. 126–128.

16. Anton Remke, "Betriebsorganisation und Arbeitsvollzüge im Eisen-Erzeugenden und Eisenverarbeitenden Betrieben des Ruhrgebiets 1840–1914," p. 63.

17. Hans Ehrenberg, *Die Eisenhüttentechnik und der deutsche Hüttenarbeiter*, pp. 146, 153.

18. Jeidels, *Methoden der Arbeiterentlohnung*, pp. 248–249.

19. *Reichsarbeitsblatt* 7 (21 December 1909):927.

20. Remke, "Betriebsorganisation und Arbeitsvollzüge," p. 61.

21. Jeidels, *Methoden der Arbeiterentlohnung*, pp. 31–32, 98.

22. Ibid., p. 126.

23. Heinemann, *Kronenorden Vierter Klasse*, p. 112.

24. Karl Wilke, *50 Jahre im Dienste des Ruhrbergbaus*, pp. 36–42.

25. Wolfram Bongartz, "Grossindustrie und Berufsqualifikation des mittleren technischen Personals," pp. 61–62; and Jeidels, *Methoden der Arbeiterentlohnung*, pp. 34–35.

26. Otto Neuloh, *Die deutsche Betriebsverfassung*, p. 172; and *Die Schwereisenindustrie im deutschen Zollgebiet*, p. 494.

27. For an example of one such work order, see Arbeitsordnung der Zeche Shamrock 1/2, Bergwerksgesellschaft Hibernia, 12 December 1892, StAM, Reg. Arnsberg 1, no. 41.

28. Jeidels, *Methoden der Arbeiterentlohnung*, p. 169.

29. *Aufsätze über den Streik der Bergarbeiter im Ruhrgebiet*, p. 20.

30. Lorenz Pieper, *Die Lage der Bergarbeiter im Ruhrrevier*, p. 76.

31. Jeidels, *Methoden der Arbeiterentlohnung*, p. 25.

32. Klaus Tenfelde, *Sozialgeschichte der Bergarbeiterschaft an der Ruhr im 19. Jahrhundert*, p. 250.

33. Report, OBA Dort., 21 January 1896, StAM, OBA Dort. B, group 119, no. 275.

34. StAM, OBA Dort. B, group 119, no. 275, pp. 276–277.

35. Ibid., pp. 280, 292.

36. See, for example, Neuloh, *Die deutsche Betriebsverfassung*, pp. 172–174; Fritz Quint, "50 Jahre Bergbau vom Kumpel gesehen," pp. 61, 68; and Werner, *Ein Kumpel*, pp. 38–39. Cf. Carl Jantke, *Bergmann und Zeche*, pp. 97–99, 132, for the same kinds of complaints being made by Ruhr miners more than a generation later.

37. Adelmann, *Quellensammlung*, 2:482.

38. Neuloh, *Die deutsche Betriebsverfassung*, pp. 156–158.

39. Ehrenberg and Racine, *Krupp'sche Arbeiterfamilien*, pp. 358–359.

Notes

40. Werner, *Ein Kumpel*, pp. 109–110.
41. Ehrenberg, *Die Eisenhüttentechnik*, pp. 121–122. See the biographies of Krupp *Meister* in Ehrenberg and Racine, *Krupp'sche Arbeiterfamilien*. See also Paul Reusch's recommendations for the training of prospective *Meister*, Reusch to F. Gohrum, 6 October 1906, HA/GHH 300 193 90/2 Reusch Nachlass: Schriftwechsel mit Verschieden 1906.
42. Bongartz, "Grossindustrie und Berufsqualifikation."
43. Donald Paul Panzera, "Organization, Authority, and Conflict in the Ruhr Coal Mining Industry," pp. 296–298; and W. Viebig, "Die technischen Grubenbeamten beim Steinkohlenbergbau im Oberbergamtsbezirk Dortmund," p. 1138.
44. Panzera, "Organization, Authority, and Conflict in the Ruhr Coal Mining Industry," pp. 293–294; and Viebig, "Die technischen Grubenbeamten," p. 1138.
45. *Glückauf* 49 (16 August 1913):1297.
46. Tenfelde, *Sozialgeschichte der Bergarbeiterschaft*, p. 297.
47. Bongartz, "Grossindustrie und Berufsqualifikation," pp. 61–62; Ehrenberg and Racine, *Krupp'sche Arbeiterfamilien*, pp. 33–72; Jeidels, *Methoden der Arbeiterentlohnung*, p. 35; and Panzera, "Organization, Authority, and Conflict in the Ruhr Coal Mining Industry," pp. 302–304.
48. Reusch to F. Gohrum, 6 October 1906, HA/GHH 300 193 90/2 Reusch Nachlass: Schriftwechsel mit Verschieden 1906.
49. Quint, "50 Jahre Bergbau," pp. 63–64; Zeche Oberhausen, Rundschreiben, 13 November 1903, and H. V. to Bergwerks-Abteilung 1, 15 September 1908, HA/GHH 30103/0 Bergwerksverwaltung: Rundschreiben und Verfügungen, 1901–1908.
50. See, for example, HA/GHH 30103/0 Bergwerksverwaltung: Rundschreiben und Verfügungen, 1901–1908. See also the accounts of two of the men responsible for these more elaborate reporting systems: Heinemann, *Kronenorden Vierter Klasse*; and Wilke, *50 Jahre im Dienste des Ruhrbergbaus*.
51. Walter Bacmeister, *Gustav Knepper*, p. 31. For traditional *Steiger* hours, see Werner, *Ein Kumpel*, p. 118.
52. Kocks, Verfügungen, 17 November 1904 and 27 June 1905, HA/GHH 30103/0 Bergwerksverwaltung: Rundschreiben und Verfügungen, 1901–1908.
53. Viebig, "Die technischen Grubenbeamten," p. 1137.
54. Neuloh, *Die deutsche Betriebsverfassung*, p. 142. Cf. Jürgen Kocka, *Unternehmensverwaltung und Angestelltenschaft am Beispiel Siemens 1847–1914*, pp. 339–347.
55. Ehrenberg, *Die Eisenhüttentechnik*, p. 116.
56. Heinemann, *Kronenorden Vierter Klasse*, pp. 95–96, 100, 179.
57. Adelmann, *Quellensammlung*, 2:328.
58. Viebig, "Die technischen Grubenbeamten," pp. 1136–1137.
59. Werner, *Ein Kumpel*, pp. 173–185.
60. Wilhelm Henning, *Geschichte der Stadtverordnetenversammlung von Essen, 1890–1914*, p. 62.
61. Bacmeister, *Gustav Knepper*, p. 48.
62. Quint, "50 Jahre Bergbau," pp. 69–71.
63. Adelmann, *Quellensammlung*, 2:302–306.
64. Ibid., p. 307.
65. *Jahresbericht des Vereins für die bergbaulichen Interessen im Oberbergamtsbezirk Dortmund für das Jahr 1900*, p. 27.

66. Stephen Hickey, "Bergmannsarbeit an der Ruhr vor dem Ersten Weltkrieg," pp. 53–54; and Pieper, *Die Lage der Bergarbeiter*, pp. 23–26.
67. HA/GHH 30100/27 Teilstreik auf Zeche Oberhausen, 1904.
68. *Aufsätze über den Streik der Bergarbeiter im Ruhrgebiet*, pp. 12–22.
69. Bacmeister, *Gustav Knepper*, p. 48; and H. A. Bueck, *Der Centralverband deutscher Industrieller, 1876–1901*, 3:627.
70. RPr Arnsberg to the Minister des Innern and to the Minister für Handel und Gewerbe, 5 December 1904, StAD, Reg. Düsseldorf, no. 15924.
71. Gert von Klass, *Hugo Stinnes*, p. 135.
72. RPr Düsseldorf to OPr Koblenz, 28 December 1904, StAM, OBA Dort. B, group 119, no. 283, p. 100.
73. Klass, *Hugo Stinnes*, p. 135.
74. *Aufsätze über den Streik der Bergarbeiter im Ruhrgebiet*, pp. 27–28.
75. Proposal for conferring the title of *Geheimer Kommerzienrat* on Emil Goecke, 14 May 1905, StAK, OP Koblenz 403/9889; and Jeidels, *Methoden der Arbeiterentlohung*, p. 273.

Chapter 8: Conflict and Readjustment

1. *Stenographischer Bericht der 47. Generalversammlung des Vereins für die bergbaulichen Interessen im Oberbergamtsbezirk Dortmund*, 2 Juni 1905, p. 6
2. Meeting of Oberberghauptmann von Velsen and Berghauptmann Baur with representatives of the Bergbau Verein, 14 January 1905, StAM, OBA Dort. B, group 119, no. 288, pp. 18–20.
3. Bergbau Verein to Johann Effert, Essen, 14 January 1905, StAM, OBA Dort. B, group 119, no. 288, pp. 38–39.
4. Alex Bein and Hans Goldschmidt, *Friedrich Hammacher*, p. 152.
5. RPr Arnsberg to Minister des Innern, 25 January 1905, StAD, Reg. Düsseldorf, Präs. Büro, no. 841.
6. Günther Brakelmann, "Evangelische Pfarrer im Konfliktsfeld des Ruhrbergarbeiterstreiks von 1905"; Donald Rosenberg, "The Ruhr Coal Strike and the Prussian Mining Law of 1905," pp. 76–92; and *Stenographische Berichte über die Verhandlungen des Reichstags*, 20, 21, and 23 January 1905, 2 Leg. Per., 1 Session, 1903–1905, vol. 5, pp. 3903–3994.
7. *Aufsätze über den Streik der Bergarbeiter im Ruhrgebiet*, p. 37.
8. *Correspondenzblatt der Generalkommission der Gewerkschaften Deutschlands* 15 (9 September 1905):587. See also Kirdorf's complaint about the failure of the south German textile industrialists in the Centralverband to appreciate the soundness of the uncompromising stance of heavy industry in 1905, quoted in Hartmut Kaelble, *Industrielle Interessenpolitik in der Wilhelminischen Gesellschaft*, p. 75.
9. Bernard Fürst von Bülow, *Denkwürdigkeiten*, 2:90; Hans Georg Kirchhoff, *Die staatliche Sozialpolitik im Ruhrbergbau, 1871–1914*, pp. 145–146; Klaus Saul, "Staatsintervention und Arbeitskampf im Wilhelminischen Reich, 1904–1914," pp. 488, 490; and Hans Jürgen Teuteberg, *Geschichte der industriellen Mitbestimmung in Deutschland*, pp. 430–433.
10. Charles Medalen, "State Monopoly Capitalism in Germany."
11. Landrat des Kreises Ruhrort to RPr Düsseldorf, 22 January 1905,

Notes

StAD, Reg. Düsseldorf, Präs. Büro, no. 841; Justizminister to Oberlandesgerichtspräsident in Hamm, 28 January 1905, StAD, Reg. Düsseldorf, no. 15925; and Minister des Innern to RPr Düsseldorf, 4 February 1905, StAD, Reg. Düsseldorf, no. 15926.

12. Karl Erich Born, *Staat und Sozialpolitik seit Bismarcks Sturz*, p. 185.

13. RPr Arnsberg to Minister des Innern, 20 January 1905, and OBA Dort. to Minister für Handel und Gewerbe, 21 January 1905, StAD, Reg. Düsseldorf, Präs. Büro, no. 841.

14. For one such demand, see Bergwerksdirektor Eugen Kleine to Gelsenkirchener Bergwerks-AG, in *Glückauf* 41 (1905):228.

15. Landrat des Kreises Ruhrort to RPr Düsseldorf, 20 January 1905, StAD, Reg. Düsseldorf, Präs. Büro, no. 841.

16. Teuteberg, *Geschichte der industriellen Mitbestimmung*, pp. 435-438.

17. *Stenographischer Bericht der 47. Generalversammlung des Vereins für die bergbaulichen Interessen im Oberbergamtsbezirk Dortmund*, 2 Juni 1905, p. 6.

18. *Stenographischer Bericht der 48. Generalversammlung des Vereins für die bergbaulichen Interessen im Oberbergamtsbezirk Dortmund*, 27 Juni 1906, p. 14.

19. Helmut Böhme, "Emil Kirdorf," pp. 28-34; and Kirchhoff, *Die staatliche Sozialpolitik im Ruhrbergbau*, p. 146. For the circumstances of Kirdorf's resignation from the leadership of the Bergbau Verein, see *Rheinisch-Westfälische Zeitung*, 28 April 1906.

20. Landrat des Kreises Ruhrort, 25 January 1905, StAD, Reg. Düsseldorf, Präs. Büro, no. 841; Landrat des Kreises Ruhrort, 11 February 1905, StAD, Reg. Düsseldorf, no. 15925; and Landrat des Kreises Ruhrort, 2 March 1905, StAD, Reg. Düsseldorf, no. 15926.

21. Landrat des Kreises Essen, 3 and 11 February 1905, StAD, Reg. Düsseldorf, no. 15925.

22. Bergbau Verein, Rundschreiben, 30 January 1905, Bergbau Archiv 18/69; and RPr Münster to Minister des Innern, 12 February 1905, StAD, Reg. Düsseldorf, no. 15925.

23. Report, RPr Arnsberg, 13 February 1905, StAD, Reg. Düsseldorf, no. 15925; and Wilhelm Henning, *Geschichte der Stadtverordnetenversammlung von Essen, 1890-1914*, p. 37.

24. Georg Werner, *Ein Kumpel*, p. 151.

25. Report, RPr Arnsberg, 13 February 1905, and Report, Polizeiverwaltung Essen, 15 February 1905, StAD, Reg. Düsseldorf, no. 15925.

26. Klaus Tenfelde and Heinrich Volkmann, eds., *Streik*, pp. 304-305.

27. Heinrich Herkner, *Die Arbeiterfrage*, 1:459; Klaus Saul, *Staat, Industrie, Arbeiterbewegung im Kaiserreich*, p. 106; and Donald Warren, *The Red Kingdom of Saxony*, pp. 41-43.

28. H. A. Bueck, *Der Centralverband deutscher Industrieller, 1876-1901*, 3:600-601; and Gerhard Kessler, *Die deutschen Arbeitgeberverbände*, p. 40.

29. Kessler, *Die deutschen Arbeitgeberverbände*, p. 47.

30. Herkner, *Die Arbeiterfrage*, 1:460; Saul, *Staat, Industrie, Arbeiterbewegung*, pp. 109-110; and Warren, *The Red Kingdom of Saxony*, pp. 44-45.

31. *25 Jahre Arbeitnordwest, 1904-1929*, p. 26.

32. *Berichte der Hauptstelle deutscher Arbeitgeberverbände*, 2:29.

33. *25 Jahre Arbeitnordwest*, p. 26.

34. Ibid., p. 36.

35. Paul Osthold, *Die Geschichte des Zechenverbandes, 1908–1933*, p. 23.
36. See Emil Kirdorf, "Das Verhältnis der Kartelle zum Staat," pp. 287–288.
37. Tenfelde and Volkmann, eds., *Streik*, pp. 308–309.
38. Willi Boelcke, ed., *Krupp und die Hohenzollern*, p. 124.
39. *Deutsche Bergwerks-Zeitung*, 27 May 1906; and Clemens Heiss, "Die gelbe Arbeiterbewegung," p. 339.
40. Adolf Weber, *Der Kampf zwischen Kapital und Arbeit*, pp. 303–305; and *25 Jahre Arbeitnordwest*, p. 23.
41. Saul, *Staat, Industrie, Arbeiterbewegung*, pp. 83–84.
42. *Geschäftsbericht des Arbeitgeberverbandes für den Bezirk der Nordwestlichen Gruppe des Vereins deutscher Eisen- und Stahlindustrieller*, 5:9–10.
43. Report, Königlicher Bergrevierbeamte, Recklinghausen, 12 March 1910, StAM, OBA Dort. B, group 119, no. 279; and Gerhard Adelmann, *Quellensammlung zur Geschichte der sozialen Betriebsverfassung Ruhrindustrie unter besonderer Berücksichtigung des Industrie- und Handelskammerbezirks Essen*, 1:277, 293.
44. Königlicher Landrat des Kreises Ruhrort to RPr Düsseldorf, 14 November 1905, StAD, Reg. Düsseldorf, no. 15933.
45. Maura Kealey, "Kampfstrategien der Unternehmerschaft im Ruhrbergbau seit dem Bergarbeiterstreik von 1889," pp. 185–188; Königlicher Landrat des Kreises Ruhrort to RPr Düsseldorf, 14 November 1905, StAD, Reg. Düsseldorf, no. 15933; and Knepper, Deutsch-Luxemburgische Bergwerks-und Hütten-AG, to Gilges, Zeche Friedlicher Nachbar, 13 June 1907, quoted in *Correspondenzblatt* 18 (13 June 1908):371.
46. For the statutes of the Zechenverband, see StAK, OP Koblenz 403/8174.
47. Heiss, "Die gelbe Arbeiterbewegung," p. 339; and Osthold, *Die Geschichte des Zechenverbandes*, p. 49.
48. *Kölnische Zeitung*, 14 October 1909.
49. *Deutsche Bergwerks-Zeitung*, 31 January 1909.
50. Rundschreiben, 12 January 1909, Bergbau Archiv 13/880 Zechenverband.
51. Kessler, *Die Arbeitsnachweise der Arbeitgeberverbände*, p. 37.
52. *Rheinisch-Westfälische Zeitung*, 30 November 1909.
53. Kessler, *Die Arbeitsnachweise der Arbeitgeberverbände*, p. 135; and *Soziale Praxis* 19 (13 January 1910), col. 380.
54. Kessler, *Die Arbeitsnachweise der Arbeitgeberverbände*, p. 176.
55. Osthold, *Die Geschichte des Zechenverbandes*, p. 81.
56. Phoenix to Hoff, 2 June 1914, Firmenarchiv Mannesmann R 8 10 26, pp. 246–247.
57. Teuteberg, *Geschichte der industriellen Mitbestimmung*, pp. 362–387, 410–415.
58. *Stahl und Eisen* 30 (1910):483.
59. Peter Rassow and Karl Erich Born, *Akten zur staatlichen Sozialpolitik in Deutschland, 1890–1914*, pp. 255–256. See also Carl Lueg quoted in Klaus Mattheier, *Die Gelben*, pp. 72, 84.
60. Teuteberg, *Geschichte der industriellen Mitbestimmung*, p. 437.
61. StAM, OBA Dort. B, group 119, no. 289, pp. 283–284, 297–298; and

Rundschreiben 46 des Bergbau Vereins, 27 October 1905, HA/GHH 301054/3 Arbeiterausschuss 1905–1919, Zeche Sterkrade.

62. Sitzung des Vorstandes des Bergbau Vereins, 20 July 1906 HA/GHH 301054/3 Arbeiterausschuss 1905–1919, Zeche Sterkrade.

63. Bergassessor Hilgenstock, "Über Lohntarife im britischen und rheinisch-westfälischen Steinkohlenbergbau," pp. 1679–1680.

64. For protocols of meetings of worker committees, see StAM, OBA Dort. B., group 119, no. 289–290; Bergbau Archiv 18/79; and HA/GHH 30 10 52/13 and 30 10 54/3.

65. Sitzung des Vorstandes des Bergbau Vereins, 20 July 1906, HA/GHH 30 10 54/3 Arbeiterausschuss 1905–1919, Zeche Sterkrade.

66. Otto Jeidels, *Die Methoden der Arbeiterentlohnung in der rheinisch-westfälischen Eisenindustrie*, p. 265.

67. See, for example, HA/GHH 300 193 009/4 Beschwerden 1910–1923.

68. *Glückauf* 41 (17 June 1905).

69. Jeidels, *Die Methoden der Arbeiterentlohnung*, p. 242.

70. Hoff to Reusch, 9 April 1909, and Reusch and Zillessen to Arbeitgeberverband, 22 April 1909, HA/GHH 300 143/1 Öffentliche Arbeiterversammlungen betreffend die Zustände in der Kaserne des Walzwerks Oberhausen 1909; and *25 Jahre Arbeitnordwest*, p. 52.

71. Gutehoffnungshütte to sämtliche Werksabteilungen, 25 May 1905, HA/GHH 30103/0 Bergwerksverwaltung: Rundschreiben und Verfügungen.

72. Besprechung der Bergbau Vereine, 6 January 1909, StAD, Reg. Düsseldorf, no. 15934, p. 10.

73. Verwaltungsbericht des OBA Dort., 1908, StAK, OP Koblenz 403/8176, p. 121.

Chapter 9: Containment

1. Hans Ehrenberg, *Die Eisenhüttentechnik und der deutsche Hüttenarbeiter*, p. 114; Great Britain, Board of Trade, *Cost of Living in German Towns*, p. 235; Otto Neuloh, *Die deutsche Betriebsverfassung*, p. 175; and *Die Schwereisenindustrie im deutschen Zollgebiet*, p. 518.

2. Gerhard Adelmann, *Quellensammlung zur Geschichte der sozialen Betriebsverfassung Ruhrindustrie unter besonderer Berücksichtigung des Industrie- und Handelskammerbezirks Essen*, 2:255; and *Reichsarbeitsblatt* 10 (21 June 1912):428.

3. VdESI, petition addressed to Reichstag and Landtag deputies and to government officials, 21 November 1912, BA, R 13 I/177, p. 2; and Vortrag Dr. Woltmann zur Frage der Arbeitsverhältnisse in der Grosseisenindustrie, Verein deutsche Eisenhütteleute, 1913, HA/GHH 300 140/16.

4. NW Gruppe des VdESI to Hochofen, Hütten- und Walzwerke der Gruppe, 28 December 1907, HA/GHH 300 140/4 Untersuchung über die Lage der Hüttenarbeiter 1906–1908.

5. *Reichsarbeitsblatt* 7 (21 December 1909):925.

6. VdESI, Generalversammlung, 23 November 1909, BA, R 13 I/139, p. 46.

7. Report, Gewerbeinspektor, Mülheim/Ruhr, 16 March 1909, StAD, Reg. Düsseldorf, no. 24582.
8. VdESI, Generalversammlung, 23 November 1909, BA, R 13 I/139, p. 45; *Die Schwereisenindustrie im deutschen Zollgebiet*, p. 613; and Reg. Köln to RPr Düsseldorf, 18 June 1909, StAD, Reg. Düsseldorf, no. 33389.
9. *Soziale Praxis* 18 (13 May 1909): col. 882.
10. VdESI, Rundschreiben, 6 March 1911, BA, R 13 I/175.
11. Hans Jürgen Teuteberg, *Geschichte der industriellen Mitbestimmung in Deutschland*, p. 457.
12. Besprechung der Bergbau Vereine über Abänderung des Allgemeinen Berggesetzes, 6 January 1909, StAD, Reg. Düsseldorf, no. 15934.
13. For examples of obstructionist tactics, see Donald Paul Panzera, "Organization, Authority, and Conflict in the Ruhr Coal Mining Industry," pp. 477–480.
14. Adelmann, *Quellensammlung*, 1:404–423 and 2:228–229, 233; and Teuteberg, *Geschichte der industriellen Mitbestimmung*, p. 461.
15. *Stenographischer Bericht der 1. ordentlichen Hauptversammlung des Zechenverbandes, 16 Mai 1908*, p. 11.
16. Teuteberg, *Geschichte der industriellen Mitbestimmung*, pp. 472–482.
17. Hartmut Kaelble, *Industrielle Interessenpolitik in der Wilhelminischen Gesellschaft*, p. 192.
18. VdESI, Generalversammlung, 10 December 1912, BA, R 13 I/83, pp. 7–8.
19. Dirk Stegmann, *Die Erben Bismarcks*, pp. 147, 160. For objections to the use of Bergbau Verein funds for electoral purposes, see Bergbau Verein to Firma Thyssen, 15 January 1907, Firmenarchiv August-Thyssen-Hütte, Sekretariat Fritz Thyssen, Kammern und Verbände, 11. Verein für die bergbaulichen Interessen, 1907–1921. Thyssen was assured that the Bergbau Verein was not using any of its own funds but was only collecting voluntary contributions. Thus placated, the company withrew its threats to quit the association and take the matter to the press.
20. Willi Boelcke, ed., *Krupp und die Hohenzollern*, p. 90. For investment by Ruhr industrialists in the *Berliner Neueste Nachrichten*, see HA/GHH 300 106/5 Berliner Neueste Nachrichten 1900–1903; and Stegmann, *Die Erben Bismarcks*, pp. 166–167.
21. Ludwig Bernhard, *Der Hugenberg-Konzern*, p. 57; Dankwart Guratzsch, *Macht durch Organisation*, pp. 187–188; and Stegmann, *Die Erben Bismarcks*, pp. 166–174.
22. Guratzsch, *Macht durch Organisation*, pp. 105, 109–110; Stegmann, *Die Erben Bismarcks*, p. 437; and Reusch to Woltmann, 19 January 1912, HA/GHH 300 193 003/11 Schriftwechsel Reusch-Woltmann.
23. Reusch to Haniel, 4 and 7 May 1914, HA/GHH 300 193 000/12 Schriftwechsel Reusch-Franz Haniel, vol. 2, 1912–1916.
24. Guratzsch, *Macht durch Organisation*, pp. 85, 117; and Stegmann, "Hugenberg contra Stresemann," p. 347.
25. Bernhard, *Der Hugenberg-Konzern*, pp. 53–56; Valeska Dietrich, "Alfred Hugenberg," p. 21; and Stegmann, *Die Erben Bismarcks*, p. 358.
26. Max Roetger, 15 October 1909, in *Verhandlungen, Mitteilungen und Berichte des Centralverbandes deutscher Industrieller*, 116:6–13. See also Kaelble, *Industrielle Interessenpolitik*, p. 76; Siegfried Mielke, *Der Hansa-Bund für*

Notes

Gewerbe, Handel und Industrie 1909–1914, pp. 60, 268–269; and Stegmann, *Die Erben Bismarcks*, pp. 190–191.

27. Mielke, *Der Hansa-Bund*, p. 249.
28. *Deutsche Bergwerks-Zeitung*, 4 September 1910; Mielke, *Der Hansa-Bund*, pp. 35, 95; and *Stenographischer Bericht über die Versammlung vom 12. 6. 1909 im Zirkus Schumann zu Berlin betreffend Reichsfinanzreform und Gründung des Hansabundes*, pp. 31–32.
29. Mielke, *Der Hansa-Bund*, p. 88; and Stegmann, "Hugenberg contra Stresemann," pp. 344–345.
30. *Deutsche Bergwerks-Zeitung*, 25 June and 2 July 1911 and 16 June 1912.
31. Wolfram Fischer, *Herz des Reviers*, p. 242.
32. Vorstandssitzung der Deutsche Vereinigung, 2 March 1912, HA/GHH 300 193 26/25 Deutsche Vereinigung, vol. 1, 1909–1915.
33. Klaus Saul, *Staat, Industrie, Arbeiterbewegung im Kaiserreich*, pp. 339–345.
34. Hans-Jürgen Puhle, *Agrarische Interessenpolitik und preussicher Konservatismus im wilhelminischen Reich, 1893–1914*, p. 163.
35. Mielke, *Der Hansa-Bund*, pp. 174, 185.
36. Kaelble, *Industrielle Interessenpolitik*, p. 135; Saul, *Staat, Industrie, Arbeiterbewegung*, p. 541; and Stegmann, "Hugenberg contra Stresemann," p. 357.
37. *Soziale Praxis* 18 (18 March 1909): col. 661, and 22 (24 April 1913): col. 867.
38. Saul, *Staat, Industrie, Arbeiterbewegung*, p. 361.
39. Karl Erich Born, Hansjoachim Henning, and Manfred Schick, *Quellensammlung zur Geschichte der deutschen Sozialpolitik von 1867 bis 1914*, p. 165; and Klaus Tenfelde and Heinrich Volkmann, eds., *Streik*, pp. 304–305.
40. Karl Gustav Werner, *Organisation und Politik der Gewerkschaften und Arbeitgeberverbände in der deutschen Baugewerbe*. See also Ernst Schröder, *Otto Wiedfeldt*.
41. David F. Crew, "Steel, Sabotage and Socialism."
42. Reusch to Woltmann, 2 November 1911, HA/GHH 300 193 003/11 Schriftwechsel Reusch-Woltmann.
43. Gerhard A. Ritter, *Die Arbeiterbewegung im Wilhelminischen Reich*, p. 70.
44. Emil Kirdorf, "Das Verhältnis der Kartelle zum Staat," p. 289; and Hauptversammlung des Zechenverbandes, 27 May 1911, Bergbau Archiv 13/511, pp. 8–9.
45. Sitzung des Geschäftsausschusses des Zechenverbandes, 5 December 1910, Bergbau Archiv 13/511.
46. *Kölnische Zeitung*, 8 December 1910.
47. Löwenstein's draft and the letters from Kleine and Stinnes, both dated 12 December 1910, Bergbau Archiv 13/511.
48. *Bergarbeiter-Zeitung*, 28 October 1911; and Akten-Notiz Löwenstein, 1911, Bergbau Archiv 13/511.
49. *Deutsche Bergwerks-Zeitung*, 16 March 1912.
50. Sitzungen des Geschäftsausschusses des Zechenverbandes, 12 and 27 February 1912, Bergbau Archiv 13/511; and Report, RPr Arnsberg, 12 March 1912, StAM, OBA Dort. B, group 119, no. 297.

51. *Deutsche Bergwerks-Zeitung*, 6 and 7 March 1912. Secretary of the Interior Clemens Delbrück reported to the Reichstag that meetings were not held at 21 mines but were held at 105 others. *Stenographische Berichte über die Verhandlungen des Reichstags*, 12 March 1912, 13 Leg. Per., 1 Session, 26 Sitzung, vol. 283, p. 642.

52. Reusch to Haniel, 12 March 1912, HA/GHH 300 193 000/0 Schriftwechsel Reusch-Haniel, 1908–1912; and Bergarbeiterausstand 1912, 12 March 1912, HA/GHH 301054/7 Zeche Sterkrade.

53. See, for example, Sitzung des Arbeiterausschusses des Schachtes Helene, 12 March 1912, Bergbau Archiv 20/312 Krupp Bergbau.

54. Sitzung des Arbeiterausschusses des Schachtes Amalie, 14 March 1912, Bergbau Archiv 20/312 Krupp Bergbau.

55. Dieter Fricke, "Eine Denkschrift Krupps aus dem Jahre 1912 über den Schutz der 'Arbeitswilligen,'" p. 1250.

56. Adelmann, *Quellensammlung*, 1:295; Krawehl to Polizeikommissar des Polizeireviers 8, Essen-West, 9 March 1912, Bergbau Archiv 20/312 Krupp Bergbau; and Reusch to Haniel, 12 March 1912, HA/GHH 300 193 000/0 Schriftwechsel Reusch-Haniel, 1908–1912. On the cooperation of the state and Ruhr employers in 1912, see Saul, *Staat, Industrie, Arbeiterbewegung*, pp. 269–282.

57. Erich Hoffmann, *Dr. Francis Kruse*, pp. 80–81.

58. Direktion, Zeche Helene & Amalie, to Kgl. Polizei-Kommissar Kappelrele, Essen-West, Polizei-Revier 8, and to Polizei-Kommissar Petersen, Altenessen, Polizei-Revier 16, 23 March 1912, Bergbau Archiv 20/312 Krupp Bergbau.

59. *Rheinisch-Westfälische Zeitung*, 18 September 1912.

60. Klaus Tenfelde, "Gewalt und Konfliktregelung in den Arbeitskämpfen der Ruhrbergleute bis 1918," p. 217; and Polizei-Präsident Essen to Krawehl, 6 and 16 January 1911, Bergbau Archiv 20/312 Krupp Bergbau.

61. Saul, *Staat, Industrie, Arbeiterbewegung*, p. 307.

62. *Deutsche Bergwerks-Zeitung*, 14 March 1912.

63. Reusch, 9 March 1912, HA/GHH 30100/6 Bergarbeiterausstand 1912.

64. Otto Krawehl to Polizei-Präsident, Essen, 12 January 1911, Bergbau Archiv 20/312 Krupp Bergbau.

65. Adelmann, *Quellensammlung*, 1:213; and Report, RPr Münster, 21 March 1912, StAD, Reg. Düsseldorf, Präs. Büro, no. 851. How frequently this fine was imposed depended upon how strong management felt vis-à-vis labor. Thus, in 1908, a recession year, the fine was used more often than in the prosperous years just past. Verwaltungsbericht des OBA Dort. für das Jahr 1908, StAK, OP Koblenz 403/8176, p. 85.

66. *Deutsche Bergwerks-Zeitung*, 12 April 1912.

67. Report, RPr Arnsberg, 18 March 1912, StAD, Reg. Düsseldorf, Präs. Büro, no. 851.

68. *Deutsche Bergwerks-Zeitung*, 13 March 1912.

69. Report, RPr Arnsberg, 18 March 1912, StAD, Reg. Düsseldorf, Präs. Büro, no. 851; *Deutsche Bergwerks-Zeitung*, 16 March 1912; and Direktion, Zeche Helene & Amalie, to Betriebsführer, 28 March 1912, Bergbau Archiv 20/312 Krupp Bergbau.

70. Adelmann, *Quellensammlung*, 1:296, 298.

71. Konferenz betreffend die Verbandsbewegung unter den Technikern, 24 October 1911, and Gutehoffnungshütte to NW Gruppe des VdESI, 27 October 1911, HA/GHH 300 10 38/1 Deutscher Techniker-Verband.

Notes

72. Gutehoffnungshütte to Oberbürgermeister Wallraff, Cologne, 11 November 1911, HA/GHH 300 193 24/0 Technikerbewegung.

73. Bericht über eine vom Gesamtverband deutsche Metallindustrieller einberufene Sitzung in Berlin, 30 October 1911, HA/GHH 300 10 38/1 Deutscher Techniker-Verband. For similar developments at Siemens see Jürgen Kocka, *Unternehmensverwaltung und Angestelltenschaft am Beispiel Siemens 1847–1914*, p. 508. Efforts in the Ruhr to increase the distance between salaried and nonsalaried employees paralleled national developments that found their most significant expression in the social insurance law of 1911 which established separate coverage for the two groups. See Kocka, *Die Angestellten in der deutschen Geschichte 1850–1980*, pp. 83–89.

74. Abt. Sch. to various Abt., 15 November 1911, HA/GHH 30 10 3/1 Rundschreiben und Verfügungen, 1908–1911.

75. Saul, *Staat, Industrie, Arbeiterbewegung*, p. 81.

76. Hoff, Arbeitgeber-Verband NW, Rundschreiben 5/12, 8 May 1912, Hoff to Poensgen, 24 July 1912, and Vielhaber, Krupp Direktorium, to Hoff, 27 July 1914, Firmenarchiv Mannesmann R 8 10 26, pp. 1, 267–268, 271–273.

Chapter 10: Unsolved Problems

1. Christoph Klessmann, "Klassensolidarität und nationales Bewusstsein," p. 156; and Klaus J. Mattheier, *Die Gelben*, pp. 133–135.

2. Gerhard Adelmann, *Quellensammlung zur Geschichte der sozialen Betriebsverfassung Ruhrindustrie unter besonderer Berücksichtigung des Industrie- und Handelskammerbezirks Essen*, 1:180; and Clemens Heiss, "Die gelbe Arbeiterbewegung," pp. 347–352.

3. Mattheier, *Die Gelben*, p. 267.

4. Verbandsversammlung, 8 December 1909, *Berichte der Hauptstelle deutscher Arbeitgeberverbände*, 7:71–72.

5. Mattheier, *Die Gelben*, p. 215.

6. *Kölnische Zeitung*, 30 May 1912; and Mattheier, *Die Gelben*, pp. 201–202. For lists of company unions in the Ruhr, see the reports of the Polizei-Präsidenten of Essen and Bochum, 25 October 1912, StAD, Reg. Düsseldorf, no. 15923.

7. See, for example, Hugenberg's speech before the Krupp company union, quoted in *Düsseldorfer Zeitung*, 3 February 1911, clipping in StAD, Reg. Düsseldorf, no. 15923.

8. Mattheier, *Die Gelben*, p. 191.

9. Krupp circular, quoted in Kurt Stenkewitz, *Gegen Bajonett und Dividende*, p. 185.

10. Hartmut Kaelble, *Industrielle Interessenpolitik in der Wilhelminischen Gesellschaft*, p. 56; and Fritz Mogs, "Die sozialgeschichtliche Entwicklung der Stadt Oberhausen (Rhld.) zwischen 1850 und 1933," pp. 135–136.

11. Klaus Saul, *Staat, Industrie, Arbeiterbewegung im Kaiserreich*, p. 143.

12. Reusch to Hasslacher, 6 April 1912, HA/GHH 300 193 90/14 Schriftwechsel Reusch-Hasslacher.

13. Otto Neuloh uses the term associative welfare to describe such efforts. See his "Sozialpolitik im grossbetrieblichen Industriesystem."

Notes

14. Bekanntmachung, 15 June 1909, HA/GHH 301052/14 Zeche Vondern: Wohlfahrtseinrichtungen 1908–1926.
15. *Deutsche Bergwerks-Zeitung*, 25 April 1912; and Verwaltungsbericht des OBA Dort. für das Jahr 1909, StAK, OP Koblenz 403/8176, p. 89.
16. Klessmann, *Polnische Bergarbeiter im Ruhrgebiet 1870–1945*, p. 270.
17. *Glückauf* 50 (1914):848.
18. Dankwart Guratzsch, *Macht durch Organisation*, pp. 93, 199; and Gregor Schöllgen, "Sozialpolitik im Kaiserreich."
19. Gutehoffnungshütte to Kgl. Staatsanwaltschaft Duisburg, 1 May 1909, HA/GHH 300 143/1 Öffentliche Arbeiterversammlung betreffend die Zustände in der Kaserne des Walzwerks Oberhausen 1909.
20. Otto Heinemann, *Kronenorden Vierter Klasse*, p. 111; and *Soziale Praxis* 22 (26 November 1912): cols. 372–373.
21. Jürgen Reulecke, "Vom blauen Montag zum Arbeiterurlaub."
22. An die Herrn Mitglieder der Unterkommission des Zechenverbandes, 8 July 1912, Bergbau Archiv 13/698 Zechenverband.
23. Report, Landrat des Kreises Ruhrort, 6 March 1906, StAD, Reg. Düsseldorf, no. 24701.
24. Vorstand Bochumer Bergwerks-AG, Zeche ver. Präsident, to Bergbau Verein, 25 March 1908, Bergbau Archiv 13/698 Zechenverband.
25. Harpener Bergbau AG to Centralverband deutscher Industrieller, 8 December 1910, Bergbau Archiv 13/698 Zechenverband.
26. Sitzung des Arbeiterausschusses der Zeche König Ludwig, Schachtanlage 1/3, 31 October 1912, Bergbau Archiv 13/698 Zechenverband.
27. Bergbau Verein, 5 January 1911, Bergbau Archiv 13/698 Zechenverband.
28. An die Herrn Mitglieder der Unterkommission des Zechenverbandes, 8 July 1912, Bergbau Archiv 13/698 Zechenverband.
29. Sitzung des Arbeiterausschusses des Schachtes Amalie, 14 March 1912, Bergbau Archiv 20/312 Krupp Bergbau.
30. Bergbau Gesellschaft Neu-Essen to Randebrock, 2 April 1912, Zechenverband to Essener Bergwerks-Verein König Wilhelm, 16 April 1912, Sitzungen des Bezirks Essen des Zechenverbandes, 25 April and 20 June 1912, and Sitzung des Vorstandes des Zechenverbandes, 15 May 1912, Bergbau Archiv 13/698 Zechenverband.
31. Sitzung des Geschäftsausschusses des Zechenverbandes, 28 October 1912, Bergbau Archiv 13/698 Zechenverband.
32. Krupp Direktorium to Vorstand des Nationalen Arbeitervereins, 5 August 1912, quoted in *Correspondenzblatt der Generalkommission der Gewerkschaften Deutschlands* 22 (17 August 1912):487.
33. *Kruppische Mitteilungen*, 15 and 29 March 1913, in Bergbau Archiv 13/698 Zechenverband.
34. Zeche Helene & Amalie to Verein für die bergbaulichen Interessen, 25 June 1914, Bergbau Archiv 13/698 Zechenverband.
35. See, for example, Zechenverband to Deutscher Kaiser, 18 March 1914, Bergbau Archiv 13/698 Zechenverband.
36. *Die Schwereisenindustrie im deutschen Zollgebeit*, p. 150.
37. Friedrich Syrup, "Die Arbeitszeit in der Grosseisenindustrie."
38. *Die Schwereisenindustrie im deutschen Zollgebeit*, pp. 618–620.
39. VdESI, petition to Reichstag, 21 November 1912, BA, R 13 I/177.

Notes

40. VdESI, circular to members, 3 June 1913, BA, R 13 I/178.
41. Reusch to Woltmann, 5 May 1914, HA/GHH 300 193 003/11 Schriftwechsel Reusch-Woltmann.
42. VdESI, Hauptvorstand, 14 January 1914, BA, R 13 I/142.
43. VdESI, Hauptvorstand, 5 November 1913, BA, R 13 I/141, p. 239.
44. VdESI, Generalversammlung, 5 November 1913, BA, R 13 I/141, pp. 51–52.
45. VdESI, Hauptvorstand, 5 November 1913, BA, R 13 I/141.
46. HA/GHH 300 140/16 Vortrag Dr. Woltmann zur Frage der Arbeitsverhältnisse in der Grosseisenindustrie, 1913, pp. 32–33; and Verhandlungen der Kommission zur Untersuchung der Frage der 24-stündigen Wechselschicht bei der Gutehoffnungshütte, 6 June 1914, HA/GHH 300 193 009/13 Abänderung der Bundesratverordnung vom 19.12.1908 betreffend Überarbeit in der Grossindustrie, 1912–1914, pp. 37–38.
47. Arbeitgeberverband für den Bezirk der NW Gruppe des VdESI, Rundschreiben 26/13, 20 November 1913, HA/GHH 300 193 24/8 Arbeiterverband, vol. 1, 1913–1915.
48. VdESI, Hauptvorstand, 14 January 1914, BA, R 13 I/142, p. 34.

Conclusions and Comparisons

1. See, for example, Wilhelm Beukenberg, "Die Entwicklung der Schwerindustrie in der Regierungszeit Wilhelms II"; Alfred Hugenberg, *Streiflichter aus Vergangenheit und Gegenwart*, pp. 209–215; and Adolf Zimmermann, *Von Haspe bis Duisburg*, pp. 17–19, 57–58.
2. For examples of foreign study and travel by members of the Ruhr elite, see Appendix B.
3. David Brody, *Steelmakers in America*, pp. 170–171.
4. Verhandlungen der Kommission zur Untersuchung der Frage der 24-stündigen Wechselschicht bei der Gutehoffnungshütte, 6 June 1914, HA/GHH 300 193 009/13 Abänderung der Bundesratverordnung vom 19.12.1908 betreffend Überarbeit in der Grossindustrie, 1912–1914.
5. *Deutsche Bergwerks-Zeitung*, 31 March 1912.
6. See, for example, Gerhard Adelmann, *Quellensammlung zur Geschichte der sozialen Betriebsverfassung Ruhrindustrie unter besonderer Berücksichtigung des Industrie- und Handelskammerbezirks Essen*, 1:289; Emil Kirdorf, "Das Verhältnis der Kartelle zum Staat"; and Zechenverband to Vorstand des Gewerkvereins christlicher Bergarbeiter, 6 December 1910, Bergbau Archiv 13/511 Zechenverband.
7. Adelmann, *Quellensammlung*, 1:294.
8. In 1907–1908, for example, of male employees of the iron and steel industry in the United States, 58 percent were foreign born, 13 percent were the native-born sons of immigrant fathers, and only 29 percent were the native-born sons of native fathers. See Daniel Nelson, *Managers and Workers*, p. 80.
9. Brody, *Steelmakers in America*; and Herbert G. Gutman, *Work, Culture, and Society in Industrializing America*.

Notes

10. See, especially, Brody, *Steelmakers in America*. Cf. Rowland Berthoff, "The 'Freedom to Control' in American Business History."

11. On theories of industrial democracy in the United States, see Milton Derber, *The American Idea of Industrial Democracy, 1865–1965*, pp. 3–140. See also David Montgomery, *Workers' Control in America*.

12. On violence in American industrial relations, see H. M. Gitelman, "Perspectives on American Industrial Violence"; and Philip Taft and Philip Ross, "American Labor Violence."

13. On the accommodation of old and new elites in the two societies, compare Lamar Cecil, "The Creation of Nobles in Prussia, 1871–1918," with Ralph E. Pumphrey, "The Introduction of Industrialists into the British Peerage." See also Sydney G. Checkland, "Cultural Factors and British Business Men, 1815–1914"; Michael R. Gordon, "Domestic Conflict and the Origins of the First World War"; James Sheehan, "Conflict and Cohesion among German Elites in the Nineteenth Century"; and David Spring, ed., *European Landed Elites in the Nineteenth Century*, pp. 1–67.

14. E. H. Phelps Brown, *The Growth of British Industrial Relations*, p. 75; and Gaston V. Rimlinger, "Welfare Policy and Economic Development."

15. On employer ideologies in the United States and England, see Reinhard Bendix, *Work and Authority in Industry*. See also W. J. Mommsen, ed., *The Emergence of the Welfare State in Britain and Germany 1850–1950*, pp. 71–163.

16. Thomas C. Cochran, *Business in American Life*, p. 238.

17. Nelson, *Managers and Workers*, p. 95.

18. Almont Lindsey, *The Pullman Strike*.

19. On industrial welfare programs in the United States, see Stuart D. Brandes, *American Welfare Capitalism, 1880–1940*; Brody, *Workers in Industrial America*, pp. 48–81; and Nelson, *Managers and Workers*, pp. 101–121. See also James Weinstein, "Big Business and the Origins of Workmen's Compensation." Specifically on United States Steel, see John A. Garraty, "The United States Steel Corporation Versus Labor." No Ruhr concern went as far in intervening in the private lives of its employees as did the Ford Motor Company after the announcement of its Americanization program in January 1914. This program was made palatable through the irresistible offer of five dollars a day. See Stephen Meyer, "Adapting the Immigrant to the Line." On Britain, see Joseph Melling, "Industrial Strife and Business Welfare Philosophy."

20. Ralf Dahrendorf, *Class and Class Conflict in Industrial Society*, pp. 61–62; Dahrendorf, *Gesellschaft und Demokratie in Deutschland*, pp. 82–86; and T. H. Marshall, *Class, Citizenship, and Social Development*, pp. 71–134. For an idealized contemporary description of this difference in approach, see Vortrag Dr. Woltmann zur Frage der Arbeitsverhältnisse in der Grosseisenindustrie, 1913, HA/GHH 300 140/16.

21. Cochran, *Business in American Life*, pp. 209, 216; and Phelps Brown, *The Growth of British Industrial Relations*, pp. 270–272.

22. On the war years, see Gerald D. Feldman, *Army, Industry and Labor in Germany 1914–1918*.

23. Peter Wulf, *Hugo Stinnes*, pp. 87–107.

24. On worker unrest in the Ruhr, see Erhard Lucas, *Zwei Formen von Radikalismus in der deutschen Arbeiterbewegung*; and Jürgen Tampke, *The Ruhr and Revolution*.

Notes

25. On Ruhr industrialists during the Weimar years, see David Abraham, *The Collapse of the Weimar Republic*; Gerald D. Feldman, *Iron and Steel in the German Inflation 1916–1923*; Hans Mommsen, "Der Ruhrbergbau im Spannungsfeld von Politik und Wirtschaft in der Zeit der Weimarer Republik"; and Bernd Weisbrod, *Schwerindustrie in der Weimarer Republik*.

Bibliography

Unpublished Sources

Bundesarchiv Koblenz
    Verein deutscher Eisen- und Stahlindustrieller (R 13 I)
Staatsarchiv Koblenz
    Oberpräsidium Koblenz (Abteilung 403)
Staatsarchiv Düsseldorf, Schloss Kalkum
    Regierung Düsseldorf
Staatsarchiv Münster
    Regierung Arnsberg
    Oberpräsidium Münster
    Oberbergamt Dortmund B, Group 119
Bergbau Archiv, Bochum
    Zechenverband (Bestand 13)
    Krupp Bergbau (Bestand 20)
Historisches Archiv der Gutehoffnungshütte, Oberhausen
    Hauptverwaltung
    Bergwerksverwaltung
    Nachlass Paul Reusch
Firmenarchiv Mannesmann, Düsseldorf
    Arbeitgeberverband Nordwest
Firmenarchiv August-Thyssen-Hütte, Duisburg-Hamborn
    Sekretariat Fritz Thyssen, Kammern und Verbände

Published Sources

Abraham, David. *The Collapse of the Weimar Republic: Political Economy and Crisis.* Princeton, 1981.
Adelmann, Gerhard. "Die Beziehungen zwischen Arbeitgeber und Arbeitnehmer in der Ruhrindustrie vor 1914." *Jahrbücher für Nationalökonomie und Statistik* 175 (November 1963):412–427.
———. "Führende Unternehmer im Rheinland und Westfalen 1850–1914." *Rheinische Vierteljahrsblätter* 35 (1971):335–352.
———. *Quellensammlung zur Geschichte der sozialen Betriebsverfassung Ruhrindustrie unter besonderer Berücksichtigung des Industrie- und Handelskammerbezirks Essen.* 2 vols. Bonn, 1960–1965.
———. *Die soziale Betriebsverfassung des Ruhrbergbaus vom Anfang des 19.*

Bibliography

Jahrhunderts bis zum Ersten Weltkrieg unter besonderer Berücksichtigung des Industrie- und Handelskammerbezirks Essen. Bonn, 1962.
Arnst, Paul. *August Thyssen und sein Werk.* Leipzig, 1925.
Aufsätze über den Streik der Bergarbeiter im Ruhrgebiet. Schriften der Gesellschaft für Soziale Reform. Vol. 2. Jena, 1905.
Bacmeister, Walter. *Emil Kirdorf: Der Mann: Sein Werk.* Essen, 1936.
——. *Gustav Knepper: Das Lebensbild eines grossen Bergmanns.* Essen, 1950.
——. *Louis Baare: Ein westfälischer Wirtschaftsführer aus der Bismarckzeit.* Essen, 1937.
Barkin, Kenneth D. *The Controversy over German Industrialization, 1890–1902.* Chicago, 1970.
Beau, Horst. *Das Leistungswissen des frühindustriellen Unternehmertums in Rheinland und Westfalen.* Cologne, 1959.
Bein, Alex, and Goldschmidt, Hans. *Friedrich Hammacher: Lebensbild eines Parlamentariers und Wirtschaftsführers, 1824–1904.* Berlin, 1932.
Bendix, Reinhard. *Work and Authority in Industry: Ideologies of Management in the Course of Industrialization.* New York, 1956.
Benz, Wolfgang. "Die Entstehung des Kruppschen Nachrichtendienstes." *Vierteljahrshefte für Zeitgeschichte* 24 (April 1976):199–212.
Berichte der Hauptstelle deutscher Arbeitgeberverbände. Berlin, 1905–1912.
Bernhard, Ludwig. *Der Hugenberg-Konzern.* Berlin, 1928.
Berthoff, Rowland. "The 'Freedom to Control' in American Business History." In *A Festschrift for Friedrich B. Artz,* ed. David Pinkney and Theodore Ropp. Durham, N.C., 1964. Pp. 158–180.
Beukenberg, Wilhelm. "Die Entwicklung der Schwerindustrie in der Regierungszeit Wilhelms II." *Nord und Süd* 37 (June 1913):390–396.
Biographisches Jahrbuch und Deutscher Nekrolog. Continued after 1917 under the title *Deutsches biographisches Jahrbuch.* Berlin, 1900–1929.
Bodenhausen-Degener, Dora Freifrau von. *Eberhard von Bodenhausen: Ein Leben für Kunst und Wirtschaft.* Düsseldorf, 1955.
Boelcke, Willi, ed. *Krupp und die Hohenzollern: Aus der Korrespondenz der Familie Krupp 1850–1916.* Berlin, 1956.
Böhme, Helmut. "Bankenkonzentration und Schwerindustrie, 1873–1896: Bemerkungen zum Problem des 'Organisierten Kapitalismus.'" In *Sozialgeschichte Heute,* ed. Hans-Ulrich Wehler. Göttingen, 1974. Pp. 432–451.
——. *Deutschlands Weg zur Grossmacht: Studien zum Verhältnis von Wirtschaft und Staat während der Reichsgründungszeit 1848–1881.* Cologne, 1966.
——. "Emil Kirdorf: Überlegungen zu einer Unternehmerbiographie." *Tradition* 13 (1968):282–300 and 14 (1969):21–48.
Bongartz, Wolfram. "Grossindustrie und Berufsqualifikation des mittleren technischen Personals: Das Beispiel Gutehoffnungshütte 1882–1914." *Zeitschrift für Unternehmensgeschichte* 24 (1979):39–63.
Born, Karl Erich. *Staat und Sozialpolitik seit Bismarcks Sturz: Ein Beitrag zur Geschichte der innenpolitischen Entwicklung des Deutschen Reiches 1890–1914.* Wiesbaden, 1957.
Born, Karl Erich; Henning, Hansjoachim; and Schick, Manfred. *Quellensammlung zur Geschichte der deutschen Sozialpolitik von 1867 bis 1914: Einführungsband.* Wiesbaden, 1966.
Brakelmann, Günther, "Evangelische Pfarrer im Konfliktsfeld des Ruhrberg-

arbeiterstreiks von 1905." In *Fabrik, Familie, Feierabend*, ed. J. Reulecke and W. Weber. Wuppertal, 1978. Pp. 297–314.

Brandes, Stuart D. *American Welfare Capitalism, 1880–1940*. Chicago, 1976.

Brandi, Paul. *Essener Arbeitsjahre: Erinnerungen des Ersten Beigeordneten Paul Brandi*. Beiträge zur Geschichte von Stadt und Stift Essen. Vol. 75. Essen, 1959.

Brepohl, Wilhelm. *Der Aufbau des Ruhrvolkes im Zuge der Ost-West-Wanderung*. Recklinghausen, 1948.

———. *Industrievolk im Wandel von der agraren zur industriellen Daseinsform dargestellt am Ruhrgebiet*. Tübingen, 1957.

Brody, David. *Steelmakers in America: The Nonunion Era*. Cambridge, Mass., 1960.

———. *Workers in Industrial America: Essays on the Twentieth Century Struggle*. New York, 1980.

Brüggemeier, Franz J., and Niethammer, Lutz. "Schlafgänger, Schnapskasinos und schwerindustrielle Kolonie: Aspekte der Arbeiterwohnungsfrage im Ruhrgebiet vor dem Ersten Weltkrieg." In *Fabrik, Familie, Feierabend*, ed. J. Reulecke and W. Weber. Wuppertal, 1978. Pp. 135–175.

Bry, Gerhard. *Wages in Germany, 1871–1945*. Princeton, 1960.

Bueck, H. A. *Der Centralverband deutscher Industrieller, 1876–1901*. 3 vols. Berlin, 1901–1905.

Bülow, Bernhard Fürst von. *Denkwürdigkeiten*. 4 vols. Berlin, 1930–1931.

Carl Funke und seine Werke. Essen, 1913.

Cecil, Lamar. *Albert Ballin: Business and Politics in Imperial Germany, 1888–1918*. Princeton, 1967.

———. "The Creation of Nobles in Prussia, 1871–1918." *American Historical Review* 75 (February 1970):757–795.

Chandler, Alfred D. *Strategy and Structure: Chapters in the History of the Industrial Enterprise*. Cambridge, Mass., 1962.

———. *The Visible Hand: The Managerial Revolt in American Business*. Cambridge, Mass., 1977.

Chandler, Alfred D., and Daems, Herman, eds. *Managerial Hierarchies: Comparative Perspectives on the Rise of the Modern Industrial Enterprise*. Cambridge, Mass., 1980.

Chandler, Alfred D., and Galambos, L. "The Development of Large-scale Organization in Modern America." *Journal of Economic History* 30 (March 1970):201–217.

Chandler, Alfred D., and Redlich, Fritz. "Recent Developments in American Business Administration and Their Conceptualization." *Business History Review* 35 (1961):1–27.

Checkland, Sydney G. "Cultural Factors and British Business Men, 1815–1914." In *Social Order and Entrepreneurship*, ed. K. Nakagawa. Tokyo, 1977. Pp. 53–82.

Class, Heinrich. *Wider den Strom: Vom Werden und Wachsen der nationalen Opposition im alten Reich*. Leipzig, 1932.

Cochran, Thomas C. *Business in American Life: A History*. New York, 1972.

Correspondenzblatt der Generalkommission der Gewerkschaften Deutschlands. Berlin, 1898–1914.

Crew, David. "Definitions of Modernity: Social Mobility in a German Town, 1880–1901." *Journal of Social History* 6 (1973):53–74.

Bibliography

———. "Steel, Sabotage and Socialism: The Strike at the Dortmunder Union Steel Works in 1911." In *The German Working Class 1888–1933*, ed. Richard J. Evans. London, 1982. Pp. 108–141.

———. *Town in the Ruhr: A Social History of Bochum, 1860–1914*. New York, 1979.

Cronin, James E. "Theories of Strikes: Why Can't They Explain the British Experience?" *Journal of Social History* 12 (Winter 1978):194–220.

Croon, Helmuth. "Bürgertum und Verwaltung in den Städten des Ruhrgebiets im 19. Jahrhundert." *Tradition* (February 1964):23–41.

———. "Die Einwirkungen der Industrialisierung auf die gesellschaftliche Schichtung der Bevölkerung im rheinisch-westfälischen Industriegebiet." *Rheinische Vierteljahrsblätter* 20 (1955):301–316.

———. *Die gesellschaftlichen Auswirkungen des Gemeindewahlrechtes in den Gemeinden und Kreisen des Rheinlandes und Westfalens im 19. Jahrhundert*. Cologne, 1960.

———. "Das Vordringen der politischen Parteien im Bereich der kommunalen Selbstverwaltung." In *Kommunale Selbstverwaltung im Zeitalter der Industrialisierung*, ed. Helmuth Croon, Wolfgang Hofmann, and Georg Christoph von Unruh. Stuttgart, 1971. Pp. 15–58.

———. "Die wirtschaftlichen Führungsschichten des Ruhrgebietes in der Zeit von 1890 bis 1933." *Blätter für deutsche Landesgeschichte* 108 (1972): 143–159.

Croon, Helmuth, and Utermann, Kurt. *Zeche und Gemeinde: Untersuchungen über den Strukturwandel einer Zechengemeinde im nördlichen Ruhrgebiet*. Tübingen, 1958.

Daebritz, Walther. *Bochumer Verein für Bergbau und Gusstahlfabrikation in Bochum*. Düsseldorf, 1934.

Daems, H., and Wee, H. v. d., eds. *The Rise of Managerial Capitalism*. The Hague, 1974.

Dahrendorf, Ralf. *Class and Class Conflict in Industrial Society*. Stanford, 1959.

———. *Gesellschaft und Demokratie in Deutschland*. Munich, 1965.

Derber, Milton. *The American Idea of Industrial Democracy, 1865–1965*. Urbana, Ill., 1970.

Desai, Ashok V. *Real Wages in Germany, 1871–1913*. Oxford, 1968.

Deutsche Bergwerks-Zeitung. Essen, 1906–1914.

Dietrich, Valeska. "Alfred Hugenberg: Ein Manager in der Publizistik." Diss., Berlin, 1960.

Domansky-Davidsohn, Elisabeth. "Der Grossbetrieb als Organisationsproblem des Deutschen Metallarbeiter-Verbandes vor dem Ersten Weltkrieg." In *Arbeiterbewegung und industrieller Welt*, ed. Hans Mommsen. Wuppertal, 1980. Pp. 95–116.

Ehrenberg, Hans. *Die Eisenhüttentechnik und der deutsche Hüttenarbeiter*. Stuttgart, 1906.

Ehrenberg, Richard, and Racine, Hugo. *Krupp'sche Arbeiterfamilien*. Jena, 1912.

Eley, Geoff. *Reshaping the German Right: Radical Nationalism and Political Change after Bismarck*. New Haven, Conn., 1980.

Evans, Richard, ed. *The German Working Class, 1888–1933: The Politics of Everyday Life*. London, 1982.

———, ed. *Society and Politics in Wilhelmine Germany*. London, 1978.

Feldenkirchen, Wilfried. *Die Eisen- und Stahlindustrie des Ruhrgebiets,*

Bibliography

1879–1914: Wachstum, Finanzierung und Struktur ihrer Grossunternehmen. Wiesbaden, 1982.

———. "Kapitalbeschaffung in der Eisen- und Stahlindustrie des Ruhrgebiets, 1879–1914." *Zeitschrift für Unternehmensgeschichte* 24 (1979):39–81.

Feldman, Gerald D. *Army, Industry and Labor in Germany 1914–1918.* Princeton, 1966.

———. *Iron and Steel in the German Inflation, 1916–1923.* Princeton, 1977.

Feldman, Gerald D., and Nocken, Ulrich. "Trade Associations and Economic Power: Interest Group Development in the German Iron and Steel and Machine Building Industries, 1900–1933." *Business History Review* 44 (Winter 1975):413–445.

Fischer, Fritz. *Krieg der Illusionen: Die deutsche Politik von 1911 bis 1914.* Düsseldorf, 1969.

Fischer, Wilfram. *Herz des Reviers: 125 Jahre Wirtschaftsgeschichte des Industrie- und Handelskammerbezirks Essen, Mülheim, Oberhausen.* Essen, 1965.

———. "Konjunkturen und Krisen im Ruhrgebiet seit 1840 und die wirtschaftspolitische Willensbildung der Unternehmer." *Westfälische Forschungen* 21 (1968):42–53.

———. "Die Stellung der preussischen Bergrechtsreform von 1851–1865 in der Wirtschafts- und Sozialverfassung des 19. Jahrhunderts." *Zeitschrift für die gesamte Staatswissenschaft* 117 (October 1961):521–534.

Franke, E. "Der Arbeitsnachweis des Zechenverbandes im Ruhrkohlenrevier." *Preussische Jahrbücher* 139 (1910):201–224.

Fricke, Dieter. "Eine Denkschrift Krupps aus dem Jahre 1912 über den Schutz der 'Arbeitswilligen.'" *Zeitschrift für Geschichtswissenschaft* 5 (1957):1245–1254.

25 Jahre Arbeitnordwest, 1904–1929: Herausgegeben aus Anlass seines 25 jährigen Bestehens vom Arbeitgeberverband für den Bezirk der nordwestlichen Gruppe des Vereins deutscher Eisen- und Stahlindustrieller. Berlin, 1929.

Fürstenberg, Hans, ed. *Carl Fürstenberg: Die Lebensgeschichte eines deutschen Bankiers, 1870–1914.* Berlin, 1931.

Garraty, John A. "The United States Steel Corporation Versus Labor: The Early Years." *Labor History* 1 (Winter 1960):3–38.

Geary, Dick. "The German Labor Movement, 1848–1919." *European Studies Review* 6 (1976):297–330.

Gebhardt, Gerhard. *Ruhrbergbau: Geschichte, Aufbau und Verflechtung seiner Gesellschaften und Organisationen.* Essen, 1957.

Geschäftsberichte des Arbeitgeberverbandes für den Bezirk der Nordwestlichen Gruppe des Vereins deutscher Eisen- und Stahlindustrieller. Düsseldorf, 1904/1905–1905/1906 and 1908/1909–1912/1913.

Gitelman, H. M. "Perspectives on American Industrial Violence." *Business History Review* 47 (1973):1–23.

Gladen, Albin. "Die Streiks der Bergarbeiter im Ruhrgebiet in den Jahren 1889, 1905 und 1912." In *Arbeiterbewegung an Rhein und Ruhr*, ed. Jürgen Reulecke. Wuppertal, 1974. Pp. 111–148.

Glückauf: Berg- und Hüttenmännische Zeitschrift: Organ des Vereins für die bergbaulichen Interessen im Oberbergamtsbezirk Dortmund. Essen, 1896–1914.

Gordon, Michael R. "Domestic Conflict and the Origins of the First World War:

The British and German Cases." *Journal of Modern History* 46 (June 1974):191–226.
Gouldner, Alvin. *Patterns of Industrial Bureaucracy*. New York, 1954.
Great Britain, Board of Trade. *Cost of Living in German Towns: Report of an Enquiry into Working Class Rents, Housing and Retail Prices, together with the Rates of Wages in Certain Occupations in the Principal Industrial Towns of the German Empire*. London, 1908.
Grebe, Paul. "Bismarcks Sturz und der Bergarbeiterstreik von Mai 1889: Ein Beitrag aus den Akten des Staatsministeriums." *Historische Zeitschrift* 157 (1938): 84–97.
Groh, Dieter. "Intensification of Work and Industrial Conflict in Germany, 1896–1914." *Politics and Society* 8 (1978):349–397.
Günther, Adolf, and Prevôt, René. *Die Wohlfahrtseinrichtungen der Arbeitgeber in Deutschland und Frankreich*. Schriften des Vereins für Sozialpolitik. Vol. 114. Leipzig, 1905.
Guratzsch, Dankwart. *Macht durch Organisation: Die Grundlegung des Hugenbergschen Presseimperiums*. Düsseldorf, 1974.
Gutman, Herbert G. *Work, Culture, and Society in Industrializing America*. New York, 1976.
Gutsche, Willibald. "Die Deutsche Bank und die Entstehung der Stahlwerks-Verband AG 1904: Dokumentation zum Verhältnis zwischen Industriemonopolen und Grossbanken im deutschen Finanzkapital." *Jahrbuch für Wirtschaftsgeschichte* 20 (1979):271–283.
Handbuch der Deutschen Aktiengesellschaften. Berlin, 1905–1906.
Hank, Manfred. *Kanzler ohne Amt: Fürst Bismarck nach seiner Entlassung, 1890–1898*. Munich, 1977.
Hardach, Karl W. *Die Bedeutung wirtschaftlicher Faktoren bei der Wiedereinführung der Eisen- und Getreidezölle in Deutschland 1879*. Berlin, 1967.
Hartmann, Heinz. *Authority and Organization in German Management*. Princeton, 1959.
———. "Managers and Entrepreneurs: A Useful Distinction?" *Administrative Science Quarterly* 3 (March 1959):429–451.
Hashagen, Justus. *Geschichte der Familie Hoesch*. 2 vols. Cologne, 1911–1916.
Heinemann, Otto. *Kronenorden Vierter Klasse: Das Leben des Prokuristen Heinemann, 1864–1944*. Düsseldorf, 1969.
Heiss, Clemens. "Die gelbe Arbeiterbewegung." *Jahrbuch für Gesetzgebung, Verwaltung, und Volkswirtschaft im deutschen Reich* 35 (1911):337–378.
Hellwig, Fritz. *Carl Ferdinand Freiherr von Stumm-Halberg*. Heidelberg, 1936.
Helmrich, Wilhelm, "August Thyssen: Ein Unternehmer des Ruhrreviers." *Tradition* 3 (1958):141–150.
Henning, Hansjoachim. "Soziale Verflechtungen der Unternehmer in Westfalen 1860–1914." *Zeitschrift für Unternehmensgeschichte* 32 (1978):1–30.
Henning, Wilhelm. *Geschichte der Stadtverordnetenversammlung von Essen, 1890–1914*. Essen, 1965.
Hentschel, Volker. *Wirtschaft und Wirtschaftspolitik im wilhelminischen Deutschland: Organisierter Kapitalismus und Interventionsstaat?* Stuttgart, 1978.
Herkner, Heinrich. *Die Arbeiterfrage*. 2 vols. 8th ed. Berlin, 1922.
Hickey, Stephen. "Bergmannsarbeit an der Ruhr vor dem Ersten Weltkrieg." In *Glück auf, Kameraden!* ed. Hans Mommsen and Ulrich Borsdorf. Cologne, 1979. Pp. 49–69.

Bibliography

———. "The Shaping of the German Labour Movement: Miners in the Ruhr." In *Society and Politics in Wilhelmine Germany*, ed. Richard Evans. London, 1978. Pp. 215–240.
Hilgenstock, Bergassessor. "Über Lohntarife im britischen und rheinisch-westfälischen Steinkohlenbergbau." *Glückauf* 43 (14 December 1907):1677–1681.
Hoffmann, Erich. *Dr. Francis Kruse: Königlich Preussischer Regierungspräsident: Ein Lebensbild*. Leipzig, 1937.
Hofmann, Wolfgang. "Preussische Stadtverordnetenversammlungen als Repräsentativ-Organe." In *Die deutsche Stadt im Industriezeitalter*, ed. Jürgen Reulecke. Wuppertal, 1978. Pp. 34–55.
Holtfrerich, Carl-Ludwig. *Quantitative Wirtschaftsgeschichte des Ruhrkohlenbergbaus im 19. Jahrhundert*. Dortmund, 1973.
Horn, Hannelore. *Der Kampf um den Bau des Mittellandkanals*. Cologne, 1964.
Hugenberg, Alfred. *Streiflichter aus Vergangenheit und Gegenwart*. 2d ed. Berlin, 1927.
Jaeger, Hans. *Unternehmer in der deutschen Politik, 1890–1918*. Bonn, 1967.
Jahresbericht des Vereins für die bergbaulichen Interessen im Oberbergamtsbezirk Dortmund. Essen, 1896–1914.
Jantke, Carl. *Bergmann und Zeche: Die sozialen Arbeitsverhältnisse einer Schachtanlage des nördlichen Ruhrgebiets in der Sicht der Bergleute*. Tübingen, 1953.
Jeidels, Otto. *Die Methoden der Arbeiterentlohnung in der rheinisch-westfälischen Eisenindustrie*. Berlin, 1907.
Kaelble, Hartmut. *Industrielle Interessenpolitik in der Wilhelminischen Gesellschaft: Centralverband deutscher Industrieller, 1895–1914*. Berlin, 1967.
———. "Long-Term Changes in the Recruitment of the Business Elite: Germany Compared to the U.S., Great Britain and France Since the Industrial Revolution." *Journal of Social History* 13 (Spring 1980):404–423.
Kaelble, Hartmut, and Volkmann, Heinrich. "Konjunktur und Streik während des Übergangs zum Organisierten Kapitalismus in Deutschland." *Zeitschrift für Wirtschafts- und Sozialwissenschaften* 92 (1972):513–544.
Kealey, Maura. "Kampfstrategien der Unternehmerschaft im Ruhrbergbau seit dem Bergarbeiterstreik von 1889." In *Glück auf, Kameraden!* ed. Hans Mommsen and Ulrich Borsdorf. Cologne, 1979. Pp. 175–197.
Kessler, Gerhard. *Der Arbeitsnachweise der Arbeitgeberverbände*. Leipzig, 1911.
———. *Die deutschen Arbeitgeberverbände*. Schriften des Vereins für Sozialpolitik. Vol. 124. Leipzig, 1909.
———. "Zur jüngsten Entwicklung der Arbeitgeberverbände." *Annalen für soziale Politik und Gesetzgebung* 1 (1911):123–132.
Kirchhoff, Hans Georg. *Die staatliche Sozialpolitik im Ruhrbergbau 1871–1914*. Cologne, 1958.
Kirdorf, Emil. "Das Verhältnis der Kartelle zum Staat." *Schriften des Vereins für Sozialpolitik* 116 (1906):272–293.
Klass, Gert von. *Hugo Stinnes*. Tübingen, 1958.
———. *Stahl vom Rhein: Die Geschichte des Hüttenwerkes Rheinhausen, 1897–1957*. Darmstadt, 1957.
Klessmann, Christoph. "Klassensolidarität und nationales Bewusstsein: Das Verhältnis zwischen der Polnischen Berufsvereinigung (ZZP) und den deutschen Bergarbeiter-Gewerkschaften im Ruhrgebiet 1902–1923." *Inter-*

Bibliography

nationale wissenschaftliche Korrespondenz zur Geschichte der deutschen Arbeiterbewegung 10 (June 1974):149–178.

———. *Polnische Bergarbeiter im Ruhrgebiet 1870–1945: Soziale Integration und nationale Subkultur einer Minderheit in der deutschen Industriegesellschaft.* Göttingen, 1978.

Knopp, Gisbert. *Die preussische Verwaltung des Regierungsbezirks Düsseldorf in den Jahren 1899–1919.* Cologne, 1974.

Koch, Max Jürgen. *Die Bergarbeiterbewegung im Ruhrgebiet zur Zeit Wilhelms II, 1889–1914.* Düsseldorf, 1954.

Kocka, Jürgen. *Die Angestellten in der deutschen Geschichte 1850–1980: Vom Privatbeamten zum angestellten Arbeitnehmer.* Göttingen, 1981.

———. "Industrielles Management: Konzeptionen und Modelle in Deutschland vor 1914." *Vierteljahrschrift für Sozial- und Wirtschaftsgeschichte* 56 (October 1969):332–72.

———. "Theoretical Approaches to Social and Economic History of Modern Germany: Some Recent Trends, Concepts, and Problems in Western and Eastern Germany." *Journal of Modern History* 47 (1975):101–119.

———. *Unternehmensverwaltung und Angestelltenschaft am Beispiel Siemens, 1847–1914: Zum Verhältnis von Kapitalismus und Bürokratie in der deutschen Industrialisierung.* Stuttgart, 1969.

———. *Unternehmer in der deutschen Industrialisierung.* Göttingen, 1975.

Köllmann, Wolfgang. *Der Bergarbeiterstreik von 1889 und die Gründung des "Alten Verbandes" in ausgewählten Dokumenten der Zeit.* Bochum, 1969.

———. *Bevölkerung in der industriellen Revolution.* Göttingen, 1974.

———. "The Process of Urbanization in Germany at the Height of the Industrialization Period." *Journal of Contemporary History* 4 (1969):59–76.

König, Max. "Über den wirtschaftlichen und politischen Einfluss der Grossindustrie auf die Gemeinde-Vertretung und -Verwaltung im Ruhrgebiet." *Kommunale Praxis* (1907): cols. 901–924.

Lambi, Ivo Nikolai. *Free Trade and Protection in Germany, 1868–1879.* Wiesbaden, 1963.

Landes, David. *The Unbound Prometheus: Technological Change and Industrial Development in Western Europe from 1750 to the Present.* Cambridge, 1969.

Lebovics, Herman. "'Agrarians' versus 'Industrializers.'" *International Review of Social History* 12 (1964):31–65.

Levenstein, Adolf. *Die Arbeiterfrage: Mit besonderer Berücksichtigung der sozialpsychologischen Seite des modernen Grossbetriebes und der psychophysischen Entwicklung auf die Arbeiter.* Munich, 1912.

Lewinsohn, Richard. *Das Geld in der Politik.* Berlin, 1930.

Lindenlaub, Dieter. *Richtungskämpfe im Verein für Sozialpolitik: Wissenschaft und Sozialpolitik im Kaiserreich, 1890–1914.* 2 vols. Wiesbaden, 1967.

Lindsey, Almont. *The Pullman Strike: The Story of a Unique Experiment and of a Great Labor Upheaval.* Chicago, 1964.

Lucas, Erhard. *Zwei Formen von Radikalismus in der deutschen Arbeiterbewegung.* Frankfurt/Main, 1976.

McCreary, Eugene C. "Essen, 1860–1914: A Case Study of the Impact of Industrialization on German Community Life." Ph.D. diss., Yale, 1964.

———. "Social Welfare and Business: The Krupp Welfare Program, 1860–1914." *Business History Review* 42 (Spring 1968):24–49.

Bibliography

Mallmann, Klaus-Michael. *Die Anfänge der Bergarbeiterbewegung an der Saar, 1848–1904*. Saarbrücken, 1981.
Marchand, Hans. *Säkularstatistik der deutschen Eisenindustrie*. Essen, 1939.
Marshall, T. H. *Class, Citizenship, and Social Development*. New York, 1965.
Martens, Oskar. "Kommerzienrat Robert Müser." *Jahrbuch für den Oberbergamtsbezirk Dortmund* 9 (1910):iii–xvi.
Martin, Rudolf. *Jahrbuch des Vermögens und Einkommens der Millionäre in der Rheinprovinz*. Berlin, 1913.
———. *Jahrbuch des Vermögens und Einkommens der Millionäre in Preussen*. Berlin, 1911.
Maschke, Erich. *Es Entsteht ein Konzern: Paul Reusch und die Gutehoffnungshütte*. Tübingen, 1969.
———. *Grundzüge der deutschen Kartellgeschichte bis 1914*. Dortmund, 1964.
Matschoss, Conrad. *Männer der Technik: Ein biographisches Handbuch herausgegeben im Auftrage des Vereins Deutscher Ingenieure*. Berlin, 1925.
Mattheier, Klaus. "Drei Führungsorganisationen der wirtschaftsfriedlich-nationalen Arbeiterbewegung: Reichsverband gegen die Sozialdemokratie, Förderungsausschuss und Deutsche Vereinigung in der Auseinandersetzung um die Gelben Gewerkschaften in Deutschland 1904 bis 1918." *Rheinische Vierteljahrsblätter* 37 (1973):244–275.
———. *Die Gelben: Nationale Arbeiter zwischen Wirtschaftsfrieden und Streik*. Düsseldorf, 1973.
Medalen, Charles. "State Monopoly Capitalism in Germany: The Hibernia Affair." *Past and Present* 78 (February 1978):82–112.
Melling, Joseph. "Industrial Strife and Business Welfare Philosophy: The Case of the South Metropolitan Gas Company from the 1880s to the War." *Business History* 21 (July 1979):163–179.
———. "'Non-Commissioned Officers': British Employers and Their Supervisory Workers, 1880–1920." *Social History* 5 (May 1980):183–221.
Merbach, Gunter. "Die leitende Angestelltenschicht in der Eisen- und Stahlindustrie des Ruhrgebiets bis 1931." Staatsexamensarbeit. Bonn, 1968.
Mews, Karl. "Otto Krawehl." *Beiträge zur Geschichte von Stadt und Stift Essen* 55 (1937):173–180.
Meyer, Stephen. "Adapting the Immigrant to the Line: Americanization in the Ford Factory, 1914–1921." *Journal of Social History* 14 (Fall 1980):67–82.
Mieck, Paul. *Die Arbeiter-Wohlfahrts-Einrichtungen der industriellen Unternehmer in den preussischen Provinzen Rheinland und Westfalen und ihre volkswirtschaftliche und soziale Bedeutung*. Berlin, 1904.
Mielke, Siegfried. *Der Hansa-Bund für Gewerbe, Handel, und Industrie 1909–1914*. Göttingen, 1976.
Mogs, Fritz. "Die sozialgeschichtliche Entwicklung der Stadt Oberhausen (Rhld.) zwischen 1850 und 1933." Diss., Cologne, 1956.
Mommsen, Hans. "Der Ruhrbergbau im Spannungsfeld von Politik und Wirtschaft in der Zeit der Weimarer Republik." *Blätter für deutsche Landesgeschichte* 108 (1972):160–175.
———, ed. *Arbeiterbewegung und industrieller Wandel: Studien zu gewerkschaftlichen Organisationsproblemen im Reich und an der Ruhr*. Wuppertal, 1980.
Mommsen, Hans, and Borsdorf, Ulrich, eds. *Glück auf, Kameraden! Die Bergarbeiter und ihre Organisationen in Deutschland*. Cologne, 1979.

Bibliography

Mommsen, W. J., ed. *The Emergence of the Welfare State in Britain and Germany, 1850–1950.* London, 1981.
Montgomery, David. *Workers' Control in America: Studies in the History of Work, Technology, and Labor Struggles.* Cambridge, 1979.
Moore, Barrington. *Injustice: The Social Bases of Obedience and Revolt.* White Plains, N. Y., 1978.
Muncy, Lysbeth W. "The Prussian Landräte in the Last Years of the Monarchy: A Case Study of Pomerania and the Rhineland in 1890–1918." *Central European History* 6 (December 1973):299–338.
Murphy, Richard C. "The Polish Trade Union in the Ruhr Coal Field: Labor Organization and Ethnicity in Wilhelmian Germany." *Central European History* 11 (December 1978):335–347.
———. "Polnische Bergarbeiter im Ruhrgebiet: Das Beispiel Bottrop." In *Glück auf, Kameraden!* ed. Hans Mommsen and Ulrich Borsdorf. Cologne, 1979. Pp. 89–108.
Muthesius, Volkmar. *Peter Klöckner und sein Werk.* 2d ed. Essen, 1959.
———. *Ruhrkohle, 1893–1943: Aus der Geschichte des Rheinisch-Westfälischen Kohlen-Syndikats.* Essen, 1943.
Nakagawa, Keiichiro, ed. *Social Order and Entrepreneurship: Proceedings of the Second Fuji Conference.* Tokyo, 1977.
Der Nationale Arbeiter-Verein Werk Krupp Essen. Essen, 1911.
Nekrologe aus dem rheinisch-westfälischen Industriegebiet, Jahrgang 1939–1951. Continued as *Lebensbilder aus dem rheinisch-westfälischen Industriegebiet, Jahrgang 1952–1954* and *Jahrgang 1958–1959.* Düsseldorf, 1955–1962.
Nelson, Daniel. *Managers and Workers: Origins of the New Factory System in the United States, 1880–1920.* Madison, Wis., 1975.
Neue Deutsche Biographie. Berlin, 1953–.
Neuloh, Otto. *Die deutsche Betriebsverfassung.* Tübingen, 1956.
———. "Sozialpolitik im grossbetrieblichen Industriesystem." In *Beiträge zur Soziologie der industriellen Gesellschaft*, ed. Walther G. Hoffmann. Dortmund, 1952.
Niethammer, Lutz. "Wie wohnten Arbeiter im Kaiserreich?" *Archiv für Sozialgeschichte* 16 (1976):61–134.
Nolan, Mary. *Social Democracy and Society: Working-class Radicalism in Düsseldorf, 1890–1920.* Cambridge, 1981.
Nussbaum, Helga. *Unternehmer gegen Monopole: Über Struktur und Aktionen antimonopolistischer bürgerlicher Gruppen zu Beginn des 20. Jahrhunderts.* Berlin, 1966.
Osthold, Paul. *Die Geschichte des Zechenverbandes, 1908–1933*: Ein Beitrag zur deutschen Sozialgeschichte. Berlin, 1934.
Panzera, Donald Paul. "Organization, Authority, and Conflict in the Ruhr Coal Mining Industry: A Case Study of the Gutehoffnungshütte, 1853–1914." Ph.D. dissertation, Northwestern University, 1980.
Phelps Brown, E. H. *The Growth of British Industrial Relations: A Study from the Standpoint of 1906–1914.* London, 1959.
Pieper, Lorenz. *Die Lage der Bergarbeiter im Ruhrrevier.* Stuttgart, 1903.
Pierenkemper, Toni. "Entrepreneurs in Heavy Industry: Upper Silesia and the Westphalian Ruhr Region, 1852 to 1913." *Business History Review* 53 (Spring 1979):65–78.

Bibliography

———. *Die westfälischen Schwerindustriellen, 1852–1913: Soziale Struktur und unternehmerischer Erfolg*. Göttingen, 1979.
Pinner, Felix (Franz Fassland). *Deutsche Wirtschaftsführer*. Charlottenburg, 1924.
Pollard, Sidney. *The Genesis of Modern Management: A Study of the Industrial Revolution in Great Britain*. Baltimore, 1965.
Porter, J. H. "Wage Bargaining under Conciliation Agreements, 1860–1914." *Economic History Review*, 2d ser., 23 (December 1970):460–475.
Pounds, Norman J. G. *The Ruhr: A Study in Historical and Economic Geography*. Bloomington, Ind., 1952.
Puhle, Hans-Jürgen. *Agrarische Interessenpolitik und preussischer Konservatismus im wilhelminischen Reich, 1893–1914*. Hanover, 1966.
Pumphrey, Ralph E. "The Introduction of Industrialists into the British Peerage: A Study of Adaptation of a Social Institution." *American Historical Review* 64 (1959):1–16.
Puppke, Ludwig. *Sozialpolitik und soziale Anschauungen frühindustrieller Unternehmer in Rheinland-Westfalen*. Cologne, 1966.
Quint, Fritz. "50 Jahre Bergbau vom Kumpel gesehen." *Beiträge zur Geschichte von Stadt und Stift Essen* 61 (Essen, 1941):57–77.
Rassow, Peter, and Born, Karl Erich, eds. *Akten zur staatlichen Sozialpolitik in Deutschland, 1890–1914*. Wiesbaden, 1959.
Redlich, Fritz. *Der Unternehmer: Wirtschafts- und sozialgeschichtliche Studien*. Göttingen, 1964.
Reichsarbeitsblatt. Berlin, 1904–1914.
Remke, Anton. "Betriebsorganisation und Arbeitsvollzüge im Eisen-Erzeugenden und Eisenverarbeitenden Betrieben des Ruhrgebiets, 1840–1914: Eine Untersuchung zur innerbetrieblichen Sozialstruktur des 19. Jahrhunderts." Diplomarbeit. Münster, 1964.
Reulecke, Jürgen. "Vom blauen Montag zum Arbeiterurlaub: Vorgeschichte und Entstehung des Erholungsurlaubs für Arbeiter vor dem Ersten Weltkrieg." *Archiv für Sozialgeschichte* 16 (1976):205–248.
———, ed. *Arbeiterbewegung an Rhein und Ruhr: Beiträge zur Geschichte der Arbeiterbewegung in Rheinland-Westfalen*. Wuppertal, 1974.
Rheinisch-Westfälische Wirtschaftsbiographien. Münster, 1931–1974.
Rimlinger, Gaston V. "Welfare Policy and Economic Development: A Comparative Historical Perspective." *Journal of Economic History* 26 (December 1966):556–571.
Risse, Joseph. "Eduard Kleine: Ein Wegbereiter des Ruhrbergbaus." *Der Anschnitt* 12 (February 1960):13–18.
Ritter, Gerhard A. *Die Arbeiterbewegung im Wilhelminischen Reich: Die Sozialdemokratische Partei und die Freien Gewerkschaften, 1890–1900*. 2d ed. Berlin, 1963.
Roberts, James S. "Drink and Industrial Work Discipline in Nineteenth Century Germany." *Journal of Social History* 15 (Fall 1981):25–38.
Röhl, J. C. G. *Germany without Bismarck: The Crisis of Government in the Second Reich, 1890–1900*. Berkeley and Los Angeles, 1967.
Rosenberg, Donald. "The Ruhr Coal Strike and the Prussian Mining Law of 1905: A Social and Political Conflict of Working Class Aspirations and Industrial Authoritarianism." Ph.D. diss., UCLA, 1971.
Rosenberg, Hans. *Grosse Depression und Bismarckzeit: Wirtschaftsablauf, Gesellschaft und Politik in Mitteleuropa*. Berlin, 1967.

Bibliography

Rostow, W. W. "Kondratieff, Schumpeter, and Kuznets: Trend Periods Revisited." *Journal of Economic History* 35 (1975):719-753.
Roth, Guenther. *The Social Democrats in Imperial Germany: A Study of Working-Class Isolation and National Integration*. Totowa, N. J., 1963.
Saul, Klaus. *Staat, Industrie, Arbeiterbewegung im Kaiserreich: Zur Innen- und Aussenpolitik des Wilhelminischen Deutschland 1903-1914*. Hamburg, 1974.
———. "Der Staat und die 'Mächte des Umsturzes': Ein Beitrag zu den Methoden antisozialistischer Repression und Agitation vom Scheitern des Sozialistengesetzes bis zur Jahrhundertwende." *Archiv für Sozialgeschichte* 12 (1972):293-350.
———. "Staatsintervention und Arbeitskampf im Wilhelminischen Reich, 1904-1914." In *Sozialgeschichte Heute*, ed. Hans-Ulrich Wehler. Göttingen, 1974. Pp. 479-494.
Saul, S. B. *The Myth of the Great Depression, 1873-1896*. London, 1969.
Schiefel, Werner. *Bernhard Dernberg, 1865-1937: Kolonialpolitiker und Bankier im Wilhelminischen Deutschland*. Zurich, 1974.
Schmidt, H. Th. "Belegschaftsbildung im Ruhrgebiet im Zeichen der Industrialisierung: Erläutet am Beispiel der Zechen Prosper 1-3 der Arenberg Bergbau GmbH in Bottrop." *Tradition* 2 (1957):265-272.
Schofer, Lawrence. *The Formation of a Modern Labor Force: Upper Silesia, 1865-1914*. Berkeley and Los Angeles, 1975.
Schöllgen, Gregor. "Sozialpolitik im Kaiserreich: Eine Denkschrift Hugenbergs aus dem Jahre 1912 zum Wohnungswesen." *Rheinische Vierteljahrsblätter* 44 (1980):232-236.
Schriften der Gesellschaft für Soziale Reform. Jena, 1901-1914.
Schröder, Ernst. *Otto Wiedfeldt: Eine Biographie*. Beiträge zur Geschichte von Stadt und Stift Essen. Vol. 80. Essen, 1964.
Schulte, Wilhelm. *Westfälische Köpfe: 300 Lebensbilder bedeutender Westfalen*. Münster, 1963.
Schumpeter, Joseph A. *Business Cycles: A Theoretical, Historical, and Statistical Analysis of the Capitalist Process*. 2 vols. New York, 1939.
Schunder, Friedrich. *Tradition und Fortschritt: 100 Jahre Gemeinschaftsarbeit im Ruhrbergbau*. Stuttgart, 1959.
Die Schwereisenindustrie im deutschen Zollgebiet, ihre Entwicklung und ihre Arbeiter: Nach vorgenommenen Erhebungen im Jahre 1910 bearbeitet und herausgegeben vom Vorstand des Deutschen Metallarbeiter-Verbandes. Stuttgart, 1912.
Seeber, Gustav, and Wittwer, Walter. "Friedrich Hammachers Aufzeichnungen über den Bergarbeiterstreik von 1889." *Jahrbuch für Geschichte* 16 (1977):403-458.
Serlo, Walter. *Bergmannsfamilien in Rheinland und Westfalen*. Rheinisch-Westfälische Wirtschaftsbiographien. Vol. 3. Münster, 1963.
———. *Die preussischen Bergassessoren*. 3d ed. Essen, 1927.
———. *Westdeutsche Berg- und Hüttenleute und ihre Familien*. Essen, 1938.
Sheehan, James. "Conflict and Cohesion among German Elites in the Nineteenth Century." In *Modern European Social History*, ed. Robert Bezucha. Lexington, Mass., 1972. Pp. 3-27.
———. *German Liberalism in the Nineteenth Century*. Chicago, 1978.
———. "Political Leadership in the German Reichstag, 1871-1918." *American Historical Review* 73 (December 1968):511-528.

Bibliography

Shorter, Edward, and Tilly, Charles. *Strikes in France, 1830–1968*. Cambridge, 1974.
Siebrecht, Fritz. *Fritz Winkhaus: Sein Leben und Wirken*. Essen, 1932.
———. *Der Köln-Neuessener Bergwerksverein: Ein Rückblick über 75 Jahre*. Essen, 1924.
Soziale Praxis: Centralblatt für Sozialpolitik. Berlin, 1908/1909–1912/1913.
Spencer, Elaine Glovka. "Between Capital and Labor: Supervisory Personnel in Ruhr Heavy Industry before 1914." *Journal of Social History* 9 (December 1975):178–192.
———. "Businessmen, Bureaucrats, and Social Control in the Ruhr, 1896–1914." In *Sozialgeschichte Heute*, ed. Hans-Ulrich Wehler. Göttingen, 1974. Pp. 452–466.
———. "Employer Response to Unionism: Ruhr Coal Industrialists before 1914." *Journal of Modern History* 48 (September 1976):397–412.
———. "Rulers of the Ruhr: Leadership and Authority in German Big Business before 1914." *Business History Review* 53 (Spring 1979):40–64.
Spethmann, Hans. *Das Ruhrgebiet im Wechselspiel von Land und Leuten, Wirtschaft, Technik und Politik*. 3 vols. Berlin, 1933–1938.
Spiethoff, Arthur. *Die wirtschaftlichen Wechsellagen: Aufschwung, Krise, Stockung*. 2 vols. Tübingen, 1955.
Spree, Reinhard. *Wachstumstrends und Konjunkturzyklen in der deutschen Wirtschaft von 1820 bis 1913: Quantitativer Rahmen für eine Konjunkturgeschichte des 19. Jahrhunderts*. Göttingen, 1978.
Spring, David, ed. *European Landed Elites in the Nineteenth Century*. Baltimore, 1977.
Stahl und Eisen: Zeitschrift für das deutsche Eisenhüttenwesen. Düsseldorf, 1896–1914.
Stearns, Peter. "Adaptation to Industrialization: German Workers as a Test Case." *Central European History* 3 (December 1970):303–331.
———. *Lives of Labor: Work in a Maturing Industrial Society*. New York, 1975.
Steffens, Horst. "Arbeiterwohnverhältnisse und Arbeitskampf: Das Beispiel der Saarbergleute in der grossen Streikzeit 1889–1893." In *Streik*, ed. Klaus Tenfelde and Heinrich Volkmann. Munich, 1981. Pp. 124–142.
Stegmann, Dirk. *Die Erben Bismarcks: Parteien und Verbände in der Spätphase des Wilhelminischen Deutschlands: Sammlungspolitik 1897–1918*. Cologne, 1970.
———. "Hugenberg contra Stresemann: Die Politik der Industrieverbände am Ende des Kaiserreichs." *Vierteljahrshefte für Zeitgeschichte* 24 (October 1976):329–378.
———. "Zwischen Repression und Manipulation: Konservative Machtelite und Arbeiter-und Angestelltenbewegung 1910–1918: Eine Beitrag zur Vorgeschichte der DAP/NSDAP." *Archiv für Sozialgeschichte* 12 (1972):351–431.
Stenkewitz, Kurt. *Gegen Bajonett und Dividende*. Berlin, 1960.
Stenographische Berichte der Generalversammlungen des Vereins für die bergbaulichen Interessen im Oberbergamtsbezirk Dortmund. Essen, 1896–1914.
Stenographische Berichte der ordentlichen Hauptversammlungen des Zechenverbandes. Essen, 1908–1914.
Stenographische Berichte über die Verhandlungen des Reichstags. Berlin, 1896–1914.

Bibliography

Stenographischer Bericht über die Gründungs-Versammlung der niederrheinisch-westfälischen Bezirksgruppe des Hansa-Bundes. Essen, 1910.
Stenographischer Bericht über die Versammlung vom 12.6.1909 im Zirkus Schumann zu Berlin betreffend Reichsfinanzreform und Gründung des Hansabundes. Berlin, 1909.
Stern, Fritz. *Gold and Iron: Bismarck, Bleichröder, and the Building of the German Empire.* New York, 1977.
Stürmer, Michael, ed. *Das kaiserliche Deutschland: Politik und Gesellschaft 1870–1918.* Düsseldorf, 1970.
Syrup, Friedrich. "Die Arbeitszeit in der Grosseisenindustrie." *Jahrbücher für Nationalökonomie und Statistik* 103 (1914):193–224.
Taeglichsbeck, O., ed. *Die Belegschaft der Bergwerke und Salinen im Oberbergamtsbezirk Dortmund nach der Zählung vom 16. Dezember 1893.* 2 vols. Dortmund, 1895–1896.
Taft, Philip and Ross, Philip. "American Labor Violence: Its Causes, Character, and Outcome." In *The History of Violence in America*, ed. Hugh Graham and Ted Gurr. New York, 1969. Pp. 281–395.
Tampke, Jürgen. *The Ruhr and Revolution: The Revolutionary Movement in the Rhenish-Westphalian Industrial Region.* London, 1979.
Tänzler, Fritz. *Die deutschen Arbeitgeberverbände, 1904 bis 1929.* Berlin, 1929.
Tegeler, Bergreferendar. "Liegt es im Interesse der Besitzer und der Arbeiter der Steinkohlenbergwerke des Bergreviers Ost-Recklinghausen, wenn die Besitzer Arbeiterwohnungen auf eigene Kosten einrichten?" Staatswissenschaftliche Arbeit, 1902.
Tenfelde, Klaus. "Gewalt und Konfliktregelung in den Arbeitskämpfen der Ruhrbergleute bis 1918." In *Gewalt und Gewaltlosigkeit*, ed. Friedrich Engel-Janosi, Grete Klingenstein, and Heinrich Lutz. Munich, 1977. Pp. 185–236.
———. "Die 'Krawalle von Herne' im Jahre 1899." *Internationale wissenschaftliche Korrespondenz zur Geschichte der deutschen Arbeiterbewegung* 15 (March 1979):71–104.
———. "Linksradikale Strömungen in der Ruhrbergarbeiterschaft 1905 bis 1919." In *Glück auf, Kameraden!* ed. Hans Mommsen and Ulrich Borsdorf. Cologne, 1979. Pp. 199–223.
———. *Sozialgeschichte der Bergarbeiterschaft an der Ruhr im 19. Jahrhundert.* Bonn, 1977.
Tenfelde, Klaus, and Volkmann, Heinrich, eds. *Streik: Zur Geschichte des Arbeitkampfes in Deutschland während der Industrialisierung.* Munich, 1981.
Teuteberg, Hans Jürgen. *Geschichte der industriellen Mitbestimmung in Deutschland.* Tübingen, 1961.
Tilly, Richard. "The Growth of Large-scale Enterprise in Germany." In *The Rise of Managerial Capitalism*, ed. H. Daems and H. v. d. Wee. The Hague, 1974. Pp. 145–169.
Tischert, Georg. "Carl Funke." *Der Niederrhein*, 3 May 1912, pp. 605–609.
Treue, Wilhelm. *Die Feuer verlöschen nie: August-Thyssen-Hütte, 1890–1926.* Düsseldorf, 1966.
———. *Die Geschichte der Ilseder Hütte.* Peine, 1960.
Ullmann, Hans-Peter. *Der Bund der Industriellen: Organisation, Einfluss und Politik klein- und mittelbetrieblichen Industriellen im Deutschen Kaiserreich, 1895–1914.* Göttingen, 1976.

Bibliography

Verhandlungen, Mitteilungen und Berichte des Centralverbandes deutscher Industrieller. Berlin, 1896-1914.
Viebig, W. "Die technischen Grubenbeamten beim Steinkohlenbergbau im Oberbergamtsbezirk Dortmund." *Glückauf* 47 (22 July 1911):1133-1142.
Volkmann, Heinrich. "Modernisierung des Arbeitskampfs? Zum Formwandel von Streik und Aussperrung in Deutschland, 1864-1975." In *Probleme der Modernisierung in Deutschland*, ed. Hartmut Kaelble. Opladen, 1978. Pp. 110-170.
Warren, Donald. *The Red Kingdom of Saxony: Lobbying Grounds for Gustav Stresemann, 1901-1909.* The Hague, 1964.
Webb, Steven B. "Tariffs, Cartels, Technology, and Growth in the German Iron and Steel Industry, 1879 to 1914." *Journal of Economic History* 40 (June 1980):309-329.
Weber, Adolf. *Der Kampf zwischen Kapital und Arbeit.* 3d ed. Tübingen, 1921.
Wegmann, Dietrich. *Die leitenden staatlichen Verwaltungsbeamten der Provinz Westfalen, 1815-1918.* Münster, 1969.
Wehler, Hans-Ulrich. *Bismarck und der Imperialismus.* Cologne, 1969.
―――. *Das Deutsche Kaiserreich, 1871-1918.* 2d ed. Göttingen, 1975.
Weinstein, James. "Big Business and the Crisis of Workmen's Compensation." *Labor History* 8 (Spring 1967):156-174.
Weisbrod, Bernd. *Schwerindustrie in der Weimarer Republik: Interessenpolitik zwischen Stabilisierung und Krise.* Wuppertal, 1978.
Wenzel, Georg. *Deutsche Wirtschaftsführer: Lebensgänge deutscher Wirtschaftspersönlichkeiten.* Hamburg, 1929.
Werner, Georg. *Ein Kumpel: Erzählung aus dem Leben der Bergarbeiter.* Berlin, 1929.
Werner, Karl Gustav. *Organisation und Politik der Gewerkschaften und Arbeitgeberverbände in der deutschen Baugewerbe.* Berlin, 1968.
Wiel, Paul. *Wirtschaftsgeschichte des Ruhrgebiets: Tatsachen und Zahlen.* Essen, 1970.
Wilke, Alfred. *Probleme der Verwaltung im Industriebezirk mit besonderer Berücksichtigung der rheinisch-westfälischen Kohlendistrikts: Eine verwaltungspolitische Studie.* Berlin, 1911.
Wilke, Karl. *50 Jahre im Dienste des Ruhrbergbaus: Erinnerungen eines 80 Jahrigen.* Kettwig, 1955.
Winkler, Heinrich, ed. *Organisierter Kapitalismus: Voraussetzungen und Anfänge.* Göttingen, 1974.
Wittwer, Walter. "Zur Taktik der herrschenden Klassen gegenüber dem Bergarbeiterstreik von 1889." In *Evolution und Revolution in der Weltgeschichte.* Berlin, 1976. 2:541-564.
Wrigley, E. A. *Industrial Growth and Population Change.* Cambridge, 1962.
Wulf, Peter. *Hugo Stinnes: Wirtschaft und Politik, 1918-1924.* Stuttgart, 1979.
Zimmermann, Adolf. *Von Haspe bis Duisburg: Industrielle Reisebriefe.* Berlin, 1912.
Zunkel, Friedrich. *Der Rheinisch-Westfälische Unternehmer, 1834-1879.* Cologne, 1962.
Zur Feier der 25-jährigen Tätigkeit des Herrn Kommerziendrats Oscar von Waldthausen im Dienste der Arenbergschen Aktien-Gesellschaft für Bergbau und Hüttenbetrieb. Düsseldorf, 1904.

Index

accidents, 50, 72, 85
agrarian-industrial relations, 15, 37–38, 45, 58, 119–121, 143
American heavy industry, 23, 47, 94, 144, 185n8
Arbeitnordwest, 104, 107, 122, 127, 138
Arbeitskammern, 117–118
Arenberg'sche AG, 149
Association of German Iron and Steel Industrialists, 14–15, 116, 137, 138; Northwest Group of, 103–104, 115, 118

Baare, Fritz, 29, 34, 151
Baare, Louis, 12, 15, 27, 29, 72
Ballin, Albert, 38
bankers, 12–13, 17, 27, 35
Behrens, Karl, 68, 151
Bergbau Verein, 14, 66, 135; and government regulation, 67, 78, 87; and politics, 118, 120, 180n19; and strikes, 64, 65, 97, 99, 107
Bergschulen, 89–90, 92
Berlepsch, Hans Freiherr von, 52, 64, 65, 68
Beukenberg, Wilhelm, 17, 30, 35, 45, 151
Beumer, Wilhelm, 57, 58
Bismarck, Otto von, 64, 66, 170n14
black lists, 105, 106–108
Bochumer Verein, 11, 17, 22, 149
Bodenhausen, Freiherr Eberhard von, 37
Brauns, Hermann, 35, 151
Brefeld, Ludwig, 68
British heavy industry, 83, 86, 142, 144
Bueck, Henry Axel, 15
Bülow, Bernhard von, 68, 99–100
Bund der Industriellen, 15, 121
Bund der Landwirte, 69, 121
Burgers, Franz, 151
business cycles, 2, 11–13, 15–17, 157–158n4

cartelization, 13–14, 23
Cartel of the Productive Estates, 121
Center party, 54, 55, 57, 61–62, 99, 122–123
Centralverband deutscher Industrieller, 15, 69, 120, 121
cities, Ruhr, 41, 42, 43–44
coal mining, Ruhr, 40; mine closures, 19–20, 42; state direction of, 26, 31; tonnage produced, 10, 11, 12, 19
coal syndicate, 13, 19, 21–22
company unions, 131–132
Concordia Bergbau AG, 149
Conservative party, 54
Consolidation, Bergwerks-AG, 149
Constantin der Grosse, Gewerkschaft, 149
corporations, Ruhr, 149–150; ownership and management, 24–28; profits and dividends, 11, 12, 16; size, 3, 18–23

Dehnke, Reinhold, 152
Delbrück, Clemens, 117
Dernberg, Bernhard, 26
Deutsche Bank, 13
Deutscher Kaiser, Gewerkschaft: growth and development of, 20, 22, 24, 149; and workers, 43, 73, 134
Deutsche Vereinigung, 55–56, 60, 123
Deutsch-Luxemburgische Bergwerks- und Hütten-AG, 22, 26, 149
Disconto-Gesellschaft, 13, 35

Index

Dortmunder Union, 22, 122, 149
Dresdner Bank, 13, 35

elections, 169n35; Landtag, 58, 131; municipal, 60–62, 122–123; Reichstag, 56–57, 66, 67, 118–119, 139
employer associations, 103–105, 121, 145
Essener Steinkohlenbergwerke AG, 26, 149
Ewald, Gewerkschaft, 149

foreign workers, 43, 44
Free Conservative party, 54, 57, 58
Funke, Carl, 5, 26, 29, 37, 96, 152

Gelsenkirchen, 43
Gelsenkirchener Bergwerks-AG, 13, 22, 23, 28, 85, 119, 149
Goecke, Emil, 29, 152
government officials, 43–44, 52–53, 134; and Ruhr industrialists, 19–20, 31–32, 45, 59–60, 68–69, 72; and strikes, 64, 65–66, 74, 99–101, 126, 143
Graf Bismarck, Gewerkschaft, 149
Gutehoffnungshütte, 126, 167n65, 169n35; growth and development of, 10, 21, 22, 24, 149; recruitment of workers, 43, 45; and supervisory personnel, 89, 91, 112, 127–128; terms of labor, 84, 95; and welfare programs, 76, 132

Hamborn, 43–44, 126
Hammacher, Friedrich, 64–65
Haniel family, 10, 38, 58
Haniel, Franz, 5, 24, 33, 59, 152
Haniel mines, 118
Hansabund, 119–120
Harpener Bergbau-AG, 13, 22, 134, 149
Hasslacher, Jacob, 35, 152
Hauptstelle deutscher Arbeitgeberverbände, 103, 121
Hibernia, Bergwerksgesellschaft, 22, 46, 100, 149, 170n14
Hilger, Ewald, 36
Hoerder Verein, 11, 12, 13, 22, 76, 77, 149

Hoesch, Albert, 25, 29, 152
Hoesch steelworks, 22, 24, 25, 106, 149
hours of work: in metallurgy, 114–117, 136–138, 141–142; in mining, 65, 94, 95–96, 101
Hueck family, 30
Hugenberg, Alfred: attitudes and expectations, 1, 53–54, 56; career, 25, 60, 152–153; and politics, 55, 119; and workers, 131, 133, 135

industrialists, American, 141–143, 144, 145
industrialists, British, 82, 143, 144, 145
industrialists, Ruhr: after 1914, 146–147; attitudes and expectations, 5–6, 37–39, 53, 66, 69–70, 72, 131–132, 139–141, 145–146; career patterns, 24–32; identity of elite, 3–5, 151–156; and politics, 53–59, 61, 168n17, 180n19; wealth and status, 33–38
industrialists, Saar, 36, 56
industrialists, Silesian, 36, 117, 132
industrialists, textile, 69, 102–103, 176n8
iron and steel industry, Ruhr, 20, 50; tonnage produced, 10, 11, 12, 19

Jencke, Hanns, 55, 65, 67; attitudes and expectations, 17, 49, 64, 69–70, 110; career, 25, 35, 153

Kamp, Heinrich, 100, 101, 104, 153
Kirdorf, Adolph, 22, 29
Kirdorf, Emil: attitudes and expectations, 38, 49, 53; career, 13, 21, 23, 28, 29, 30, 33, 34, 35, 153; and politics, 39, 45, 55, 59, 120; and workers, 85, 87, 97, 99, 101
Kleine, Eduard, 57, 117, 123; attitudes and expectations, 20–21, 53; career, 4, 29–30, 153
Kleine, Eugen, 30, 153
Kloeckner, Peter, 27, 54, 153
Klönne, Karl, 35
Knappschaften, 75–76, 113
Knepper, Gustav, 93, 96
Kölnische Zeitung, 123
Köln-Neuessener Bergwerksverein, 150

Index

König Ludwig, 26, 134, 150
Kost, Heinrich, 153–154
Krabler, Emil: attitudes and expectations, 20–21, 72; career, 29, 154; and workers, 78, 91, 98, 101, 112
Krawehl, Otto, 26, 29, 125, 135–136, 154
Krupp, Bertha, 25, 33
Krupp, Friedrich Alfred: career, 25, 29, 154; and politics, 45, 54, 55, 57, 59; and Stumm, 36; and William II, 38–39, 66; and workers, 93–94
Krupp steelworks: growth and development of, 10, 21, 22, 24, 25, 150; and politics, 32, 120, 168n17; and supervisory personnel, 89, 128; and welfare programs, 73, 76, 78, 133, 135, 172n11; and workers, 47, 82, 85, 86, 91, 92, 93, 106, 131
Krupp von Bohlen und Halbach, Gustav, 25, 28, 31, 59, 125, 154
Kruse, Francis, 137

labor: after 1914, 146–147; opportunities for advancement, 50, 167n65; productivity, 94; recruitment of, 40–46, 77, 81; turnover, 46–47, 74
labor exchanges, 105, 108–110
legislation: antilabor, 57–58, 68–70; mining, 100, 101, 110; regulating working conditions, 66–67, 116–117; social, 144, 183n73
Liebrich, Wilhelm, 78
lockouts, 105–106, 122, 147
Lothringer Hüttenverein, 27, 150
Löwenstein, Hans von und zu, 123
Lueg, Carl, 24, 29, 54, 59, 154

managerial hierarchies, 91–92
military, use of in strikes, 64, 68, 100–101, 125
Miquel, Johannes, 68
Moabit riots, 126
Möller, Theodor Adolf von, 99, 100
Müser, Robert, 13, 29, 154

National Liberal party, 54, 57, 58, 70
Navy League, 55
Neumühl, Gewerkschaft, 24, 83, 102, 150

newspapers, 112, 119
Nordstern, AG Steinkohlenbergwerk, 22, 150

Oberbergamt Dortmund, 9–10, 45, 66, 95
Ostmarkenverein, 45

Pan-German League, 55
Phoenix steelworks, 21, 22, 96, 109, 150
Pieper, Hermann, Sr., 29, 154–155
Pieper, Hermann, Jr., 29, 155
police, use of in strikes, 125–126
Polish workers, 44–46, 68
Posadowsky-Wehner, Arthur Graf von, 52, 99
prices, 11, 16

Randebrock, Paul, 4, 45, 117, 124, 155
Reichsverband gegen die Sozialdemokratie, 55
Reusch, Paul: career, 24, 155; and politics, 55, 119, 120–121; and strikes, 122, 124–125, 126; and supervisory personnel, 127, 128; and workers, 116, 137
Rheinbaben, Georg Freiherr von, 60
Rheinische Stahlwerke, 12, 22, 116, 150
Rheinpreussen, Gewerkschaft, 24, 25, 150
Röchling family, 36
Roetger, Max: attitudes and expectations, 54, 167n1; and politics, 55, 120; and supervisory personnel, 131; and workers, 128, 133
Ruhr industrial region, 9, 10–11, 41–44

Saar heavy industry, 36, 67
safety inspectors, 116–117
Schaaffhausen'scher Bankverein, 12–13
Schalker Verein, 22, 150
Schmieding, Theodor, 30, 58
Schorlemer-Lieser, Klemens Freiherr von, 60
Servaes, August, 57, 155
Silesian heavy industry, 10, 36, 43, 46, 47, 48, 81, 139–140
Social Democratic party, 56–57, 58, 61–62, 66, 67, 139, 145
Spaeter, Carl, 27

Index

Springorum, Friedrich, 25, 35, 59, 106–107, 155
Stahlwerksverband, 14
Steigerverband, 127
Stinnes, Hugo: career, 23, 26–27, 28, 29, 155–156; and politics, 55; and strikes, 96–97, 122, 124, 126; wealth and status, 33, 34, 38; and workers, 92, 123–124, 146
strikes, 48, 49, 67, 68, 102–103, 104, 106–107, 121–122, 134; coal strike, 1889, 63–65, 86; coal strike, 1905, 97–102; coal strike, 1912, 124–127, 142; employer response to, 74, 143
Studt, Konrad von, 60
Stumm-Halberg, Carl Ferdinand Freiherr von, 36, 38, 67
subcontracting, 87
supervisory personnel: organizations, 127–129; recruitment and training, 89–90; salaries and benefits, 85, 89, 90, 183n73; and workers, 82, 83, 84–85, 87–89, 91–92, 111–112, 126

tariffs, 14–15, 69
Tengelmann, Ernst, 96, 156
Thyssen, August, 33, 34, 37–38; career, 5, 22, 23, 24, 28, 29, 156; and politics, 54, 55, 59, 61, 180n19; and strikes, 100, 101, 126
Thyssen & Co., 24, 150
trade unions: after 1914, 146–147; Catholic, 122–124; and employers, 51, 113, 142, 143; growth and development of, 48–49, 139; Polish, 45; publicizing abuses, 112
Tull, Matthias, 54, 156

unemployment, 42, 76–77

vacations, 125, 133–136
Verein deutscher Arbeitgeberverbände, 103, 121
Verein für Sozialpolitik, 167n1
Vereinigung deutscher Arbeitgeberverbände, 121

wages: determination of, 64, 82–85, 111, 125, 142; differentials, 50, 80–82; fines withheld from, 85–86, 101, 126–127, 182n65; real, 80, 173n1; reductions in, 12, 116
Waldthausen family, 38
Waldthausen, Oskar von, 26, 156
welfare programs, 186n19; government regulation of, 133; health care, 78; housing, 73–75, 100, 132–133, 172n11; insurance and pensions, 75–78, 126, 133; motives for, 71–72, 78–79, 132, 144
Werner, Georg, 92
William II, 38–39, 64, 66, 67, 69, 125
Winkhaus, Fritz, 21, 29, 31–32, 156
Woltmann, Arnold, 138
women, employment of, 46
worker committees, 65, 66–67, 101, 110–111, 124–125, 182n51
work rules, 92–94

Zechenverband, 104–105, 107–109, 123–124, 134–135
Zollverein, Gewerkschaft, 24, 150
Zuckthausvorlage, 69–70